To Hal & Phyllis
Bon appetit! Hope
you enjoy many m[...]
meals. Laurie

MW00380853

Carrots to Caviar

Copyright © 1983 by
Stephan Kasouris and Lavonne Szany

All rights reserved. No part of
this publication may be reproduced or
transmitted in any form or by any means,
electronic or mechanical, including photocopy,
recording, or any information storage and
retrieval system, without permission
in writing from the publisher.

Requests for permission to make copies of
any part of the work should be mailed to:
Permissions, Gourmet Wizardry Publications
16 East Broad Street
Columbus, Ohio 43215

Design by Paul Russell
Introduction and Forward by James Zaferopoulos
Inside Jacket by Therese Nolan
Food Photography by Craig Smith
Special Photography and Cover Photography by
Tom Watson

ISBN 0-9611616-0-4

First Edition

We dedicate this book to our
mothers, Electra and
Florence who taught us the
most important ingredient in
any recipe...love.

Table of Contents

Introduction

A Guide To A New Style of Cooking and Entertaining

Dining is much more than eating. Dining is an event. An experience. An entertainment. And such dining must facilitate enjoyment. It must do that unobtrusively, yet dramatically... with quiet flair and simple elegance. For something flashy doesn't really entertain...it titilates. Something involved and cumbersome makes you a slave to food. It locks you in the kitchen; and, thereby, it hinders your enjoyment of your guests, while it deprives them of your company. Your guests are in your home because they care for you—if they had wanted just the food, they would have eaten out. Honor them with an event...with an experience...an entertainment worthy of the tribute they pay you by their presence in your home.

Good food, well prepared and gracefully presented should be an extension of the host. It should be tasteful, colorful and simple to prepare. Since the food should act as catalyst to bring you and your guests together, pick something that all would like. Think not only of what to serve for your guests but how you will present it. Nothing can focus the attention of your guests like tableside cookery can. But, if you will recall the Maitre'd working his tableside magic with a chafing dish, you realize that most of what he does it quick and simple, though artistically prepared. The secret of his artistry is in the critical selection of ingredients and in the proper blending with that certain flair that is as much a pleasure as the food itself.

In *Carrots to Caviar,* the emphasis is on simplicity and grace. Painstaking preparation has been simplified to basic ingredients, and tableside cookery procedures. How to select a menu, basic ingredients, combining of tastes, and presentation of food are topics dealt with in this book in a concise, sensible manner that places a premium on taste and satisfaction also. We wish you great success with *Carrots to Caviar.* We wish you many treasured evenings ...and we hope that, through our book you and your guests will share the joys that we have known through our years of entertaining.

About the Authors

Although they were born on separate continents and during different decades, Chef Stephan and Lavonne have been brought together in America by their common love for food and entertaining. As the many devotees of their famous "Gourmet Wizardry" can attest, they provide a fresh concept of cookery for professionals and novices alike. *Carrots to Caviar* demonstrates what they have learned about cuisine and entertaining through their many years of work and practice in the hospitality industry.

Through television, radio, and newsprint media, Chef Stephan and Lavonne have conveyed a unique approach to flambé techniques and recipe creation. Their artistry has been brought together here in a concise, colorful and systematic manner.

Chef Stephan Kasouris comes from a close-knit family in which good food and entertaining have long been a tradition. The hardships of World War II brought him to America, and a combination of accident and opportunity placed him in the restaurant business. The period of his arrival was the "Romantic Era" of the late 1940's, when restaurants were showplaces for their guests, as well as their cuisine. Silver, starched linens and mink stoles created an ambiance which, in our day only the silver screen preserves. It wasn't hard for the impressionable young man's enthusiasm to be stimulated by the glitter and grace of the restaurant life as a career, and he has worked devotedly to capture and preserve its spirit and its art, since that beginning. Fortune has taken him to many restaurants, throughout the United States and Europe, and in each, Chef Stephan learned his craft and art from new perspectives.

What he learned and practiced were distilled into his own focus...a system he applied in his own restaurant, "Le Gourmet", and in his famous demonstrations.

Lavonne Szany is an Ohio native of Hungarian and Canadian parentage. She brings to the team of Chef Stephan and Lavonne the balancing influence of traditional hospitality which compliments perfectly Stephan's more continental perspective. The warm and hospitable atmosphere of the traditional Sunday dinner influences profoundly her approach to entertaining. Her memories of youth were filled with childhood parties, picnics and the warm, easy fellowship of family and friends at holidays. At 15, she secured her first job in the large kitchen of a country club, and with its chefs in tall white hats and its unusual foods and its excitement. This whetted her appetite and she decided from that point to devote herself to restauranteering as a career, and set out asiduously to study and learn her craft. Though her parents had wanted her to use her interest in a different manner, Lavonne decided—after three years of study in home economics—to devote herself to a career in catering and restaurant hospitality instead. It was a happy compromise. Her career has taken her across the country. She has studied under the best European chefs in America...and, of course, she met Stephan.

Chef Stephan and Lavonne have forged a synthesis. They took his European training and her roots in the traditional midwestern conception of hospitality to create a new emphasis in the art of entertaining. *Carrots to Caviar* is its compendium.

Appetizers

Melon Kabobs

Yield: about 24

One canteloupe　　　Granulated sugar
One honey-dew melon　Pastel cupcake liners
One pint strawberries　Large frill tooth-picks

With a small melon scooper, make as many canteloupe and honey-dew balls as possible. Sprinkle the strawberries with granulated sugar. To assemble the melon kabobs, take a toothpick and spear one canteloupe ball, then one honey-dew ball and finally one strawberry, leaving the stem exposed on the end. Place in a cupcake liner, and arrange on a tray with other hors d'oeuvres if desired.

Roquefort Mushroom Caps

Makes 12

4 ounces Roquefort cheese　12 large fresh mushroom
2 ounces butter　　　　　　　caps
2 teaspoons chopped　　　　 1 teaspoon chopped
　chives　　　　　　　　　　　parsley
1 teaspoon Cognac

Cream Roquefort, butter, chives and Cognac together and fill mushroom caps with this mixture. Sprinkle parsley over the stuffed mushrooms.

BLEU OR ROQUEFORT CHEESE?

Because of the likeness of the taste of bleu cheese and Roquefort cheese, many people mistakenly assume they are the same.

Roquefort cheese, by law, is made from ewe's milk in the Roquefort area of France.

Bleu cheese, made in many countries, is produced from cow's milk.

Proscuitto and Lox Canapés

1 ounce butter　　　　　 1-4 ounce jar of Lox,
1 ounce cream cheese　　　drained
8 paper-thin slices　　　 1 teaspoon fresh ground
　proscuitto　　　　　　　white pepper

Cream butter and cream cheese together until light and smooth and spread on proscuitto slices with a spatula. Top with enough lox to cover the proscuitto. Roll very tightly and cut into rolls 1 inch long. Spear with toothpicks and sprinkle with ground pepper. Chill before serving.

Spanikopita

Makes about 32

2 pounds fresh spinach	1 cup melted butter
1 pound Feta cheese	½ teaspoon tarragon
1 large onion, minced	Salt and fresh ground
6 eggs, beaten	white pepper to taste
1 pound phyllo leaves	

Clean spinach, and chop fine after discarding stems. Heat 1 tablespoon butter over moderate heat in a sauté pan and sauté onion until tender and transparent. Add spinach and sauté 2 minutes, or until spinach is slightly wilted. Place spinach-onion mixture in a mixing bowl and add eggs, Feta cheese, tarragon and salt and pepper to taste. Mix well.

Place half of phyllo sheets in a 10×16×2-inch baking pan, brushing each individual sheet with melted butter. Spread spinach mixture on phyllo sheets and then top with remaining phyllo sheets, buttering each sheet individually as before. Bake in a preheated 350°F. oven for 30 minutes or until golden brown. Cut into 2-inch squares or triangles.

Spanikopita may be prepared ahead of time, frozen and baked before serving.

Be sure to place a damp towel on unused phyllo leaves while you are preparing spanikopita or the phyllo will dry and crumble.

Chicken Liver Paté

Serves four

¼ pound butter	1 teaspoon thyme
2 cloves garlic, minced	2 tablespoons Brandy
1 medium onion, chopped fine	1½ ounces Burgundy wine
1 apple, peeled and chopped fine	3 tablespoons butter
1 pound chicken livers, rinsed and drained	Salt and fresh ground pepper to taste

Melt 3 tablespoons butter in a sauté pan. Sauté onion and apple over moderate heat. Remove onion and apple from the pan and set aside. In the same pan, sauté chicken liver until browned, about 3 minutes. Season with salt and pepper to taste, along with thyme. Heat Brandy and wine in a saucepan, ignite with a match and pour the flaming Brandy over the chicken livers; add the onion, apple, garlic, combining well. Cream ¼ pound butter in a food processor. Add chicken liver mixture and pureé until smooth. Put in small crocks or molds and chill until ready to serve.

Clams Capri

Serves two

12 fresh clams, shells scrubbed	2 ounces chopped red pimento
¼ cup butter	1 tablespoon oregano
½ cup olive oil	6 garlic cloves, pressed
2 ounces chopped parsley	1 cup breadcrumbs

Remove clams from shells, chop and replace in shells. In a small mixing bowl, blend butter, oil, chopped parsley, pimento, oregano, garlic and bread-crumbs to make a paste. Place 1 teaspoon of mixture on each clam. Bake at 375°F. for 15 minutes. Serve with lemon wedges.

When clams and oysters are purchased, the shells must be tightly closed; when dead, the shells open automatically and the shellfish are no longer edible.

Oysters on Horseback

Serves four

2 dozen oysters, shucked and drained	Salt and white pepper to taste
12 strips bacon, cut in half crosswise	4 pieces toast, crusts removed
4 wooden skewers	Pinch of cayenne pepper
¼ cup fine breadcrumbs	1 lemon quartered
¼ cup butter	

Season each oyster with salt and pepper to taste. Wrap each oyster in a ½ slice of bacon then thread on skewers, 6 bacon-wrapped oysters per skewer. Broil in a baking pan turning once. Mix breadcrumbs, butter and cayenne pepper over moderate heat. When oysters have cooked and bacon is crisp, unskewer each set on a piece of toast, sprinkle with breadcrumbs and serve garnished with a lemon quarter.

Crab Villa Levanté

Serves two as an entrée
Serves four as an appetizer

8 crab legs, shells off	4 garlic cloves, pressed
¼ cup grated horseradish	Juice of one lemon
¼ cup mustard	2 cups Italian bread-
1 cup butter	crumbs

Blend horseradish and mustard in a small bowl and dip the crabmeat into the mixture to coat thoroughly. Grease a baking casserole and place the crabmeat attractively in the casserole. Melt the butter over low heat and add the garlic. Pour over crab legs, and squeeze lemon juice over this. Sprinkle with breadcrumbs, and bake for 20 minutes at 375° F. Garnish with parsley and lemon wedges.

Garlic lends a unique savory flavor, but must be blended properly with the other ingredients in a recipe so it will not be overbearing. The proper method is to use a garlic press. This is a utensil which crushes out the juice of the clove which you scrape off and use. Discard the tough pulp remaining inside the garlic press.

Escargots Champignons à la Pierre

Serves two

½ cup butter	1½ ounces Burgundy
3 cloves garlic, pressed	wine
2 tablespoons chives	Juice of ½ lemon
½ teaspoon Worchester-	2 tablespoons Parmesan
shire sauce	cheese, grated
12 escargots	Salt and fresh ground
½ cup sliced fresh	pepper to taste
mushrooms	

Melt butter in a skillet or chafing dish, add garlic, chives and Worchestershire sauce. Season with salt and fresh ground pepper. Add escargots and fresh mushrooms, and cook until escargots are thoroughly heated and mushrooms are tender. Add the Burgundy wine and sprinkle the lemon juice over the mixture. Cook 2 minutes longer. Add the Parmesan cheese and stir well. Serve immediately.

Be sure to serve lots of French bread for dunking in the sauce.

Shrimp Treena Flambé

Serves four

4 tablespoons butter	1 tablespoon flat parsley,
3 cloves garlic, pressed	chopped
3 scallions, sliced	¼ teaspoon dill weed
20 shrimp; peeled,	1 ounce Dry Sherry
deveined and boiled	1 ounce Vodka
1 cup fresh sliced	Salt and pepper to taste
mushrooms	

Melt butter in a saute pan over moderate heat. Add garlic and scallions and sauté until tender. Add shrimp; stir in Sherry, and mushrooms, parsley and dill weed. Cook for 3 more minutes. Pour Vodka towards front of pan and ignite. Season with salt and pepper to taste. Serve with lemon wedges.

Escargots à la Juli

Serves two

3 tablespoons butter	½ teaspoon fresh ground
3 scallions, minced	pepper
1 apple, peeled, cored,	2 tablespoons Sherry
and chopped	2 tablespoons Brandy
12 escargots	Juice of ½ lemon
½ teaspoon thyme	¼ cup chopped walnuts
⅛ teaspoon salt	

Melt butter in a sauté pan over moderate heat. Sauté scallions and apple, add escargots, thyme, pepper, salt and Sherry. When the escargots are thoroughly heated, push mixture to the side of the pan. Pour Brandy towards the front of the pan and ignite. Squeeze the juice of ½ lemon over the mixture and add the chopped walnuts. Stir and serve immediately.

Danish Ham Rolls

2 teaspoons Dijon-style mustard
2 teaspoons mayonnaise

12 thin slices Danish ham
12 white asparagus

Blend mustard and mayonnaise together and spread on Danish ham slices. Roll around asparagus spears and cut into 1-inch rolls. Secure with a toothpick and chill before serving.

Shrimp Canapés

½ cup butter, creamed
¼ cup mayonnaise
24–2½ " toast rounds

24 large shrimp
Chopped parsley

Blend butter and mayonnaise together and spread on toast rounds. Decorate with shrimp and parsley.

Terrine Maison Pierre

Serves twelve

½ pound sliced bacon
½ pound chicken livers
½ pound ground lamb's
  liver
½ pound lean ground veal
½ cup ground pork
¼ cup butter
1 small onion, peeled and
  minced
3 cloves garlic, pressed
1½ ounce Brandy

Juice of ½ lemon
¼ teaspoon oregano
1 bay leaf
¼ teaspoon rosemary
¼ teaspoon thyme
½ teaspoon minced
  parsley
¼ teaspoon marjoram
2 eggs, beaten
Salt and fresh ground
  pepper to taste

Line a terrine with all bacon except 3 slices. Mix veal, lamb's liver and pork together. Melt butter in a large skillet over moderate heat. Add onion and garlic and sauté until onion is transparent. Remove onion from skillet with a slotted spoon and add to meat mixture. Sauté chicken livers until lightly browned. Remove from pan and chop. Set livers aside. Stir Brandy and lemon juice into remaining juices in pan; then add to meat mixture. Blend herbs, eggs, and salt and pepper to taste into meat mixture. Place half of meat mixture in terrine and cover with chicken livers. Add remaining meat and smooth over top. Cover with remaining bacon slices and place bay leaf on top. Cover terrine with foil; then a tight-fitting lid and place in a roasting pan. Add enough boiling water to the pan to come halfway up the sides of the terrine. Bake in a preheated 350°F. oven for 2 hours or until firm. Place a weight on top of the mixture in the terrine and allow to cool. Serve at room temperature.

Sardine Canapés

Yield: 24

2 tablespoons butter
3 tablespoons mustard
⅛ teaspoon garlic salt
24 oblong toast fingers

2 tins boneless, skinless
  sardines, packed in
  olive oil
4 tablespoons chopped egg

Cream butter with mustard and garlic salt. Spread on toasts. Top with 1 sardine and garnish with chopped egg.

Shrimp à la Moutard

Serves four

24 Shrimp, peeled and
  deveined (21–25 count)
4 tablespoons olive oil
2 green onions minced
4 springs fresh dill,
  minced
½ cup whipping cream
½ cup butter, cut in
  small bits

1 tablespoon Dijon-style
  mustard
1 tablespoon minced
  tarragon leaves
1 tablespoon chopped
  chives
Salt and fresh ground
  pepper to taste
1 ounce cooking Sherry

In a very large sauté pan heat olive oil over high heat until it begins to smoke. Sauté shrimp until opaque. Transfer shrimp to a heated serving platter and keep warm.

Lower heat to medium and add tarragon and green onion to sauté pan and sauté until onion is tender. Add sherry to pan. Whisk in whipping cream and reduce mixture by one-fourth. Season with salt and pepper to taste. Whisk in whipping cream and then swirl in butter a bit at a time. Whisk in mustard and dill and then lace shrimp with sauce. Sprinkle with chives before serving.

Mushrooms à la Grecque

Serves six

30 large fresh
  mushrooms, stems
  removed
Juice of 1 lemon
1 onion minced
6 tablespoons olive oil
2 tomatoes peeled,
  seeded, and chopped
1 clove garlic, pressed

½ green pepper, seeded
  and minced
⅛ teaspoon thyme
½ teaspoon oregano
1 bay leaf
½ cup dry white wine
Salt
Fresh ground pepper

Clean and place mushrooms in a mixing bowl. Squeeze juice of lemon over mushrooms and toss. Heat olive oil over moderate heat and sauté onion and green pepper until tender and transparent. Add tomato, oregano, garlic, thyme, and bay leaf, stock, and white wine. Bring mixture to a boil and cook until reduced by one-fourth. Season with salt and pepper to taste.

Add mushrooms and cook them for 10 minutes or until tender. Place mixture in a mixing bowl and refrigerate for 4 hours or overnight.

Seafood Crepes Flambé with Champagne Sauce

Serves four

8 crepes (recipe follows)
½ cup chopped shallots
½ cup fresh sliced
  mushrooms
¾ cup butter
3 tablespoons flour
½ cup Champagne
1 quart half and half
4 egg yolks, well beaten

½ pound cooked lobster
  meat
½ pound shrimp, boiled,
  peeled and deveined
½ pound crabmeat,
  cooked
1½ ounce Cognac
1 tablespoon chopped
  parsley

Melt butter over moderate heat and sauté shallots
until tender and transparent. Sprinkle with flour and
cook, stirring constantly until flour turns light brown.
Whisk in Champagne and half and half. Remove pan
from heat and whisk in beaten egg yolks. Simmer until
slightly thickened, stirring constantly.

In another pan melt remaining ¼ cup butter over
moderate heat and sauté seafood and mushrooms until
well heated. Pour Cognac towards front of pan and
ignite. When flames have extinguished, add half of
sauce to seafood. Divide evenly among crepes and roll
up. Cover crepes with remainder of sauce. Sprinkle
with parsley before serving.

Basic Crepes

Yield: 20 Crepes

1 cup flour
2 eggs
¼ teaspoon salt

1½ cups milk
1 tablespoon clarified
  butter

Place flour in a mixing bowl and make a well in the
center. Add the eggs and whisk until well blended.
Add salt and half of the milk, beating to make a
smooth batter. Gradually beat in the remaining milk.
Stir in the melted butter.

Rub the bottom of a crepe pan with melted butter.
Spoon enough of the batter into the pan to barely cover
the bottom. Quickly tilt the pan so that the batter coats
the entire pan and cook until the crepe starts to turn
golden brown on the bottom. Using a spatula, turn the
crepe over to "set" the other side. (Do not allow it to
brown.) Place the finished crepes between sheets of
waxed paper.

Cucumber Cups

2 medium-sized cucumbers	½ teaspoon salt
1½ cup crabmeat	1 tablespoon sour
2 tablespoons mayonnaise	cream
2 tablespoons chopped	½ teaspoon lemon
chives	juice

Wash cucumbers thoroughly and score lengthwise with a fork. Slice into 1½-inch slices and scoop out the seedy center of each slice.

Mix crabmeat with mayonnaise, sour cream, chives, salt and lemon juice and fill the cucumber cups.

Crabmeat Ravigote

Serves four

1 pound crabmeat	12 strips pimento
⅓ cup tarragon vinegar	2 avocados, cut in half
1½ tablespoons dill	lengthwise, seeds
pickles, minced	removed
½ cup mayonnaise	1 tablespoon capers
1 head Bibb lettuce	Salt and fresh ground
4 tablespoons chopped	pepper to taste
pimento	

Place crabmeat in a bowl, with tarragon vinegar and refrigerate for 20 minutes. Strain crabmeat and add salt and pepper to taste to the crabmeat. Add remaining ingredients to crabmeat with the exception of pimentos, capers and avocados. Place equal amount of mixture in avocado halves and top with pimentos and capers. Serve on a bed of Bibb lettuce.

Lobster or Shrimp Cocktail

Serves four

4 Romaine lettuce leaves	24 shrimp, boiled,
1 pound cooked lobster OR	peeled and deveined
meat diced	12 small capers
	4 lemon wedges

Place 1 lettuce leaf in each of 4 crystal coupes or small glass bowls. Divide lobster meat or shrimp among the coupes and cover with Cocktail Sauce (below). Garnish each with three capers and a lemon wedge. Place each coupe in a small bowl filled with crushed ice if desired.

Lobster or Shrimp Cocktail Sauce

1 egg yolk	1½ tablespoons
2 tablespoons olive oil	horseradish
½ teaspoon lemon juice	1 tablespoon Brandy
½ teaspoon salt	4 drops hot red pepper
¼ teaspoon pepper	sauce
8 tablespoons tomato	1 tablespoon whipping
ketchup	cream

Mix egg yolk with oil and lemon juice. Season with salt, pepper and hot red pepper sauce; beating well to obtain a smooth mixture. Whisk in tomato ketchup, horseradish, Brandy and cream. Place on lobster or shrimp.

Mermaid Mousse

Serves six

2 envelopes unflavored	¼ teaspoon red hot
gelatin	pepper sauce
½ cup cold water	2 pounds cooked shrimp
1½ cup mayonnaise	pieces
⅓ cup lemon juice	1 pound Alaskan king
2 teaspoons dry mustard	crabmeat, drained
2 teaspoons sugar	1 cup whipping cream
1 cup minced celery	

Stir gelatin into cold water, and dissolve over boiling water. Combine mayonnaise, lemon juice, mustard, sugar and red pepper sauce in a mixing bowl. Add gelatin and mix well. Stir in celery, crabmeat, and shrimp. Whip cream and fold in seafood mixture. Spoon into an 8 cup mold. Chill until set. Unmold onto a serving dish lined with salad greens.

Canapés Louise

Serves four

2 ounces paté de foie gras	1 teaspoon chopped chives
or goose liver paste	12 slices cooked roast
⅛ teaspoon salt	beef (thin)

Blend paté, salt, and chives until creamy and spread on roast beef with a spatula. Roll tightly and cut into one-inch rolls. Secure with a toothpick and chill before serving.

Cheese Puffs Hors d'Oeurves

Serves twelve

12 bread rounds	1 tablespoon chives
1 cup grated Cheddar	⅛ teaspoon of Worchester-
cheese	shire sauce
1 teaspoon baking powder	¼ pound butter, at room
1 egg, separated	temperature

Toast the bread rounds on 1 side only. In a mixing bowl, blend the Cheddar cheese and baking powder. Add to a lightly beaten egg yolk and a stiffly beaten egg white. Fold in the chives and Worchestershire. Spread this mixture on buttered toast rounds, mounding high in the center. Put under the broiler until melted, puffy and lightly browned.

Oysters Paul

Serves four

½ cup butter
⅔ cup chopped onions
2 tablespoons chopped chives
3 cups crabmeat
½ teaspoon Pernod
Juice of 2 lemons

48 asparagus tips
24 oysters on the half-shell
½ cup chopped pimentos
2 cups Hollandaise sauce
Salt and fresh ground pepper to taste

Melt butter in a sauté pan over moderate heat and sauté onions and chives until onions are tender and transparent. Add crabmeat, Pernod, salt, pepper and ⅔ of pimentos. Cook, stirring constantly until all ingredients are thoroughly warmed. Place two asparagus tips on top of each oyster and top asparagus with crabmeat mixture. Squeeze lemon juice over oysters. Place a teaspoon of Hollandaise sauce over each oyster and garnish with remaining pimento. Place oysters under a broiler for 30 seconds or until Hollandaise sauce is golden brown.

Hot Ham Appetizer Flambé

Serves two

3 tablespoons brown sugar
3 tablespoons white wine vinegar
½ teaspoon cornstarch dissolved in 1 tablespoon water
½ cup smoked ham cut in julienne

4 tablespoons capers
2 tablespoons white raisins
1 tablespoon candied fruit, minced
2 tablespoons pine nuts
1½ ounce Brandy
8 toast points

Place brown sugar, vinegar and constarch mixture in a sauté pan over moderate heat and cook, stirring constantly until mixture becomes transparent and thickened. Add capers, ham, raisins, candied fruits and pine nuts and cook until sauce thickens. Pour Brandy towards the front of pan and ignite. When flames have extinguished, place mixture on toast points and serve.

Tarama Salata (Greek Caviar)

Makes 2 cups

4 pieces white bread, crusts removed
4 ounce jar tarama (cod fish roe)
Juice of 1 lemon
¼ cup minced onion
1 cup olive oil

2 teaspoons minced parsley
Greek olives for decoration
Fresh Greek bread or sesame crackers

Dip bread in water, then squeeze out excess moisture. Place bread, tarama, lemon juice, and onion in a blender or food processor and process until smooth. Add oil, 1 teaspoon at a time and process after each addition until well blended. Do this until all the oil has been added and the mixture is fluffy. Pour into a serving bowl, sprinkle with parsley and decorate with olives and serve with bread or sesame crackers.

Asparagus Crepes

Serves four

16 crepes
16 fresh asparagus spears
½ cup butter
1 teaspoon salt
½ teaspoon of black pepper

6 paper-thin slices ham or proscuitto
2 cups Hollandaise sauce

Wash asparagus well and melt butter over low heat in a small saucepan. Cook over low heat until tender. Sprinkle with salt and pepper. Wrap each spear with a slice of ham. Fill each crepe with a wrapped asaragus spear, fold over and place in a shallow buttered baking dish. Bake in a 350°F. oven for 20 minutes or until tender and heated. Top with Hollandaise sauce before serving.

Shrimp Stuffed Mushroom Caps

Serves four

1 cup finely chopped, cooked shrimp
1 tablespoon breadcrumbs
1 tablespoon minced onion
1 tablespoon minced parsley
1 tablespoon butter
1 teaspoon minced tarragon

1 egg
16 large, cleaned mushroom caps with stems removed
3 tablespoons grated Parmesan cheese
Salt and fresh ground pepper to taste
½ ounce dry cooking Sherry

Mix shrimp, breadcrumbs, onion, parsley, butter, egg tarragon together. Fill the mushrooms caps with the mixture, sprinkle with cheese and season with salt and pepper to taste. Place in a greased casserole and bake in a 350° F. oven for 15-20 minutes. Sprinkle with Sherry before serving.

Oysters Rockefeller

Serves four

20 oysters on the half shell
2½ cups cooked or drained canned spinach
¼ cup chopped shallots
¼ cup breadcrumbs
¼ cup crumbled cooked bacon
2 teaspoons chopped parsley

½ teaspoon salt
½ teaspoon fresh ground white pepper
⅛ teaspoon red hot pepper sauce
¼ cup melted butter
Juice of one lemon
1 teaspoon Pernod

Preheat oven to 475°F. Blend all ingredients except oysters and Pernod in a mixing bowl. Place about one teaspoon of spinach mixture on each oyster. Embed shells on rock salt in a shallow pan. Sprinkle with Pernod and bake for 10-15 minutes or until ingredients are thoroughly heated and oysters are plump. For a special touch, dot each oyster with Hollandaise sauce and return to broiler to lightly glaze top.

Soups

Snow Pea Soup

Serves six

3 tablespoons butter	1 pound fresh snow peas;
1 cup sliced leeks	strings and tips
3 tablespoons flour	removed, and chopped
4 cups chicken stock	1 tablespoon butter
1-12 ounce package	1½ cups half and half
frozen baby peas	Salt and white pepper to
1½ cups water	taste
1 scallion, minced	

Melt butter over moderate heat in a sauté pan and sauté leeks until tender, about 10 minutes. Stir in flour. Add chicken stock, salt and frozen peas and purée in a blender or food processor. Set mixture aside. Meanwhile bring water to a boil. Add pea pods, scallions and butter. Boil until pea pods are tender, about 10 minutes. Remove from heat. Add to purée base and blend in half and half. Chill and season with salt and white pepper before serving.

Sherried Chicken Soup

Serves six

1-3 pound chicken	1 teaspoon tarragon
2½ quarts water	1 bay leaf
1 carrot, chopped	½ cup uncooked rice
1 stalk celery, chopped	½ teaspoon curry powder
1 onion cut in half	¼ cup cooking Sherry
1 tablespoon butter	1 cup whipping cream
4 whole cloves	2 teaspoons salt

Melt butter over moderate heat in a Dutch oven or large saucepot. Add carrot, celery, onion studded with cloves and sauté 5 minutes. Add chicken, water, salt, bay leaf and tarragon and bring to a boil. Cover pan slightly and simmer for 1½ hours. Skim skum floating to top.

Transfer chicken to a cutting board. Remove meat from carcass and discard skin and bones. Discard bay leaf and cloves from stock. Return chicken to stock and add rice, curry, Sherry and cream. Simmer for 30 minutes or until rice is tender.

Vichysoisse

Serves four

3 medium-sized leeks,	4 cups chicken stock
minced	1½ cups whipping cream
1 medium onion, minced	Salt and white pepper to
2 tablespoons butter	taste
4 medium potatoes, peeled	2 tablespoons chopped
and sliced thin	chives

Melt butter over moderate heat in a saucepan and sauté onion and leek until tender and transparent. Add potato and chicken stock and bring mixture to a boil. Simmer covered for 20 minutes. Place ingredients in a blender or food processor and purée. Add cream, and salt and pepper to taste. Serve chilled, garnished with chives.

Quick Vichysoisse

Serves six

3 tablespoons minced	¼ cup instant mashed
onion	potato mix
1 cup half and half	1 can cream of chicken
2 cups milk	soup
½ teaspoon salt	2 tablespoons dried
¼ teaspoon fresh ground	chives
pepper	

Add onion to half and half. Combine milk, soup, salt and pepper in a heavy saucepan over low heat. Bring to scalding point and add mashed potato. Cook stirring constantly until mixture begins to thicken. Combine with half and half and onions. Before serving, beat until smooth and creamy. Serve garnished with chives.

Creamy Vegetable Soup

Serves four

2 tablespoons unsalted butter
¾ cup chopped, peeled turnips
½ cup chopped, peeled carrots
¼ cup chopped scallions
½ head broccoli, broken into small florets
4½ cups boiling water
1½ teaspoons salt
¼ teaspoon fresh ground pepper
½ cup whipping cream

Melt butter over moderate heat in a 4–quart saucepan. Stir in vegetables, cover and cook 6 minutes or until vegetables begin to soften but do not brown. Increase heat to high; add boiling water, salt and pepper. When mixture comes to a boil, cover pan, reduce heat to moderate low and simmer for 20 minutes. Place cream and 2 cups soup into blender, cover and purée 15 seconds. Pour into another saucepan. Repeat process with remaining soup. Heat puréed mixture to serving temperature and ladle into soup bowls.

Cock-A-Leekie Soup

Serves six

1 three-pound chicken
2½ quarts water
Bouquet garni (in cheese cloth)
   2 sprigs parsley
   1 bay leaf
   ¼ teaspoon thyme leaves
2 teaspoons salt
1 tablespoon chopped parsley
¼ cup pearl barley
7 leeks, sliced
2 stalks celery, chopped

Place chicken in a large saucepan with water and bouquet garni. Bring to a boil over high heat and skim off scum that rises to the surface. Add leeks, celery, barley and salt. Reduce heat to low and simmer for 2 hours.

Transfer chicken to a cutting board. Remove and discard bouquet garni. Remove the meat from the carcass and discard the skin and bones. Slice meat and return to broth. Simmer soup over moderate heat for 5 minutes. Sprinkle with parsley before serving.

Chicken Curry Soup

Serves six

4 teaspoons butter
4 teaspoons curry powder
3 tablespoons flour, blended with
6 cups chicken broth
1 cup whipping cream
½ teaspoon paprika
6 tablespoons crushed pineapple, drained
4 egg yolks
1½ cups cooked chicken, diced fine
1½ tablespoons chives, chopped
6 tablespoons toasted sliced almonds

Melt butter in a heavy Dutch oven. Add curry and stir until well-blended. Stir in chicken broth and flour mixture. Bring to a boil, stirring constantly, and add paprika and pineapple. Reduce heat. Beat eggs and cream together in a mixing bowl. Add a small amount of soup to the egg mixture and blend well. Add egg mixture to soup and stir over low heat until slightly thickened. Add chicken, chives and almonds. Stir until thoroughly heated and serve.

Quick Shrimp Bisque in Aspic

Serves four

2 cans cream of shrimp soup (10 ounce)
1 can clam consommé (10 ounce)
2 tablespoons clear gelatin
1 tablespoon Dry Sherry
½ cup tomato juice
6 ounces tiny shrimp
1 cucumber, sliced thin

Dissolve gelatin in consommé and bring to a boil. Add remaining ingredients except cucumber. Place soup in bouillon cups and chill until set. When ready to serve, slice cucumbers decoratively and place in soup.

Cream of Carrot Soup

Serves eight

1 cup grated carrots	3 cups milk
3 tablespoons onion, grated	1 tablespoon lemon juice
3 tablespoons butter	1 tablespoon minced parsley
3 tablespoons all-purpose flour	Fresh ground pepper to taste

In a heavy Dutch oven, sauté carrots and onion in butter until carrots are tender and soft, being careful not to over-cook. Sprinkle flour over carrots and stir mixture thoroughly. Slowly add milk to mixture, stirring well to prevent lumping. Stir until thickened. Add lemon juice, parsley and fresh ground pepper to taste. Stir and serve immediately.

Black Bean Soup

Serves six

2 cups dried black beans	1 garlic clove, pressed
3 quarts water	2 ounces Dry Sherry
1 ham bone	½ cup chopped hard boiled egg
½ cup chopped onion	½ cup minced onion
1 teaspoon beef extract	
1 green pepper, minced	

Wash beans, cover with cold water, soak overnight, and drain. Add 3 quarts fresh water and ham bone. Boil gently until beans are softened and liquid thickened. Add more water if necessary. Add the beef base, green pepper, garlic, onion and Sherry. Simmer ½ hour. Remove ham bone. Serve in heated soup crocks or bowls. Allow each guest to garnish his soup with chopped egg and onion, as desired.

Watercress Soup

Serves six

3 bunches fresh watercress
3 leeks, white part only
6 tablespoons unsalted
  butter
2 large potatoes peeled
  and diced
6 cups chicken stock

2 cups whipping cream
2 tablespoons yogurt
  (plain)
1 teaspoon salt
Juice of ½ lemon
½ teaspoon fresh ground
  white pepper

Remove any bruised leaves and stalks from
watercress. Wash in cold water and shake off excess
water. Wash the leeks and cut into small pieces. Melt
butter over moderate heat and sauté leeks until tender.
Add watercress and sauté until wilted. Add potatoes
and chicken stock. Bring mixture to a boil and simmer
for 20 minutes or until potatoes are tender. Pureé soup
in a blender or food processor. Strain and add cream
and yogurt. Return to low heat and cook until soup
begins to boil. Season with salt and pepper and juice
of lemon. Serve hot or cold. If re-heating do not allow
to boil.

French Onion Soup

Serves six

6 medium-sized onions cut
  in rings
6 tablespoons butter
2 tablespoons flour
½ teaspoon salt
¼ teaspoon fresh ground
  pepper

4 cups beef stock
1½ ounce red wine
6 toasted slices French
  bread
3 garlic cloves, pressed
½ cup grated Parmesan
  cheese

In a medium sized flameproof casserole or Dutch
oven, melt the butter over moderate heat. Reduce the
heat to low and add onions and cook stirring constantly
until onions are golden brown. Season with salt and pepper.
Add flour to pan and stir until smooth. Stir in stock
and red wine. Bring mixture to a boil; then reduce heat
and simmer for 30 minutes.
Preheat broiler. Rub each toast slice with garlic.
Place toast slices on the surface of soup and sprinkle
with Parmesan cheese. Broil soup until cheese is
bubbling and golden. Transfer to individual bowls and
serve immediately.

Sweet Potato Soup

Serves four

2 medium sized sweet
  potatoes
1 quart chicken broth
¼ cup whipping cream

⅛ teaspoon fresh ground
  pepper
2 tablespoons fresh
  chopped chives

Heat oven to 350° F., and bake sweet potatoes for
1½ hours. Remove from oven, and when cooled
enough to handle, peel sweet potatoes and cut into 1
inch chunks. Pureé with broth in a food blender or
processor, until smooth. Pour mixture into a saucepan,
stir in cream. Heat to serving temperature, but not
boiling. Ladle into soup bowls and sprinkle with
chopped chives and pepper.

Fresh Spinach Soup

Serves eight

2 pounds fresh spinach
¼ cup butter
¼ cup minced onion
1 quart chicken broth
2 tablespoons chives

2 tablespoons lemon juice
2 tablespoons chopped
  hard boiled egg
Salt and fresh ground
  pepper to taste

Clean spinach and drain thoroughly. Chop spinach
finely. Melt butter in a large Dutch oven or soup kettle.
Sauté onion until tender. Add spinach and coat well
with butter. Cook covered until spinach is tender. Add
chicken broth, chives, lemon juice and salt and pepper
to taste. Bring soup to a boil and then simmer covered
for 20 minutes. Ladle into soup bowls and sprinkle
with chopped egg.

Mushroom Soup

Serves four

1 pound fresh mushrooms,
  cleaned and chopped
2 cloves garlic, pressed
2 tablespoons unsalted
  butter
¼ teaspoon thyme
5 drops red hot pepper
  sauce

1 teaspoon salt
½ teaspoon fresh ground
  white pepper
2 cups whipping cream
2 cups chicken stock
1 tablespoon minced
  parsley
Juice of one lemon

Sprinkle chopped mushrooms with lemon juice. Melt butter over moderate heat in a heavy saucepan and sauté garlic and mushrooms until tender and liquid disappears. Add thyme, red hot pepper sauce, salt, pepper, chicken stock and whipping cream. Simmer uncovered for 20 minutes. Pureé mixture in a blender or food processor. Place in warmed soup cups and sprinkle with parsley before serving.

Shrimp Bisque Christine

Serves four

2 pounds raw shrimp,
  shelled and deveined
4 tablespoons butter
¼ cup minced onion
¼ cup minced celery
2 tablespoons grated carrot
3 cups chicken stock

⅛ teaspoon thyme
1 teaspoon minced parsley
4 dashes of bitters
1 cup whipping cream
¼ cup dry white wine
Salt and fresh ground
  pepper to taste

Place shrimp in blender or food processor and process until chopped fine. Melt the butter in heavy saucepan or Dutch oven and cook the vegetables until wilted. Add the shrimp and cook 4 minutes, stirring constantly. Add the chicken stock, thyme, parsley, cream, wine, bitters, and salt and pepper to taste. Taste for seasoning, and top with minced parsley.

Avgolemono Soup

Serves six

3 cups chicken broth
½ cup washed rice
2 egg yolks
2 whole eggs

Juice of one lemon
Salt and fresh ground
  pepper to taste

Bring the broth to a boil and add the rice. Cook until tender. Add salt and pepper to taste. Beat the eggs and egg yolks until light and frothy and add the lemon juice slowly, blending well. Add a little of the hot broth to the egg mixture, blending it in well. Slowly add the egg to the broth, stirring constantly. Heat through, but do not boil or the eggs will ''curdle'' the soup.

Avgolemono Soup Uvarlakia

Serves six

6 cups clear chicken broth
1 pound lean ground beef
½ cup white uncooked rice
¼ teaspoon oregano

¼ teaspoon dried parsley
Salt and pepper to taste
Juice of one lemon
2 whole eggs

Mix all above ingredients together except chicken broth, egg and lemon and make into small meatballs. Place in a saucepan with chicken broth and simmer for 30 minutes. Remove from heat and follow the same procedure by adding egg-lemon mixture explained in Avgolemono Soup.

Borscht

Serves four

½ cup minced carrots
1 cup minced onion
1 cup minced beet
1 tablespoon butter
2 cups beef stock

1 cup finely shredded
  cabbage
1 tablespoon vinegar
½ cup sour cream
Salt and pepper to taste

Place carrots, onion and beet in a saucepan with 2
cups of water and bring to a boil. Simmer covered for
15 minutes. Add beef stock, butter, cabbage and
vinegar. Season with salt and pepper to taste and
simmer 15 minutes longer. Place soup in bowls and top
with a dollop of sour cream before serving. Soup may
be chilled and served cold.

Chilled Turtle Soup

Serves six

2 cans clear turtle broth
3 tablespoons unflavored
  gelatin
1 cup water
2 tablespoons sweet
  Sherry

Juice of ½ lemon
4 tablespoons sour cream
1 tablespoon black caviar
Salt and fresh ground
  pepper to taste

Heat turtle soup in a saucepan and dissolve gelatin.
Add a cup of water, Sherry and lemon juice. Add salt
and pepper to taste. Pour into bouillon cups and chill
until set. Top with equal amount of sour cream and
sprinkle with caviar.

Beer Soup Germany

Serves four

4 tablespoons butter
4 tablespoons flour
1½ quarts German beer
1 teaspoon sugar
1 teaspoon salt

½ teaspoon white pepper
⅛ teaspoon cinnamon
¾ cup whipping cream
½ cup croutons

Melt butter over moderate heat in a heavy saucepan
and stir in flour to make a roux, cooking until mixture
is golden. Add beer, sugar, salt, pepper and cinnamon.
Whisk in whipping cream and then ladle into soup
bowls. Garnish with croutons.

Sauces

Basic White Sauce

2 tablespoons butter
¼ cup flour
2½ cups milk or half and half
½ teaspoon salt
White pepper to taste

Melt butter slowly in a small saucepan over low heat. Do not let it become brown or it will change the color of the sauce. Remove the pan from the heat and stir in flour to form a smooth paste—this is called roux. Return mixture to heat and stir for 1–2 minutes or until smooth.

Meanwhile heat the milk in a separate saucepan until bubbles form around edge of the pan. (Do not allow to boil.)

Remove the roux saucepan from the heat and add a little of the milk at a time, stirring continuously. When the mixture is blended thoroughly, return the pan to the heat and bring the mixture to a boil, stirring continuously. Add salt and pepper to taste. Reduce heat to low and cook the sauce for 5–7 minutes longer (uncovered). If the sauce is not cooked enough, it will taste like flour. It should be smooth and shiny.

Buerre Blanc

¾ cup white wine vinegar
2 shallots, minced
½ cup butter, room temperature
1 tablespoon minced parsley

Place wine, vinegar and shallots in a saucepan and boil until reduced to one tablespoon. Remove from heat and beat in butter a teaspoon at a time. Stir in parsley. The buerre blanc should be thick, not liquid. If it is too liquid, chill for a few minutes, then stir again.

Blender Hollandaise Sauce

Yield: Approximately ¾ cup

1 egg
3 tablespoons lemon juice
¼ teaspoon salt
Pinch white pepper
½ cup melted butter

Combine egg, lemon juice and seasonings in a blender container. Blend egg mixture until well mixed. Add hot butter very gradually, blending until thickened and smooth.

Blender Hollandaise is practically fool-proof and a real time-saver. The consistency is somewhat thinner than Basic Hollandaise, but it will thicken after it is poured over hot foods.

Chicken Stock

5 pounds chicken scraps and bones
2 onions, sliced
2 carrots, sliced
2 quarts water
1 stalk celery
½ green pepper, chopped
1 bay leaf
3 sprigs parsley
1 teaspoon salt

Place all ingredients in a large soup or stockpot. Simmer for 4 hours, skimming the fat and scum that rises to the top, from time to time. Strain.

Veloute Sauce

Yield: 2 cups

¼ cup butter
¼ cup flour
3 cups chicken stock
Salt and pepper to taste

Melt butter over low heat in a saucepan and stir in flour. Cook, stirring constantly until flour is lightly browned. Stir in stock a little at a time. Continue stirring until sauce thickens. Simmer until sauce is reduced to 2 cups. Season with salt and pepper to taste.

Aurore Sauce

2 cups Veloute sauce
3 tablespoons tomato
  puree

Add tomato pureé to veloute sauce and cook over low heat in a saucepan for 5 minutes.

Sauce Parisienne

2 egg yolks
⅓ cup Veloute sauce
1 hard boiled egg, riced
2 tablespoons whipping
  cream

Beat egg yolks and cream together in a small mixing bowl. Heat Veloute sauce over moderate heat in a saucepan. Add Veloute sauce to egg mixture a small amount at a time, stirring well after each addition. Pour mixture in saucepan and cook until very hot. Sprinkle boiled egg over sauce before serving.

Hollandaise Sauce

4 egg yolks, well beaten
1 cup butter, melted
2 tablespoons lemon juice
Pinch of salt
Pinch of cayenne pepper
2 drops red hot pepper
  sauce

Place the egg yolks in the top of a double boiler over hot water and whisk until they begin to thicken. When the egg yolks thicken, add the butter in very small amounts, whisking well after each addition. When all the butter has been added, and the sauce is fluffy, add the lemon juice in small amounts, along with the salt, pepper and red hot pepper sauce. Serve immediately.

A perfect Hollandaise sauce depends largely upon how the butter is added. The egg yolks will absorb only a small quantity of butter at a time so it must be added very slowly in small amounts. The water in the bottom of the double boiler should be hot, but never boiling. Boiling water will cause the Hollandaise to separate.

Bearnaise Sauce

1 cup Hollandaise sauce
1 tablespoon minced green
  onion
¼ teaspoon white pepper
½ teaspoon tarragon
  leaves
½ teaspoon chervil
2½ tablespoons red wine
  vinegar
2½ tablespoons dry white
  wine
¼ cup finely chopped
  parsley

Combine onion, pepper, tarragon, chervil, vinegar and wine in the top of a double boiler and place over direct heat. Simmer until almost all the liquid has evaporated. Cool to lukewarm and beat into the Hollandaise in the top of a double boiler with a whisk. Add the parsley and stir until well blended.

Bechamel Sauce

2 cups milk	5 tablespoons butter
1 bay leaf	¼ cup flour
6 peppercorns	½ teaspoon salt
⅛ teaspoon grated nutmeg	¼ teaspoon white pepper

Place milk, bay leaf, peppercorns and nutmeg in a small saucepan over low heat. Warm the mixture for 10 minutes, but do not allow it to boil. Strain into a mixing bowl and allow to cool.

Meanwhile in a separate saucepan melt the butter over low heat. (Do not allow butter to sizzle or brown.) Remove the saucepan from the heat and stir in the flour with a wooden spoon, mixing to form a smooth paste.

Return the saucepan to low heat and stir mixture for 1–2 minutes. Now add the flavored milk gradually and salt and pepper to taste, mixing constantly with the spoon. Bring the sauce to a boil, stirring constantly. Reduce heat to low and cook 5–7 minutes to thoroughly cook flour. Sauce should be thick and shiny.

Aioli Sauce (Garlic Mayonnaise)

8 cloves garlic, mashed	1¼ cup olive oil
¼ teaspoon salt	Juice of ½ lemon
2 egg yolks	

Place mashed garlic cloves in a bowl with salt and egg yolks, and mix thoroughly. Add a few drops of olive oil, mixing thoroughly after each addition. Add remainder of oil in the same manner, beating thoroughly after each addition. Add the lemon juice and mix well. Serve with hot or cold vegetables, fish or beef.

Mornay Sauce

Yield: 2½ cups

2 cups Bechamel sauce	¼ cup whipping cream
2 egg yolks, well beaten	⅓ cup grated Gruyere cheese

Heat Bechamel sauce in a saucepan over low heat. Beat in egg yolks a little at a time. Stir in cheese and cream, and continue to stir until cheese has melted.

Creamy Basil Sauce (For Poached Fish or Fresh Vegetables)

Yield: 2 cups

2 egg yolks	⅓ cup water
½ cup dry white wine	3 tablespoons fresh chopped basil or 2 teaspoons dried basil
½ teaspoon salt	
¼ teaspoon fresh ground pepper	
1 cup vegetable oil	½ cup minced fresh parsley

Place yolks, wine, salt and pepper in a blender; cover and blend 15 seconds at high speed. With blender still running, slowly pour in ¾ of the oil in a thin stream. When mixture is thick, add water, basil and remaining oil and blend about 30 seconds longer, or until mixture is very pale green. Whisk in parsley.

Madeira Sauce

2 tablespoons butter	1 clove garlic, pressed
2 celery stalks, minced	1 tablespoon minced parsley
1 carrot, minced	
1 small onion, minced	½ teaspoon dried thyme
1 tablespoon chopped cooked ham	2 cups brown stock
2 tablespoons flour	2 cups Madeira wine
2 tomatoes, peeled, seeded and chopped	Salt and fresh ground pepper to taste

Melt the butter in a large skillet over moderate heat. Add celery, carrot, onion and ham and saute' until all ingredients are golden brown. Add the flour and stir constantly until the flour is brown. Reduce the heat to low and add the tomatoes, garlic, parsley and thyme, and simmer for 5 minutes. Add brown stock and simmer for 30 minutes. Strain the sauce and return the liquid to the saucepan. Stir in the Madeira and simmer for 5 minutes. Add salt and pepper to taste.

Brown Stock

½ pound cracked soup bones
1 pound lean soup beef, cubed
1 tablespoon butter
8 ounces ham, diced
1 large onion, diced
1 stalk celery, chopped
1 clove
1 bay leaf
1 clove garlic
4 sprigs parsley
½ teaspoon thyme
1 teaspoon salt
8 cups water
1 carrot, minced

Place bones and beef cubes on a baking sheet and brown in a preheated 450°F. oven for 15 minutes. Melt butter over moderate heat in a heavy large pot and add ham, carrot, celery, and onion. Place meat and bones on top, add ½ cup of water and simmer until water has evaporated. Add remaining water and ingredients. Bring to a rapid boil, reduce heat and simmer 5 hours. Skim scum from top and replenish water when needed. Remove from heat and strain immediately. Chill and discard fat.

Espagnole Sauce

Yield: 2 cups

¼ cup butter
1 onion, stuck with a clove and quartered
1 carrot, diced
¼ pound lean ham, cooked and diced
¼ pound veal, diced
¼ cup flour
4 cups beef stock, heated
3 sprigs parsley, minced
1 bay leaf
⅛ teaspoon thyme
Salt and fresh ground pepper to taste

Place butter in a heavy saucepan and heat over moderate heat until melted. Add onion, carrot, ham and veal. Cook, stirring for 8-10 minutes, or until meat is lightly browned.
Reduce heat to low, add flour to the mixture and stir until it is a rich brown, about 5 minutes. Remove the pan from the heat and stir in the beef broth. Add parsley, bay leaf and thyme and simmer for 30 minutes or until sauce is reduced to 3 cups.
Strain sauce through a fine sieve and add salt and pepper to taste.

Bordelaise Sauce

1 marrow bone
1 tablespoon butter
2 shallots, minced
½ cup dry red wine
2 cups Espagnole sauce

Simmer marrow bone in enough water to cover, long enough that marrow can easily be removed. Remove marrow and press it through a sieve. Sauté shallots in butter over moderate heat in a saucepan. Add marrow and red wine. Simmer until mixture is reduced to 1 tablespoon. Stir in Espagnole sauce, and continue to cook until well heated.

Sauce Chausseur

2 tablespoons butter
½ pound mushrooms, sliced thin
1 shallot, minced
1½ ounce white wine
¼ teaspoon tarragon
2 cups Espagnole sauce
1 tablespoon minced parsley

Melt butter over moderate heat in a saucepan. Add mushrooms and shallot and cook until shallot is wilted. Add wine and tarragon and continue to cook mixture until reduced to 1 tablespoon. Stir in Espagnole sauce and parsley. Heat until sauce begins to simmer.

Eggs

Henri's Dessert Omelette Flambé

Serves four

8 eggs	½ cup plums, drained
¼ teaspoon salt	½ cup fruit cocktail,
2 tablespoons butter	drained
½ cup apricot halves,	3 ounces Anisette liqueur
drained	¼ cup confectioner's sugar

Beat eggs and salt with a whisk until well blended. Melt butter in a large omelette pan over moderate heat. Place eggs in pan as butter begins to foam, and cook, lifting edges of omelette and tilting pan to allow unset portion to run under omelette. When omelette has set, add drained fruits, and ⅓ of Anisette. Fold omelette in half and continue cooking until omelette raises. Transfer omelette to a serving platter. In a separate pan, heat remaining Anisette. Pour over omelette and ignite. When flames have extinguished, sprinkle with confectioner's sugar and serve.

Seafood Quiche

Serves four

1–9″ unbaked pie shell	½ pound baby shrimp or
4 eggs	shrimp pieces
2 cups heavy cream	1 cup shredded
2 tablespoons minced onion	Mozzarella cheese
1 teaspoon salt	2 tablespoons chopped
⅛ teaspoon cayenne pepper	parsley
½ pound crabmeat,	
chopped	

Preheat oven to 425° F. Beat eggs until well blended. Stir in cream, onion, salt and pepper. Sprinkle crabmeat, shrimp pieces and cheese in the pie shell. Pour egg mixture over seafood and cheese; sprinkle with parsley. Bake 15 minutes, then reduce heat to 300° F. and bake for 30 minutes longer or until knife inserted in center comes out clean.

Quiche is a sophisticated French pizza, excellent for lunch, brunch, or with a salad for a light dinner.

Poached Eggs Cape Cod

Serves four

3 tablespoons butter	4 English muffin halves,
4 scallions, chopped fine	toasted
½ pound precooked	4 poached eggs
lobster meat, cubed	¼ cup Bearnaise sauce
1 ounce Madeira wine	½ teaspoon salt
½ cup half and half	½ teaspoon fresh ground
1 tablespoon cornstarch	pepper

Melt butter in chafing dish over moderate heat and sauté scallions until tender. Add lobster, salt and pepper to taste and sauté until lobster is thoroughly heated. Add wine, half and half and cornstarch. Cook mixture, stirring constantly until slightly thickened. Divide mixture evenly on English muffin halves and top each with a poached egg. Top with Bearnaise sauce. Place under broiler for 30 seconds to lightly brown top and serve.

Oeufs Florentine

Serves four

¼ cup butter	1½ tablespoon Parmesan
1–8 ounce can spinach,	cheese, grated
drained	Salt and fresh ground
8 eggs	pepper to taste
1 cup Mornay sauce	

Melt butter in a saucepan over moderate heat. Add spinach, salt and pepper to taste and cook until heated. Divide spinach into 4 small greased baking ramekins or casseroles, forming a nest in the middle. Place eggs in nest. Top with Mornay sauce and sprinkle with Parmesan cheese. Bake in a 350° F. oven until eggs set and Mornay sauce is golden brown. Serve in baking casseroles with toast, muffins or bagels.

Poached Eggs in Red Wine Sauce

Serves four

8 eggs	½ teaspoon thyme
4 slices bacon	1 bay leaf
4 shallots, minced	1 teaspoon chopped
1 garlic clove, pressed	chives
1 tablespoon cornstarch	Salt and fresh ground
3 tablespoons unsalted	pepper to taste
butter	8 toasted bread rounds
½ bottle dry red wine	or English muffin halves
2 tablespoons beef stock	

Cook bacon until lightly browned over moderate heat in a sauté pan. Remove bacon from pan and allow to drain on paper towels. Add shallots to pan and cook until tender. Add garlic and stir well. Remove pan from heat and stir in cornstarch and butter. Return pan to heat and cook stirring constantly until mixture begins to thicken. Heat wine and beef stock together in a saucepan and whisk into the cornstarch mixture. When ingredients are well blended add bacon, thyme, bay leaf and salt and pepper to taste. Simmer sauce for 10 minutes. Meanwhile poach eggs in gently simmering water for 3 minutes. Place eggs on top of toasted bread rounds or English muffin halves on a serving platter. Pour red wine sauce over eggs. Garnish with chopped chives.

Eggs Continental

Serves two

¾ cup grated Cheddar	1 tablespoon chives
cheese	4 English muffin halves
½ cup half and half	4 poached eggs
1 ounce dry Sherry	Minced parsley
3 tablespoons butter	Salt and fresh ground
3 tablespoons chopped	pepper to taste
onion	

In a double boiler, place cheddar cheese with salt, pepper, half and half and Sherry. Blend well with a whisk until mixture is smooth. Meanwhile melt butter in a sauté pan and sauté onion and chives until tender. Blend onions with cheddar cheese mixture. Top each muffin half with a poached egg and pour cheddar cheese mixture over eggs. Garnish with minced parsley and serve.

Whether eggshells are brown, white, or spotted makes no difference to the quality of the egg.

Mushroom Quiche

Serves four

4 tablespoons butter	½ teaspoon fresh ground
1 small onion, minced	pepper
2 cloves garlic, pressed	1–9″ unbaked pie shell
1 small potato, sliced thin	3 eggs
1 cup sliced fresh	½ cup sour cream
mushrooms	½ cup heavy cream
¼ cup green pepper, diced	¾ cup grated Mozzarella
½ teaspoon salt	cheese

Melt the butter in a large skillet over moderate heat; sauté the onions, green pepper, garlic and potato for 3 minutes and then add the mushrooms, salt and pepper to taste. Beat eggs; add heavy cream, sour cream and blend with a whisk. Pour the mixture in the pie shell. Add the mixture over the vegetables. Sprinkle the Mozzarella cheese on the top and bake 450° F. for 20 minutes or until a knife inserted 1-inch from the edge of the pastry comes out clean.

Eggs with Caviar

Serves four

4 toasted English muffin	1 tablespoon minced dill
halves	4 tablespoons red or
8 eggs	black caviar
4 tablespoons whipping	Fresh ground white
cream	pepper to taste
4 tablespoons unsalted	
butter	

Whisk together eggs and heavy cream until thoroughly blended. Season with pepper to taste.
Melt two tablespoons of butter in a sauté pan over low heat. Pour in the eggs and cook until they begin to thicken slightly, mixing with a spatula. Stir in the dill and cook until creamy. Remove from heat and add remaining butter. Place English muffins on serving dishes. Spoon eggs on muffins and top with caviar. Serve at once.

Scrambled Egg Pita

Serves two

2 tablespoons butter	1 tablespoon Cheddar
1 tablespoon minced green	cheese, grated
pepper	2 half slices Pita bread
1 green onion, minced	¼ cup taco sauce
3 eggs, well-beaten with 2	Salt and pepper to taste
tablespoons half and half	2 tablespoons chopped
2 tablespoons chopped	ripe black olives
tomato	

Melt butter in a sauté pan, and add green pepper and green onion. Sauté until tender. Pour in egg-cream mixture and cook eggs stirring constantly. While eggs are still runny, add tomato, cheese, olives, and salt and pepper to taste. Cook until all ingredients are thoroughly heated and eggs are set. Fill pita bread with egg mixture and top with taco sauce. Serve immediately.

Oeufs Provençale

Serves four

2 tablespoons butter	8 eggs
1 tablespoon minced	2 tablespoons grated
parsley	Parmesan cheese
1 small onion, minced	Salt and fresh ground
4 large ripe tomatoes	pepper to taste

Melt butter in sauté pan and cook parsley, and onion until tender. Cut one inch off tomato tops and scoop out the insides. Chop the scooped tomato and add to the sautéed onion. Fill the tomato cavities with this mixture and place in a greased baking dish. Bake in a 350° F. oven for 8 minutes. Remove tomatoes from oven and break 2 eggs into each tomato. Season with salt and pepper and sprinkle with Parmesan cheese. Return to oven and bake for 10 minutes longer. Serve immediately.

Eggs en Brioche

Serves four

4 small brioches, warmed	6 eggs
4 tablespoons unsalted butter	3 tablespoons whipping cream
2 tablespoons minced onion	Fresh ground white pepper
4 ounces pastrami, julienned	

Cut off tops of brioches and scoop out insides leaving a shell. Heat 2 tablespoons of butter in a sauté pan over moderate heat and sauté onion until tender and transparent. Combine eggs and whipping cream in a mixing bowl using a whisk. Season with fresh ground pepper to taste.

Reduce heat to low and melt remaining butter in sauté pan which onion has been sautéed. Pour in eggs and cook, stirring constantly until eggs begin to thicken. Add pastrami and cook until eggs are soft and creamy. Place brioches on warmed individual serving plates and fill with egg pastrami mixture. Replace tops and serve.

Quiche Lorraine

Serves four

1 unbaked 8″ pie shell	½ teaspoon salt
6 slices of bacon	¼ teaspoon pepper
1 medium onion, chopped	1 tablespoon chopped chives
¼ cup ham, cut in julienne strips	Pinch of cayenne pepper
¾ cup half and half	Pinch of nutmeg
4 eggs, well beaten	Paprika
½ cup grated Cheddar cheese (or Swiss cheese)	

Chill the pie shell or place in the freezer for 5 minutes. Fry the bacon in a skillet until crisp. Remove the bacon from the skillet and drain. Add the onion, and ham to the bacon dripping and sauté until the onions are transparent. Combine the cream, eggs, ¼ cup of cheese, salt, pepper, chives, cayenne and nutmeg in a large mixing bowl. Stir in the bacon, onion and ham, and then pour into pie shell. Sprinkle with remaining cheese, then with paprika. Bake at 350° F. for 25 minutes or until light and puffy, and a knife inserted in the center comes out clean.

This is a excellent brunch or luncheon dish. It can be combined with a bowl of soup for a dinner. It can be served hot or cold. For a special touch, top hot quiche with Hollandaise sauce.

Kahlua-Coffee Soufflé

Serves four

6 lady fingers broken in pieces	¾ cup hot milk
3½ ounces Kahlua	¼ cup strong black coffee
4 tablespoons confectioner's sugar	1 tablespoon sugar
3 tablespoons butter	5 egg yolks
¼ cup flour	7 egg whites
	1 cup chopped pecans

Place lady fingers in a mixing bowl and sprinkle with 2 ounces Kahlua. Let soak for one minute then mash mixture with a fork to paste.

Preheat oven to 350°F. Grease a soufflé dish then sprinkle with confectioner's sugar.

In a saucepan, melt butter over moderate heat and sprinkle in flour. Cook, stirring constantly until mixture turns golden and smooth. Slowly stir in milk to make a thick sauce. Cook, stirring constantly for 3 minutes.

Stir in remaining liquor, coffee and lady finger paste. Set aside to cool a little. Beat the sugar and egg yolks until light and add gradually to the cooled sauce.

Beat the egg whites until stiff and fold into the sauce. Spoon into the soufflé dish and sprinkle with pecans. Bake for 40 minutes or until soufflé is well risen and lightly browned. Serve immediately.

Omelette Soufflé Grand Marnier

Serves four

8 eggs separated	1½ ounces Grand Marnier
1½ cup granulated sugar	1 cup drained mandarin orange sections
¼ cup confectioner's sugar	¼ teaspoon salt
2 tablespoons grated orange rind	

Preheat oven to 400°F. Grease the sides of a soufflé dish with butter and dust with granulated sugar. In a small mixing bowl, beat egg yolks and sugar until smooth and frothy. Add orange rind and half of the Grand Marnier; blend well. In another bowl, using a wire whisk, beat egg whites until foamy, add salt and beat until stiff. Gently fold egg whites into egg yolk mixture. Place mixture in soufflé dish and build high in center. Bake for 30 minutes. Remove from oven and pour remaining Grand Marnier over soufflé. Sprinkle with confectioner's sugar and arrange orange sections decoratively around soufflè. Serve immediately.

Prune Nut Soufflé

Serves two

1½ cups prunes	⅔ cup pecans, chopped fine
⅛ teaspoon salt	6 egg whites stiffly beaten
1 tablespoon lemon juice	⅔ cup water
½ teaspoon grated orange rind	Confectioner's sugar
¼ cup sugar	½ teaspoon grated lemon zest

Place prunes in enough water to cover in a sauce pan and simmer until prunes are plump and moist. Drain prunes, remove pits and pureé in a food processor or blender. Add lemon juice, orange and lemon rind, salt, sugar and mix well. Fold nuts into egg whites and then fold into prune mixture. Pour mixture into a buttered, sugared soufflé dish and bake in a preheated 350°F. oven for 40 minutes. Remove and sprinkle with additional confectioner's sugar if desired.

Banana Soufflé

Serves two

½ cup milk	4 bananas, peeled
½ teaspoon vanilla extract	1 tablespoon butter
3 tablespoons sugar	2 egg yolks, beaten
1 tablespoon flour	2 egg whites, stiffly beaten
⅛ teaspoon salt	

Butter a soufflé dish, sprinkle with sugar. Preheat oven to 325°F. In a small saucepan heat milk, vanilla and sugar to scalding point. Blend in flour and salt, stirring constantly, to form a thin paste.

Pureé bananas in a food processor or blender. Blend bananas with butter and egg yolks and add to milk mixture. Gently fold in egg whites. Pour mixture into prepared soufflé dish and bake for 15 minutes. Serve immediately.

Crabmeat Omelette

Serves two

4 scallions minced
3 tablespoons butter
1 cup crabmeat
6 eggs beaten well
8 asparagus spears, cooked
   al denté and warmed

½ cup Hollandaise
   sauce
Salt and fresh ground
   pepper to taste

Melt 2 tablespoons butter in a sauté pan over moderate heat and sauté scallions until tender. Add crabmeat and salt and pepper to taste. Cook until crabmeat is thoroughly heated. In another pan melt 1 tablespoon butter over moderate heat. Pour in ½ eggs and cook omelette, lifting edges of omelette and tilting pan to allow unset portion to run under omelette. Repeat the same process with remaining butter and eggs. Place an equal amount of crabmeat mixture in each omelette and fold omelettes. Place 4 asparagus spears on each omelette and top with Hollandaise sauce.

A perfect omelette is moist inside, plump in the middle and golden brown on the outside.

French Toast Elegante

Serves four

1 day-old loaf French
   bread
5 eggs
3 tablespoons sugar
⅛ teaspoon salt

1½ cups half and half
1½ ounce Grand Marnier
Grated zest of 1 orange
2 tablespoons butter

Cut eight 1½ inch slices from French bread. In a bowl beat eggs with sugar, salt, half and half, Grand Marnier and orange rind. Soak bread slices in egg mixture until they are very wet.

Melt butter on a griddle or large fry pan and cook soaked bread slices until golden. Transfer to heated plates and top with orange syrup.

Orange Syrup

1 cup maple syrup
1 tablespoon grated
   orange rind

2 tablespoons Brandy
⅛ teaspoon cinnamon
1 teaspoon grated lemon
   rind

Heat ingredients in a small saucepan over low heat. Serve with French Toast Eleganté.

Chicken Soufflé

Serves four

2 tablespoons butter
3 tablespoons flour
1 cup hot milk
⅛ teaspoon grated
   nutmeg

5 eggs, separated
2 cups cooked white
   chicken, chopped very
   fine
Salt to taste

Butter and lightly flour a soufflé mold. Preheat oven to 350°F. Melt butter in a heavy saucepan over low heat and add flour. Cook, stirring constantly, until mixture is golden brown. Stir in ¼ cup hot milk mixture and whisk mixture until thickened. Season with nutmeg and salt to taste. Remove pan from heat.

Beat egg yolks until light and add chopped chicken and ¼ cup hot sauce. Beat egg whites until stiff and very gently fold into egg yolk mixture. Gently fold in remaining sauce. Pour mixture into prepared mold and bake for 30 minutes. Serve immediately.

Breakfast Custard

Serves four

3 tablespoons butter
1 onion, peeled and sliced
   thin
1 cup sliced green onion
½ cup cooked ham,
   chopped fine
6 eggs

1 cup whipping cream
¼ cup milk
½ teaspoon salt
½ teaspoon fresh ground
   white pepper
Pinch cayenne

Generously butter 4 baking custard cups or ramekins. Preheat oven to 300°F. Melt butter in a saucepan over moderate heat. Add onions and sauté until tender. Beat eggs with whipping cream and milk until well blended. Add onion, salt, pepper, cayenne and ham and mix well. Spoon mixture into custard cups. Place custard cups in a pan filled with 1½ inches with boiling water and bake in preheated oven for 45 minutes or until lightly browned and puffy. Let stand for 5 minutes before serving.

Salads

Potato Salad Roquefort

Serves six

Viniagrette Dressing:
- 3 tablespoons red wine vinegar
- ½ teaspoon salt
- ½ teaspoon fresh ground pepper
- 3 shallots, minced
- 1 teaspoon Worchestershire sauce
- 1 teaspoon dried mustard
- ¼ cup olive oil
- 1 egg, well beaten
- 2 tablespoons minced parsley

Salad Ingredients:
- 6 large leaves Romaine lettuce, rinsed and blotted dry
- 2 pounds small new potatoes, boiled and sliced thin
- ½ cup crumbled Roquefort cheese
- ¼ cup whipping cream
- 10 slices bacon, broiled until crisp, and crumbled

Place vinegar, salt, pepper, shallots, Worchestershire, and mustard in a small bowl. Stir until salt dissolves. Slowly pour in oil, whisking continuously until well blended. Add egg and whisk until blended. Sprinkle with parsley and set aside.

Place Romaine lettuce on a large platter. Arrange potato slices in long, even rows. Sprinkle potatoes with Roquefort and bacon. Whisk cream into dressing and spoon over potatoes.

This dish is excellent served at room temperature or chilled.

Avocado Strawberry Salad

Serves four

- ¾ cup confectioner's sugar
- 8 ounces cream cheese
- ½ cup slivered almonds
- 2 tablespoons Amaretto
- 2 ripe avocados, peeled and seeds removed
- 1 pint fresh strawberries, cleaned and hulled
- ⅓ cup orange juice
- 1 Bermuda onion, sliced
- Lettuce for garnish

Combine 1/2 cup confectioner's sugar and cream cheese in a wooden bowl and beat until fluffy. Stir in the almonds and Amaretto. Place mixture in avocado halves. Arrange strawberries on avocados. In another bowl, mix remaining confectioner's sugar and orange juice. Spoon over the strawberries. Garnish the avocados with Bermuda onion slices and serve on a bed of lettuce.

Believe it or not, the avocado is a fruit. Look for avocados that are firm and dark green and black in color. Allow avocado to soften and ripen at room temperature for 2–5 days. Test the avocado by pressing with your index finger. If it feels a little soft, it is ready. To speed the ripening process, place avocados in a brown paper sack in a warm place for 1–2 days.

Store ripened avocados in the refrigerator to slow the ripening process. When ready to use your avocado, halve it lengthwise and twist the halves to separate. Carefully lift the seed out with the tip of a sharp knife. To peel, use the tip of a knife to loosen the skin. Lift and strip the skin. To preserve the green color, brush the avocado with lemon juice—otherwise it will brown. Store unused portions tightly wrapped in plastic wrap in the refrigerator.

Pasta Salad

Serves four

2 cups roast duck cut in julienne strips	⅔ cup mayonnaise
2 celery stalks, chopped	1 teaspoon Worchestershire sauce
2 cups pasta shells cooked al dente'	Juice of 1 lemon
1 medium zucchini, cubed	½ teaspoon salt
¼ cup black olives	⅛ teaspoon cayenne pepper
2 anchovy fillets	½ teaspoon dill weed
	Fresh ground pepper to taste

In a serving bowl mix together; duck, celery, pasta, zucchini and olives. In another bowl mix together, until well blended; anchovy, mayonnaise, Worchestershire sauce, lemon juice, salt, cayenne pepper, dill weed and fresh ground pepper to taste. Toss dressing with pasta mixture and chill before serving.

Special Spinach Salad

Serves four

1 pound raw spinach	6 green onions, minced
1 cup fresh sliced mushrooms	½ clove garlic, pressed
6 slices bacon, broiled and crumbled	⅛ cup red wine vinegar
½ pound flaked Alaskan King crabmeat	½ teaspoon dry mustard
½ cup salad oil	4 tablespoons brown sugar
	Juice of ½ lemon
	Salt and fresh ground pepper to taste

Place spinach in a large salad bowl and gently blot dry with a towel. Heat oil in a sauté pan or chafing dish over moderate heat. Sauté onions until golden brown; add garlic, vinegar, dry mustard, brown sugar, salt and pepper to taste. Stir mixture until it is well blended and syrupy. Meanwhile toss the spinach, mushrooms, bacon and crabmeat. Pour the dressing over the salad and toss so that all ingredients are well coated. Sprinkle with lemon juice and serve.

To keep bacon from curling while broiling or frying, snip edges with shears before cooking.

Fruit Salad Flambé

Serves four

2 ounces butter	3 tablespoons orange juice
1 ounce Grand Marnier	3 ounces whipping cream
½ ounce Kirsch liqueur	
1–32 ounce jar citrus salad, drained	

Melt butter over moderate heat and add fruit salad. Cook until fruit salad is thoroughly heated. Pour liqueur towards the front of the pan and ignite. When flames have extinguished, place fruit in serving dishes. Add juice to the pan, blend in cream and pour sauce over the fruit.

Orange Pomegranate Salad

Serves four

2 oranges, peeled	One head Romaine lettuce, cleaned and torn into bite-size pieces
Seeds of one pomegranate	
½ cup orange juice	
3 tablespoons olive oil	Salt and fresh ground pepper to taste

Slice oranges very thin and place in serving bowl. Add pomegranate seeds. In a small mixing bowl, pour in orange juice, and blend in salt and pepper. Stir until salt is dissolved. Whisk in oil in a thin steady stream. Pour over oranges and pomegranate seeds. Add lettuce and toss lightly before serving.

Mermaid Salad

Serves four

2 cloves garlic, pressed
½ teaspoon dried mustard
1 teaspoon Worchestershire sauce
½ cup olive oil
⅛ cup red wine vinegar
1 head Romaine lettuce, washed and broken into bite-size pieces
12–1½" pieces hearts of palm
½ cup Alaskan King crabmeat
16 pitted black olives
Juice of ½ lemon
Salt and fresh ground pepper to taste

Place garlic in a wooden bowl, and press into the wood. Add dried mustard, fresh ground pepper to taste, Worchestershire, and mix. Add olive oil and vinegar and blend again. Add lettuce, hearts of palm, crabmeat and black olives and toss well. Squeeze the juice of the lemon on the salad and toss once more. Serve on chilled salad plates.

Salad Fantastica

Serves four

4 heads Bibb lettuce, washed and cleaned
1–8 ounce can of hearts or palm, drained
1–8 ounce can of hearts of artichoke, drained
1 cup plain yogurt or sour cream
1 tablespoon pimento strips
1 tablespoon Dijon-style mustard
1 tablespoon soy sauce
1 tablespoon chopped parsley
8 thin slices cucumber
Salt and fresh ground pepper to taste

Place the heads of Bibb lettuce on chilled dinner plates, spreading the leaves slightly to make a hollow center. Remove the hearts of the Bibb lettuce and chop coarsely. In a wooden bowl place sour cream or yogurt, pimento and mustard, soy sauce, ½ of parsley and salt and pepper to taste. Stir well. Add the hearts of palm and artichoke and chopped lettuce. Toss mixture and place in the hollowed Bibb lettuce. Garnish with cucumber slices and remaining parsley.

Cucumber Pineapple Salad Suzanne

Serves four

1 pineapple, peeled, cored and cubed
2 cucumbers, peeled and cubed
¾ cup roasted cashews

Dressing:
¼ cup honey
½ cup half and half
Juice of one lemon
Salt and fresh ground pepper to taste

Place pineapple, cucumber and cashews in an attractive bowl. Whisk dressing ingredients with salt and pepper to taste and pour over salad. Toss and chill before serving.

Lettuce Crepes

Serves four

1 head Iceberg lettuce
12 slices bacon, broiled and crumbled
1 cup chopped raw cauliflower
1 cup Roquefort or Thousand Island dressing

Reserve 8 outer leaves of the Iceberg lettuce. Shred enough remaining lettuce to make 1½ cups. Toss the lettuce, bacon and cauliflower with ¾ cup of the dressing. Place 2 tablespoons of the mixture in each lettuce leaf, then roll and secure with a toothpick. Top with the remaining dressing and serve.

Salad Cherise

Serves four

1 large head Romaine lettuce, cleaned and torn in bite-size pieces	½ teaspoon sugar
	1 teaspoon chervil
	⅛ teaspoon dry mustard
16 dark red ripe cherries, pitted	4 tablespoons olive oil
	½ teaspoon salt
Juice of ½ lemon	⅛ teaspoon white pepper
Juice of ½ orange	

Squeeze the juice of ½ lemon and orange into a wooden bowl and add sugar, chervil, salt, pepper and dry mustard. Stir until well blended, and then whisk in olive oil. Add lettuce, cherries and toss. Serve on chilled plates.

Salad Espagnole

Serves four

1 pound fresh spinach	4 cantaloupe wedges ⅜″ thick
2 small bunches fresh basil leaves	
	8 ounces poached salmon fillet
1 small bunch fresh sorrel leaves	
	1 tablespoon mayonnaise
3 fresh peaches, pitted and sliced	1 cup whipping cream
	2 tablespoons sour cream
16 strawberries, hulled and sliced	Salt and fresh ground pepper to taste

Place salmon in a food processor or blender along with basil, sorrel, mayonnaise, whipping cream and sour cream. Process to form a smooth dressing. If mixture is too thick add additional cream. Season with salt and pepper to taste.

Attractively arrange spinach on salad plates. Surround with peaches, strawberries and canteloupe wedges. Pour salad dressing over spinach and serve.

Spinach Salad

Serves four

1 pound raw spinach	8 drops Worchesterhire
½ cup fresh sliced	sauce
mushrooms	3 tablespoons brown sugar
6 tablespoons olive oil	½ cup bacon, broiled and
¼ cups chopped onions	crumbled
2 tablespoons cider	Salt and fresh ground
vinegar	pepper to taste
¼ teaspoon dry mustard	

Heat olive oil over a moderate flame in a flat skillet or chafing dish and sauté onions until tender. Add vinegar, dry mustard, Worchestershire, brown sugar, and salt and pepper to taste—stir until well blended. When mixture begins to boil, add bacon and stir well. Sprinkle mushrooms over spinach and pour the hot dressing over the greens. Toss and serve immediately.

Spinach salad may be garnished with chopped hard boiled egg if desired.

Hearts of Artichoke Salad

Serves four

4 cooked artichoke hearts	2 cups chopped Romaine
¾ cup minced celery	lettuce
¾ cup minced parsley	4 slices tomato, halved
¾ cup minced green onion	1 hard boiled egg chopped
12 anchovy fillets	3 teaspoons caviar
½ teaspoon salt	1½ cups Viniagrette
⅛ teaspoon ground	Dressing
white pepper	(see Dressings)

Mince anchovy fillets and combine with celery, parsley, green onion and salt and pepper in a mixing bowl. Form the mixture into 4 balls.

Cover 4 salad plates with the chopped lettuce. Place an artichoke heart in the center and garnish with minced vegetable-anchovy mixture. Garnish each plate with 2 halves of tomato slice.

Pour Viniagrette Dressing over artichokes and sprinkle with chopped egg and caviar.

Mushroom Salad Juli

Serves four

2 garlic cloves, pressed
½ teaspoon grated lemon
  rind
½ teaspoon grated orange
  rind
3 tablespoons olive oil
Juice of ½ lemon

⅛ teaspoon nutmeg
1 tablespoon minced parsley
3 cups fresh sliced
  mushrooms
Salt and fresh ground
  pepper to taste

Rub inside of a wooden bowl with pressed garlic. Discard excess garlic pulp. Add lemon and orange rind, oil, lemon juice, nutmeg and salt and pepper to taste and whisk ingredients together. Add mushrooms and toss gently to coat with dressing. Sprinkle with parsley and marinate in refrigerator for 20 minutes. Serve on a bed of lettuce.

Mushrooms:
When buying mushrooms, look for those with firm caps and beige stems. Fresh mushrooms are slightly moist with the underside gills not yet exposed.

Nouvelle Potato Salad

Serves four

1 pound small new
  potatoes
¼ cup sour cream
½ cup mayonnaise
1 tablespoon lemon juice
1 teaspoon olive oil

½ teaspoon salt
½ teaspoon fresh ground
  pepper
4 tablespoons fresh
  chopped chives

Boil potatoes until fork tender and cool. Place potatoes in a mixing bowl along with mayonnaise, sour cream, lemon juice, oil, salt, pepper and 1 tablespoon chives. Carefully toss mixture until well blended. Transfer to serving bowl. Sprinkle with remaining chives.

Difference between black and white pepper:
Black and white pepper come from the same plant. Black pepper is the dried immature berry which is picked before it is fully ripened. Its appearance is black on the outside and white on the inside. Its flavor is sharper than white pepper. White pepper is a fully mature berry with the dark outer coat removed. Its flavor is more delicate and mild. Ground pepper looses flavor rapidly so use fresh ground pepper whenever possible.

Cold Fava Bean Salad

Serves eight

2 pounds dry fava beans
8 tablespoons olive oil
4 cloves garlic, pressed
1 tablespoon butter
½ cup minced onion
½ cup minced celery

2 tablespoons chopped
  parsley
2 tablespoons chopped
  fresh basil
2 tablespoons wine vinegar
Salt and pepper to taste

Shell the beans and cook in enough boiling water to cover, until tender. Drain and rinse with cold water. Heat oil, garlic, and butter over moderate heat in a large skillet. Add beans, and toss well. Add onions, celery, parsley, basil, vinegar and salt and pepper to taste. Toss well and place in a serving bowl. Chill well.

***You may use 3 one-pound cans of fava beans, instead of fresh fava beans. Rinse them well before adding to oil and butter.

Green Bean Salad

Serves four

1 pound fresh green beans
1 clove garlic, pressed
½ cup ham, chopped
3 tablespoons olive oil
3 tablespoons lemon juice

1 teaspoon basil
½ cup chopped black
  olives
Salt and fresh ground
  pepper to taste

Cook beans in boiling salted water until tender. Rub garlic in a wooden bowl. Add lemon juice and whisk in olive oil gradually. Add beans, ham, black olives and basil and toss lightly. Season with salt and pepper and chill before serving.

Beef Salad

Serves six

1 pound strip sirloin, trimmed	Juice of ½ lemon
⅓ cup olive oil	1 teaspoon oregano
¼ cup red wine vinegar	⅛ teaspoon salt
3 large garlic cloves, pressed	¼ teaspoon ground pepper
	1 scallion, minced

Trim and cut the sirloin into ¾-inch julienne strips. In a large skillet, sear the sirloin in 3 tablespoons of the olive oil over high heat for 30 seconds. Transfer the beef to a large mixing bowl.

To make the dressing, combine all remaining ingredients, except the olive oil, in a small mixing bowl. Add the olive oil in a thin stream, whisking and continue to whisk until all the oil is added. Add the dressing to the beef and let it marinate for 30 minutes, tossing occasionally. Serve on a plate lined with Romaine lettuce and garnish with watercress or parsley sprigs.

Caesar Salad

Serves four

3 cloves garlic, pressed	1 egg
4 anchovies, drained	Juice of 1 lemon
½ teaspoon Worchestershire sauce	2 heads Romaine lettuce
1 teaspoon dry mustard	4 tablespoons Parmesean cheese, grated
½ cup olive oil	¼ cup croutons
2 tablespoons red wine vinegar	Salt and fresh ground pepper to taste

Rub the pressed garlic into a wooden bowl, add the anchovies, and rub them into the bowl until a paste is formed. Remove any large bits of anchovy or garlic.

Add the Worchestershire, dry mustard, and fresh ground pepper, blending ingredients into the bowl. Add any salt that is desired. Pour the oil and vinegar into the bowl and mix well. Add the egg and squeeze the lemon juice into the mixture. Mix all ingredients until they are well blended and dressing is smooth.

Add the Romaine lettuce and toss so that it is well coated. Add the Parmesean cheese and toss lightly. Add the croutons and toss again.

Serve on well chilled salad plates.

Caesar Salad — created in Tijuana, Mexico by a restaurant owner who was entertaining a hungry crowd.

Orange Watercress Salad

Serves four

1 large bunch watercress	4 tablespoons olive oil
1 head Bibb lettuce, torn into bite-size pieces	⅛ teaspoon sugar
1 seedless orange, peeled with all pith removed	Juice of ½ lemon
	¼ teaspoon fresh ground pepper

Slice orange into very thin circles. Place oil, sugar and pepper in a wooden bowl. Stir until well blended. Add lettuce, orange slices and watercress and toss well. Squeeze juice of ½ lemon over the salad and toss again. Serve on chilled plates and season with additional pepper if desired.

Cucumber Salad

Serves four

6 cucumbers, peeled and sliced ¼″ thick	½ cup red wine vinegar
1 carrot, peeled and sliced ⅛″ thick	⅓ cup superfine sugar
1 Bermuda onion, thinly sliced into rings	½ cup oil

Combine vinegar and sugar, mix well. Whisk in oil in a slow stream. Pour over vegetables and toss. Chill 30 minutes and serve.

Cucumbers—buy medium sized, smooth and firm to the touch, preferably unwaxed.

Mexican Fiesta Salad

Serves four

1 head, Iceberg lettuce, chopped	¼ cup green or red pepper strips
1 head, Romaine lettuce, chopped	¾ cup ripe pitted olives, green or black
¼ cup alfalfa sprouts	¼ cup toasted sunflower seeds
4 green onions, sliced thin	2 tablespoons sesame seeds
1 cup cooked chicken, cubed	4 eggs, hard boiled, and halved
1 cup pineapple chunks, fresh or canned	Salt and fresh ground pepper to taste
8 tomato wedges	
1 cup zucchini, thinly sliced	

Dressing:

1 cup oil	½ teaspoon salt
¼ cup hot taco sauce	4 garlic cloves, pressed
¼ cup cider vinegar	⅛ teaspoon oregano

Arrange ingredients for salad attractively on serving plates. For dressing combine ingredients with a wire whisk and chill. Pour over salad before serving.

When preparing salad greens for a salad, wash them, then *tear* into bite-sized pieces. Cutting bruises the tender leaves. Never serve *wet* lettuce; it dilutes the dressing, if not ruining it.

Avocado Dressing

Yield one cup

2 avocados peeled and pitted	2 tablespoons olive oil
¾ cup half and half	1 teaspoon salt
1 garlic clove, pressed	Dash cayenne pepper
1 tablespoon tarragon vinegar	4 drops red hot pepper sauce

Place all ingredients in a blender or food processor and process until smooth.

French Dressing

Yield: ½ cup

2 tablespoons wine vinegar	1 teaspoon black pepper
1 teaspoon salt	5 tablespoons olive oil

In a small mixing bowl, beat vinegar, salt and pepper with a fork until salt is dissolved. Add oil gradually and whisk until dressing is thickened.

Chutney

Makes one quart

2 cups sugar	1½ ounces crystallized ginger, diced
1¼ cup white vinegar	1 pound peaches, peeled and diced
¼ cup Sauterne wine	
2 ounces Brandy	1 pound pears, unpeeled and diced
2 oranges, diced with rind	
1 lemon, diced with rind	1 pound apricots, peeled and diced
1 lime, diced with rind	
1 medium onion, diced	
1 clove garlic, minced	
1 cup seedless white raisins	

Bring sugar, vinegar, wine and brandy to a boil and cook for 15 minutes. Add remaining ingredients and simmer 30 minutes longer.

Cauliflower Salad

Serves four

3 cups cauliflower florets	1 cup sliced pitted olives
½ cup olive oil	Juice of one lemon
½ teaspoon garlic powder	½ teaspoon fresh ground white pepper
1 cup mayonnaise	

Steam cauliflower florets for 5 minutes or until crisp-tender. Immediately rinse under cold water to stop the cooking process.

Blend olive oil, garlic powder, pepper, lemon juice and mayonnaise in a salad bowl. Toss cauliflower and olives in dressing and chill salad before serving.

Greek Salad

Assorted greens
Tomatoes, chilled, peeled
  and quartered
Cucumber, peeled and
  sliced
Green onions, thinly
  sliced

Anchovies
Greek Kalamata olives
Feta cheese
Olive oil
Red wine vinegar
Fresh mint or oregano

One should be more concerned with the arrangement
of the ingredients in this salad, than with the
proportions. The Greek Salad should delight the eye as
well as the taste buds.

Wash, dry and tear the greens and arrange them in a
large wooden bowl, platter or glass bowl. Cover the
salad with a row of sliced cucumber, sprinkle with
chopped onions. Place the tomato wedges around the
perimeter of the serving dish. Put the anchovies on the
top center of the salad in a criss-cross manner to form
"x"s. Use the Feta cheese and olives as a final
garnish. Serve the salad with olive oil and vinegar with
a sprinkle of fresh mint or oregano.

You can use the proportions to suit your own
personal taste. Isn't it as pretty as a picture?

Olive oil is oil from the flesh of ripe olives. Virgin
olive oil is that which is first extracted and is much
better in flavor and appearance than oil from a second
or third pressing.

Roquefort Dressing

Yield: 2 cups

¼ pound Roquefort
  cheese
1 cup sour cream
¼ cup mayonnaise
¼ cup Sherry
¼ cup red wine vinegar
1 tablespoon minced
  onion

½ teaspoon salt
2 cloves garlic, pressed
¼ teaspoon paprika
Fresh ground pepper to
  taste

Crumble cheese into a mixing bowl. Add remaining
ingredients and stir until well blended. Refrigerate until
well chilled, at least 2 hours.

Cucumber Dressing

Yield: 1½ cups

¼ cup olive oil
3 tablespoons tarragon
  vinegar
1 cup grated, peeled,
  seeded, cucumber

¼ teaspoon dry mustard
Fresh ground pepper to
  taste

Mix salt, dry mustard and fresh ground pepper to
taste with vinegar. Whisk in oil, a small amount at a
time. Add cucumber and chill for at least 2 hours.

Thousand Island Dressing

Yield: 1 pint

1 cup mayonnaise
¼ cup chili sauce
2 tablespoons sweet pickle
  relish
2 tablespoons chopped
  pitted black olives
1 tablespoons minced
  pimento

Juice of ½ lemon
¼ teaspoon Worchester-
  shire sauce
¼ teaspoon red hot
  pepper sauce

Blend all ingredients thoroughly and chill.

Green Goddess Dressing

Yield: ½ cup

1 egg	4 scallions, minced
1 tablespoon chopped parsley	2 tablespoons tarragon vinegar '
3 anchovy fillets	¼ cup oil

Place egg, parsley, anchovy, scallion and vinegar in a blender container and whip to a pureé consistency. Gradually add oil, blending until all oil has been blended, and mixture becomes thick. Continue to blend for 1 minute after oil has been added.

Viniagrette Dressing

Yield: ½ cup

1 garlic clove, pressed	1 egg
1 teaspoon kosher salt	6 tablespoons olive oil
½ teaspoon fresh ground white pepper	2 tablespoons wine vinegar
½ teaspoon dry mustard	Juice of ½ lemon

Mash garlic and salt in a wooden bowl until a paste is formed. Add mustard, pepper, egg and 2 tablespoons of olive oil and mix with a whisk. Add vinegar and lemon juice, whisking slowly. Continue to whisk in remaining olive oil, a couple drops at a time, until all has been absorbed.

Mint Leaf Dressing

Yield: 2 cups

½ cup tarragon vinegar	Fresh ground pepper to taste
Juice of ½ lemon	
1 cup salad oil	½ cup chopped fresh mint leaves
½ teaspoon salt	
⅓ cup sugar	

Combine all ingredients and mix well. Chill 1 hour. Shake well before serving.

Honey Poppy Seed Dressing

Yield: 1½ cups

1 cup honey	5 teaspoons cider vinegar
1 teaspoon dry mustard	1 teaspoon lemon juice
1 teaspoon paprika	1 teaspoon grated onion
¼ teaspoon salt	1 cup oil
2 teaspoons poppy seeds	

Blend all ingredients except oil in a mixing bowl. Gradually add oil and whisk until mixture thickens.

Seafood

Lobster Emmanuel

Serves two

1–2½ pound live lobster	1 tablespoon chopped
1 tablespoon olive oil	parsley
2 ounces cooking Sherry	⅛ teaspoon cayenne
1 cup whipping cream	pepper
2 tablespoons butter	¼ teaspoon white pepper
2 tablespoons flour	½ teaspoon salt
¼ cup peeled shrimp,	¼ onion, peeled and
chopped	minced
¼ cup Alaskan King	½ ounce Brandy
crabmeat	2 egg whites
1 clove garlic, pressed	3 egg yolks

Boil lobster for 15 minutes in salted water. Remove meat from tail and claws, leaving shell intact. Cube lobster meat and mix with crabmeat and shrimp.

Heat olive oil in a skillet over moderate heat and sauté onions and garlic until golden. Add seafood mixture and parsley; cook until seafoods are thoroughly heated and opaque. Add cream and flour and mix until a smooth paste is formed. Add butter, salt, pepper, cayenne pepper, Sherry and Brandy. Continue to cook over low heat until mixture is thickened. Strain ⅓ cup sauce into a mixing bowl.

Place lobster shell in a shallow baking pan and divide seafood mixture equally into cavities of lobster shell.

Beat egg yolks and stir into sauce in mixing bowl. Beat egg whites until stiff and fold into yolk mixture. Spread sauce over seafood in lobster cavities. Bake in a preheated 400°F oven for 15 minutes.

Lobster and Scallop Croquettes

Serves six

1 pound lobster meat,	3 hard boiled eggs, chopped
chopped fine	2 tablespoons flour
1 pound scallops, chopped	1 cup half and half
fine	⅛ teaspoon nutmeg
1 medium onion, chopped	6 tablespoons butter
2 ounces cooking Sherry	1½ tablespoons parsley
2 eggs beaten	½ cup breadcrumbs
1 teaspoon lemon juice	1 cup oil
Salt and fresh ground	
pepper to taste	

Mix lobster and scallops and set aside. Heat butter in a skillet over moderate heat and sauté onions until golden. Add flour and stir until flour is light brown. Blend in half and half and stir until mixture is thickened. Add seafood mixture salt and pepper and cook, stirring constantly for 3 minutes.

In a mixing bowl, blend Sherry, hard boiled eggs, lemon juice, nutmeg, parsley and add to fish mixture. Form into croquettes 2″×4″ each. Dip croquettes into beaten egg then roll in breadcrumbs. Heat oil over high heat and fry croquettes until golden brown. Drain on absorbent paper.

Baked Scrod with Parsley-Vermouth Sauce

Serves four

2 pounds scrod fillets	⅛ teaspoon thyme
½ teaspoon fresh ground	⅛ teaspoon paprika
pepper	¼ teaspoon prepared
1 cup butter	mustard
4 shallots, minced	½ cup grated Gruyere
1 tablespoon parsley,	cheese
minced	1 cup Dry Vermouth
	½ cup clam juice

Generously sprinkle scrod with salt and pepper. Sauté onions in ¼ cup butter over moderate heat until tender and transparent. Add parsley, thyme, mustard and remove from heat.

Spread 1 tablespoon of the onion mixture on each fillet. Sprinkle the cheese on top and roll each fillet like a jelly roll, fastening with a toothpick.

Arrange on a buttered baking dish and pour the Vermouth and clam juice over the fish and sprinkle with paprika. Bake at 350°F. for 20–25 minutes. Before serving, remove the toothpicks.

Curried Shrimp Flambé

Serves four

24 large shrimp, peeled	1 clove garlic, pressed
and deveined	2 ounces Brandy
2 tablespoons olive oil	2 tablespoons curry
2 tablespoons chopped	powder
green onions	2¼ cup heavy cream
2 tablespoons minced	2 egg yolks
carrot	Salt and fresh ground
2 tablespoons chopped	pepper to taste
celery	

Heat oil in a large frying pan over moderate heat; add chopped onion, celery, carrot and garlic and cook until vegetables are soft. Add shrimp and season with salt and pepper to taste. Sauté shrimp until golden. Pour Brandy towards the front of the pan and ignite. When flames have extinguished transfer shrimp to a heated serving platter and keep warm.

Beat yolks and heavy cream in a small mixing bowl and add to pan. Blend in curry powder and cook, stirring constantly until mixture is thickened slightly and pour sauce over shrimp.

Jambalaya

Serves four

½ pound boiled ham, diced
1 pound shrimp, peeled and deveined
½ pound cooked chicken, diced
1 medium onion, chopped
2 tablespoons butter
1–8 ounce can tomatoes
1 green pepper, chopped
1 tablespoon chopped parsley
2 cloves garlic, pressed
1 stalk celery, chopped
1 teaspoon thyme
½ tespoon saffron
2 cups cooked rice
⅛ teaspoon cayenne pepper
Salt and fresh ground pepper to taste
4 tablespoons tomato paste

Melt butter in a Dutch oven over moderate heat and sauté onion, green pepper and celery until tender. Season with cayenne pepper and salt and fresh ground pepper to taste. Add garlic, parsley, thyme, saffron, tomato paste and canned tomatoes. Simmer for 30 minutes, stirring frequently. Add ham, shrimp and chicken and cook for 10 minutes. Add rice and stir well.

Seafood Gumbo

Serves six

1½ pounds peeled and deveined shrimp
1 pound crabmeat
½ pint oysters with juice
6 tablespoons flour
8 tablespoons butter
6 cloves garlic, pressed
½ cup chopped onion
¼ cup diced green pepper
½ cup chopped celery
1 cup tomato sauce mixed with 3 quarts water
2 tablespoons chopped parsley
1 cup chopped okra
3 bay leaves
½ teaspoon thyme
½ teaspoon dill
Salt and fresh ground pepper to taste

Melt butter over moderate heat and mix in flour to form a paste. Add garlic and cook until golden brown. Add onion, pepper, celery and cook until tender. Add shrimp and tomato sauce and simmer until shrimp are tender. Add parsley, bay leaves, thyme, dill, salt and pepper, okra, crabmeat and oysters and cook 20 minutes longer. Serve gumbo over steamed rice.

Shrimp Creole

Serves four

6 tablespoons olive oil
½ cup chopped green pepper
½ cup chopped onion
½ cup chopped celery
1½ pound fresh shrimp, peeled and deveined
6 drops red hot pepper sauce
½ teaspoon Worchestershire sauce
2 tomatoes, skinned and chopped
2 cups prepared tomato sauce
¼ cup dry white wine
2 tablespoons minced parsley
Salt and fresh ground pepper to taste
2 cloves garlic, pressed

Heat olive oil and garlic in a sauté pan over moderate heat. Add onion, green pepper and celery and sauté until onions are tender. Add shrimp, red hot pepper sauce, Worchestershire and salt and pepper to taste. Cook mixture for 2 minutes longer, stirring constantly. Add tomatoes and tomato sauce. Stir in white wine and cook 5 minutes. Sprinkle with parsley before serving.

Fresh shrimp with heads removed are sold by the pound either fresh or frozen. Shrimp are graded by the number per pound:

Jumbo:	Under 25
Large:	25–30
Medium:	30–42
Small:	42 and over

Cooked shrimp with shells removed are sold by the pound; the meat is pink. Canned shrimp with shells removed are available in several sizes of cans and may be used in place of cooked shrimp.

Shrimp Flambe'

Serves two

2 tablespoons butter
2 tablespoons oil
6 shallots, minced
½ cup fresh sliced mushrooms
16 medium sized shrimp, boiled, peeled and deveined
1½ ounce dry white wine
1½ ounce Brandy
1 cup whipping cream
½ cup sour cream
1 tablespoon chopped parsley
⅛ teaspoon thyme
Salt and fresh ground pepper to taste

Melt butter with oil over moderate heat and sauté shallots until tender and transparent. Add mushrooms and wine; sauté until mushrooms are tender. Add shrimp. Pour Brandy towards the front of pan and ignite. When flames have extinguished, blend in whipping cream and sour cream. Add parsley and thyme. Season with salt and pepper to taste.

Squid Amsterdam

Serves four

2 pounds squid	1 lemon
2 cups olive oil	2 eggs, beaten
½ cup Burgundy wine	Flour for dredging
½ cup red wine vinegar	2 tablespoons chopped
1 teaspoon oregano	parsley
2 cloves garlic, pressed	

Place squid, 1 cup olive oil, vinegar, wine and oregano in a shallow pan and marinate squid for 45 minutes.

In a large skillet, heat remaining oil over high heat until it begins to smoke. Slice squid into rings and season with salt and pepper to taste. Dredge squid in flour and dip into egg. Dredge once again in flour and fry squid until golden brown. Transfer squid to a heated serving platter. Add lemon, garlic and parsley to skillet and cook until garlic is golden. Pour sauce over squid and serve.

Lobster Rena' Flambé

Serves four

2 fresh or frozen lobster tails, thawed and cut into 1½ " cubes, (about 2 pounds)	1 16-ounce can tomatoes, chopped
2 tablespoons olive oil	1 cup white wine
1 stalk celery, chopped fine	1 tablespoon chopped parsley
1 onion, finely chopped	¼ cup chopped pitted olives
½ teaspoon thyme	1½ ounces Vodka
½ teaspoon oregano	Salt and fresh ground pepper to taste
2 cloves garlic, pressed	

Heat olive oil in a saute' pan over moderate heat. Add celery, onion, thyme, oregano, garlic and salt and pepper to taste. Saute' the mixture, stirring occasionally, until lightly browned. Add tomatoes and wine. Season with salt and pepper to taste, and simmer 15 minutes, covered. Add lobster and olives, combining well with sauce. Cover pan again and simmer for 8–10 minutes. Pour Vodka towards the front of pan and ignite. Sprinkle with parsley on top and serve with white rice, when flames have extinguished.

Frog Legs Meuniere

Serves four

12 pairs medium frog legs	1½ tablespoons chopped parsley
8 tablespoons butter	½ ounce Cognac
¼ cup chopped green onions	Juice of one lemon
¼ pound sliced fresh mushrooms	Salt and fresh ground pepper to taste
1½ ounces dry white wine	

Separate frog legs and season with salt and pepper to taste. Melt butter in a skillet over moderate heat and saute' onion until tender. Add frog legs and mushrooms and saute' until frog legs are browned. Stir in white wine and Cognac. Squeeze lemon juice over frog legs and sprinkle with chopped parsley.

Shrimp Hongroise Flambé

Serves four

½ cup butter	¼ teaspoon paprika
2 tablespoons olive oil	2 ounces Sherry
1 cup chopped green onions	1½ pounds shrimp, peeled and deveined
1 pound fresh sliced mushrooms	1 cup sour cream
¼ cup chopped parsley	Fresh ground pepper to taste
½ teaspoon salt	1 ounce 151 Proof Rum

Heat butter and olive oil over moderate heat in a large sauté pan. Add green onions and sauté until tender. Add mushrooms and cook 5 minutes. Mix in parsley, Sherry, paprika, and shrimp. Cook until shrimp turns pink. Season with salt and pepper to taste. Pour 151 Rum towards the front of the pan and ignite. When flames have extinguished lower heat.

Blend in sour cream and stir until heated and serve.

Trout Marinara

Serves six

1 6½ pound whole trout, dressed	1 tablespoon tomato paste diluted with 1 cup water
1½ cup olive oil	3 bay leaves
½ cup white wine vinegar	4 teaspoons flour plus flour for dredging fish
1 lemon	Salt and fresh ground pepper to taste
2 garlic cloves, pressed	
1 teaspoon sugar	

Season trout with salt and pepper to taste. Squeeze lemon juice on fish, then dredge in flour.

Heat olive oil in a large sauté pan until it begins to smoke. Sauté trout until golden brown on both sides. Remove fish and add remaining flour to pan, stirring until blended. Add vinegar, tomato paste, garlic, sugar and bay leaves. Simmer covered for 10 minutes. Replace fish and simmer for 5 minutes longer. Transfer fish to a heated serving platter and pour sauce over fish.

Dover Sole Veronique

Serves four

4 Dover sole fillets	¼ cup whipping cream
½ cup butter	¼ cup milk
2 tablespoons flour	⅛ teaspoon cayenne pepper
2 bay leaves	1 cup seedless white
2 shallots, chopped	grapes
1 teaspoon whole	Juice of 1 lemon
peppercorns	⅔ cup dry white wine
1 carrot, peeled and	Salt and white pepper to
chopped	taste

Preheat oven to 350°F. Wash fillets and pat dry with a towel. Melt 2 tablespoons butter in a large baking casserole. Line casserole with sole and add 1 cup of water, salt and pepper to taste and bay leaves. Poach sole until tender and opaque. In a saucepan melt remaining butter over moderate heat and sprinkle flour in pan. Cook, stirring constantly until mixture turns golden. Add wine, shallots, peppercorns, cream, milk and carrot and cook 15 minutes over low heat. Strain liquid and place in a clean pan; add cayenne pepper, grapes and lemon juice. Cook, stirring constantly until grapes are heated. Place sole on serving plates and place sauce over sole.

Trout Hungarian

Serves four

4 medium sized trout,	½ teaspoon salt
dressed	¼ teaspoon fresh ground
½ cup flour	pepper
½ cup butter	Juice of 1 lemon
2 tablespoons vegetable	1 teaspoon paprika
oil	1¼ cup sour cream
3 cups fresh, sliced	1 tablespoon chopped
mushrooms	parsley

Lightly dredge fish with flour. Melt half of butter in a large skillet over moderate heat. Add fish and fry for 5 minutes on each side or until flaky and lightly browned. Transfer to a serving platter and keep warm. Add remaining butter and oil to pan and sauté mushrooms for 3 minutes. Add salt, pepper, lemon juice, paprika and sour cream. Cook, stirring constantly until all ingredients are well blended. Pour over fish and sprinkle with parsley.

Trout Fromage

Serves four

4 10-ounce boneless trout	16 asparagus spears
½ pound Roquefort	cooked al dente'
cheese, crumbled	¼ cup pitted black olives,
1 onion, chopped	chopped
1 teaspoon chopped parsley	1 cup olive oil
½ teaspoon dill weed	Salt and fresh ground
	pepper to taste

Heat ½ cup of olive oil in a skillet over moderate heat and sauté onion until tender. Season with salt and pepper. Remove skillet from heat and add parsley, dill, black olives, Roquefort cheese and blend well. Stuff each trout with 4 asparagus spears and ¼ of onion cheese mixture.

Pour remaining olive oil in a baking casserole and place stuffed trout in casserole. Cover casserole and bake in a preheated 375°F. oven for 25 minutes or until trout is flaky.

Trout with Sauce Verte

Serves four

4 trout, dressed	¼ cup olive oil
12 slices lemon, paper	4 tablespoons flour
thin	Salt and fresh ground
½ cup butter	pepper to taste

Sauce Verte

4 tablespoons olive oil	2 fillets of anchovy, mashed
Juice of one lemon	2 teaspoons capers,
2 garlic cloves, pressed	drained and chopped

Combine all ingredients for Sauce Verte and whisk together until slightly thickened. Melt butter with olive oil over high heat in a large skillet. Wash trout and blot dry with paper towels. Dust with flour and season with salt and pepper to taste. Fry trout for 10 minutes, turning over only once. Drain on paper towels, then transfer to a warmed serving platter. Top with lemon slices and Sauce Verte.

Lobster Thermidor

Serves four

4 two-pound live lobsters	4 tablespoons Sherry
6 tablespoons butter or margarine	1½ cups light cream
3 tablespoons flour	¼ cup grated Cheddar cheese
⅛ teaspoon nutmeg	Lemon wedges
Dash paprika	Parsley
1 teaspoon salt	

Grasp each lobster by body, holding the claws away from you. Then plunge it, head first, into boiling salted water, 3 tablespoons salt to 3 quarts water. Cover, let boil 12–15 minutes, then remove from the water. Cut heads, with large claws, from the tails. Remove meat in large chunks from the tails and remaining heads, 3 cups in all. (Save the shells for refilling with finished dish.)

In double-boiler top, melt the butter. Stir in flour, nutmeg, paprika, salt, Sherry, and cream; mixing well. Add lobster meat, cook over hot water, stirring, until just thickened. Arrange the empty tails on a broiler rack, then fill with the lobster mixture and sprinkle with cheese. When filling is heated through, and cheese is melted, turn oven to broil and brown the cheese lightly. Serve over rice pilaf and garnish with parsley and lemon wedges.

To remove fish odors from utensils, add 2 tablespoons baking soda to the dishwashing water.

Scallops Curry

Serves four

¼ cup butter	1 tablespoon chopped shallots
1½ pound medium scallops	2 cups Chablis wine
Bouquet garni:	1 tablespoon curry powder
1 bay leaf	½ cup whipping cream
2 sprigs parsley	Salt and fresh ground pepper to taste
½ teaspoon thyme	

Melt 4 tablespoons butter in a heavy saucepan over moderate heat, add shallots and sauté until golden. Add scallops and stir 2 minutes. Add wine, bouquet garni and curry powder. Cover pan and bring to a boil, reduce heat and simmer for 10 minutes. Transfer scallops to a warmed serving platter and keep warm. Reduce cooking liquid to ½ original amount. Remove bouquet garni, add cream and stir mixture well until completely warmed. Do not allow mixture to boil. Add salt and fresh ground pepper to taste and pour over scallops.

Fillet of Sole Montego Bay

Serves two

1 pound sole fillets	¼ teaspoon paprika
2 eggs, well beaten	¼ teaspoon curry powder
⅓ cup almonds	3 tablespoons butter
3 tablespoons grated Parmesan cheese	3 tablespoons olive oil
½ teaspoon salt	2 bananas, peeled and cut in quarters
¼ teaspoon dill weed	1 tablespoon lemon juice

Grind almonds and mix with cheese, salt, dill, paprika, and curry powder on waxed paper. Dip fish fillets in egg then dredge in almond cheese mixture. Heat butter and oil in a large skillet over moderate heat and sauté fillets until browned on both sides, turning only once. Place fish on a heated platter. Place bananas in skillet and cook for 1 minute on each side. Sprinkle with lemon juice and arrange on sole fillets.

Frog Legs Polonaise

Serves four

20 medium-sized pairs frog legs	2 tablespoons chopped pimento
1½ cups half and half	1 ounce dry cooking Sherry
½ cup flour	Juice of 1 lemon
½ cup butter	Salt and fresh ground pepper to taste
2 hard cooked eggs, peeled and riced	
2 tablespoons chopped parsley	

Season frog legs with salt and pepper to taste. Pour half and half in a shallow pan and dip frog legs in half and half and then in flour. Melt butter in a large skillet over moderate heat and add the frogs legs. Sauté them for about 12 minutes, or until they are golden on both sides. Transfer frogs legs to a heated serving platter and keep warm.

Deglaze juices in skillet with Sherry and lemon juice. Add egg, parsley and pimento and pour over frogs legs before serving.

Salmon Marquery

Serves four

4 salmon steaks, each 1½″ thick	1½ cups half and half
1½ cups white wine	12 oysters, shucked
½ cup water	6 shrimp, peeled and deveined
½ teaspoon tarragon leaves	Salt and fresh ground pepper to taste
4 tablespoons cornstarch	2 tablespoons butter
½ cup fresh sliced mushrooms	

Place salmon steaks in a large skillet and cover with wine and water. Add tarragon leaves and salt and pepper to taste. Cover skillet tightly and simmer over low heat until salmon is tender. Drain salmon and place in a greased oven-proof baking dish. Keep warm.

Meanwhile, melt butter in a sauté pan over moderate heat and stir in mushrooms. Sauté until mushrooms are tender. Stir in cornstarch and half and half. Cook, stirring constantly until mixture begins to thicken. Add oysters and shrimp and cook, stirring constantly for 5 minutes longer. Season with salt and pepper to taste. Spoon sauce over salmon, arranging 3 oysters and 1 shrimp on each salmon steak. Place baking dish under a broiler until the sauce turns golden.

Lime Baked Halibut

Serves four

4 halibut steaks 1½″ thick	1 can minced clams (7½ ounce) undrained
2 tablespoons butter	1 fresh lime, sliced thin
1 small onion, minced	½ cup Rhine wine
2 cups pitted olives, chopped	2 tablespoons chopped parsley
1 carrot, minced	Salt and fresh ground pepper to taste
1 cucumber, sliced paper thin	

Place fish in a baking casserole. Dot with butter and sprinkle with salt and pepper. Cover with onion, olives, carrot and cucumber slices. Pour minced clams over vegetables. Arrange lime slices decoratively on clams and pour wine over all ingredients. Bake in a 400° F. oven for 20 minutes, or until fish flakes with a fork. Sprinkle with parsley before serving.

Scallops Nouvelle

Serves two

1 pound sea scallops,
   rinsed and drained
½ cup chicken broth
½ cup demi-sec white
   wine
½ cup whipping cream
2 tablespoons butter

2 carrots peeled and cut in
   thin julienne strips
¼ zucchini, cut in thin
   julienne strips
1 scallion, cut in thin
   julienne strips

If scallops are large, quarter them. In a large sauté
pan, bring broth and wine to a boil over high heat.
Add scallops and cook 1½ minutes, stirring constantly
until broth is milky white and scallops are opaque.
Remove cooked scallops. Add cream to broth and boil
until liquid has the consistency of cream and is reduced
to ½ cup.

In another skillet melt butter over moderate heat and
sauté carrot and zucchini strips until they begin to
soften. Add scallion and sauté 15 seconds longer.
Remove from heat.

Stir scallops into cream sauce and then arrange on
serving plates. Sprinkle with sautéed vegetables.

French Mussels

Serves three

3 pounds mussels
½ teaspoon minced onion
½ cup dry white wine
3 teaspoons chopped
   parsley

2 tablespoons butter or
   margarine
Salt
Pepper
Cayenne pepper

Wash and scrape mussels well in cold water,
washing all sand out. Place in a large kettle. Add the
onion, wine, 1½ teaspoon parsley, and 1 tablespoon
butter. Sprinkle with salt, pepper, and cayenne. Cover,
boil until mussels open, about 10–12 minutes. Pour
off stock carefully without disturbing sediment. Boil
down stock to 2 cups. Discard half of shell to which
the meat is not attached. Arrange the remaining open
side up in deep soup dishes. To the hot stock, add 1
tablespoon butter and seasonings to taste. Pour over
mussels. Sprinkle with remaining parsley.

Oysters Newburg Flambé

Serves four

24 oysters	1½ cups whipping cream
¼ cup oyster broth	¼ teaspoon Worchester-
1 teaspoon Dijon-style	shire sauce
mustard	4 egg yolks, beaten
4 tablespoons butter	1½ ounces Sherry
2 tablespoons flour	1 ounce 151 Proof Rum
1 teaspoon salt	Fresh ground pepper to
⅛ teaspoon nutmeg	taste

Melt butter in a large sauté pan over moderate heat. Blend in flour, salt, nutmeg and pepper. Heat until mixture begins to turn golden and gradually whisk in cream and Worchestershire sauce. Blend mustard and oyster broth into sauce. Cook, stirring constantly for 2 minutes.

Vigorously stir 3 tablespoons of hot cream mixture into eggs. Place egg mixture in sauce and cook, stirring constantly until sauce thickens. Add oysters and Sherry. Cook until oysters are heated and their edges begin to curl. Pour 151 Rum towards front of pan and ignite. When flames have extinguished serve with crisp toast points.

Salmon En Croûte

Serves eight

1 6-pound whole salmon,	3 pounds fresh spinach,
skinned and filleted	chopped and blanched
1½ pounds puffed pastry	1 pound bacon, very
dough	lightly browned
1 large onion chopped	¼ pound butter
⅓ cup chopped parsley	1 cup white wine winegar
2 cloves garlic, chopped	1 cup olive oil
fine	1 cup dry red wine
½ teaspoon chopped	
tarragon leaves	

Place salmon in a pan along with garlic, oil, wine, vinegar, and salt and pepper to taste. Marinate for ½ hour.

Heat ½ of butter over moderate heat in a skillet and sauté onions and garlic until tender. Add tarragon, parsley and spinach to onions and cook for 5 minutes.

Remove fish from marinade and stuff with spinach mixture. Wrap salmon with bacon strips. Roll out puffed pastry so it is large enough to envelope salmon. Place salmon in puffed pastry sealing edges well, and place on a greased baking sheet. Bake in a preheated 375° F. oven for 1½ hours. Allow salmon to cool for 20 minutes before serving. Slice into 2-inch slices and serve. May be topped with Bearnaise sauce if desired.

Frog Legs Gourmande

Serves four

16 pairs medium-sized	½ pound chicken livers
frog legs	1 cup Brown sauce
¼ cup flour	1 tablespoon chopped
½ cup butter	parsley
¼ cup oil	½ cup Madeira Wine
3 cloves pressed garlic	Salt and fresh ground
4 shallots, chopped	pepper to taste
1 cup fresh sliced	
mushrooms	

Dredge frog legs in flour. Melt butter and oil over high heat and sauté frog legs until golden brown. Add garlic, shallots, mushrooms and chicken livers. Cook, stirring constantly until shallots are golden brown. Add Brown sauce, parsley and Madeira and simmer 20 minutes or until chicken livers and frog legs are tender. Season with salt and fresh ground pepper to taste.

Scallops Christopher

Serves four

2 tablespoons butter	2 tablespoons flour
1 large onion, minced	1½ pounds raw sea
1½ tablespoon curry	scallops
powder	4 six inch rounds puffed
½ cup half and half	pastry dough
1 tablespoon shredded	Salt and pepper to taste
coconut	

Melt butter over moderate heat in a large skillet and sauté onion until tender. Add curry powder, half and half, coconut, flour and salt and pepper to taste. Cook, stirring constantly, until mixture begins to thicken. Add scallops and cook for 5 minutes. Place ¼ of scallop mixture on the pastry sheets. Bring all ends of pastry together and twist. Place on a greased baking sheet and bake at 350° F. until dough is puffed and golden brown.

Oysters Caruso

Serves two

1 teaspoon garlic powder
2 eggs, well beaten
12 oysters, shells scrubbed
1 cup breadcrumbs
1 pound raw spinach,
  cleaned and chopped

1 cup Hollandaise sauce
Juice of 1 lemon
Oil for deep frying
Salt and fresh ground
  pepper to taste

Add salt, pepper and garlic powder to egg and mix well. Dip oysters in egg batter, then in breadcrumbs and deep fry until golden brown. Place spinach in oyster shells, and top with fried oysters. Bake 15 minutes at 375° F. uncovered. Remove from oven and turn setting to broil. Top oysters with Hollandaise sauce and squeeze lemon juice over the Hollandaise. Place under broiler for 1 minute, then serve immediately.

To open oyster shells, wash them thoroughly and rinse in cold water but do not soak. Insert a strong thin knife between shells near the thick end and run it along the back of the shell until muscle holding shells is cut. Discard flat shell, save liquor from oysters and remove any small pieces of shell from oysters. Serve oysters on the deep half of the shell.

Stuffed Lobster

Serves four

4 live 1½ pound lobsters
½ pound Alaskan King
  crabmeat
2 onions, chopped fine
2 tablespoons chopped
  parsley
1 cup chopped fresh
  mushrooms

1 tablespoon flour
¼ cup chicken broth
¼ cup Dry Sherry
½ cup dry breadcrumbs
½ cup Parmesan cheese
Salt and fresh ground
  pepper to taste
¼ cup butter

Split lobsters and remove meat, reserving shells. Cut lobster and crabmeat in small pieces. Melt 3 tablespoons of butter over moderate heat in a sauté pan and cook onions until tender and transparent. Add mushrooms and sauté 3 more minutes. Sprinkle flour over mixture and cook, stirring constantly until flour turns golden. Add Sherry and broth and cook, stirring constantly, until mixture begins to boil. Add lobster, crabmeat and parsley. Cook until lobster is opaque. Season with salt and pepper to taste.

Divide seafood mixture among lobster shells. Sprinkle with breadcrumbs and cheese and dot with remaining butter. Place on a baking sheet and lightly brown top under a preheated broiler.

Sole Oriental

Serves four

4 fillets of sole
2 tablespoons sesame oil
2 tablespoons fresh grated
  ginger-root
2 tablespoons grated
  orange rind

1 tablespoon soy sauce
1 tablespoon dry white
  wine
1 tablespoon water
2 scallions, cut in julienne
  strips

Fill a 12-inch skillet with 1-inch water and bring to a boil over high heat. Meanwhile fold sole fillets into thirds and secure with a toothpick. Add fillets to skillet, cover and simmer 10 minutes or until fish is opaque white in color. Place all other ingredients in a small saucepan, and bring to a boil. Stir sauce until well blended. Remove toothpicks from sole fillets and place on a serving platter. Spoon sauce over cooked fillets.

Shrimp with Curry Sauce

Serves four

24 peeled and deveined
  shrimp
⅓ pound butter
1 tablespoon fresh parsley
½ clove garlic, pressed
2 scallions, chopped fine

2½ tablespoons curry
  powder
½ cup chopped pecans
⅔ cup whipping cream
Salt and fresh ground
  pepper to taste

In a chafing dish or skillet, melt butter over moderate heat. Add garlic, scallions and sauté until tender. Add shrimp, pecans, curry, parsley and salt and pepper to taste. Cook shrimp for 8 minutes stirring occasionally, until shrimp are opaque. Add whipping cream and blend well. Bring mixture to slow boil and serve on toast points or on rice.

Baked Red Snapper

Serves four

One 2½ pound whole red
  snapper, dressed
2 onions, peeled and
  sliced thin
2 cloves garlic, pressed
1⅓ cup olive oil
1½ pounds ripe tomatoes,
  quartered

1 tablespoon tomato sauce
½ cup parsley,
  chopped
½ cup white wine
1 lemon
Salt and fresh ground
  pepper to taste

Wash fish and pat dry with paper towels. Season
with salt and pepper to taste and squeeze lemon juice
over fish. Preheat oven to 375°F.

Heat 1 cup of olive oil in a large skillet over
moderate heat and sauté onion and 1 clove of garlic
until golden. Add parsley to mixture. Spread remaining
garlic over fish.

Grease an oven-proof casserole with remaining oil,
and place onion mixture in bottom of casserole. Place
red snapper on top of onion mixture. Mix wine and
tomato sauce together and pour over snapper. Top with
tomatoes. Bake for 45 minutes or until tender and
flaky.

Sole Epinard

Serves four

2 pounds sole fillets
1 cup fish stock
½ cup white wine
⅛ teaspoon cayenne
  pepper
½ cup butter
¼ cup flour
3 egg yolks, well beaten

½ cup whipping cream
2 cups cooked, drained
  spinach
2 tablespoons Parmesan
  cheese
1 teaspoon chives
Salt and fresh ground
  pepper to taste

Preheat oven to 350°F. Wash sole and pat dry with
a towel. Grease a large baking casserole and line with
sole. Add 1 cup of water, salt and pepper to taste
and poach until sole is tender and opaque. In a saucepan place fish stock, wine, chives, cayenne, butter and
salt and pepper to taste and cook over moderate heat
for 5 minutes. Add flour, mixed with a little water
and stir constantly until thickened. Beat eggs and cream
together, and add to sauce. Simmer, stirring constantly,
for 5 more minutes. Place sole on serving platter and
top with spinach. Sprinkle with Parmesan cheese and
pour sauce over sole. Serve immediately.

To store fresh fish, wrap the whole fish or fillets or
steaks in moistureproof, vapor-proof material or waxed
paper. Use fish the same day if possible. Place in
freezer if fish is not to be used in two days. Fish
should *never* be refrozen after thawing.

Shrimp Manuel Flambé

Serves four

4 tablespoons butter
½ cup green onions,
  minced
1 stalk of celery, minced
1 tablespoon chopped
  chives
½ teaspoon salt
½ teaspoon white pepper

4 teaspoons Dijon-style
  mustard
½ teaspoon horseradish
Juice of ½ lemon
1½ pound boiled, peeled
  and deveined shrimp
1½ ounce Vodka

Heat the butter in a sauté pan over moderate heat;
add onions, celery and chives. Sauté until celery and
onions are tender. Add salt and pepper, mustard and
horseradish. Mix well, add shrimp and stir until shrimp
are heated through. Add Vodka and flambé. Squeeze
the lemon juice over the shrimp and serve.

Sole Parmesan

Serves four

8 fillets sole dusted with
  3 tablespoons flour
4 tablespoons grated
  Parmesan cheese
2½ tablespoons whipping
  cream

¼ cup chicken stock
½ teaspoon minced parsley
4 tablespoons butter
2 tablespoons olive oil
Salt and white pepper to
  taste

Season sole fillets with salt and pepper to taste. Melt
butter with oil over moderate heat and sauté sole fillets
until golden brown, turning only once. Sprinkle sole
fillets with grated Parmesan. Transfer fillets to a
warmed serving platter and keep warm. Whisk chicken
stock and whipping cream together and add to juices in
the pan. Cover and simmer for 5 minutes. Pour the
sauce over sole fillets and sprinkle parsley over all.

Scallops Provençale

Serves four

1 pound fresh raw sea
  scallops
5 tablespoons butter
½ cup green onion,
  minced
4 cloves garlic, pressed
1 tablespoon chives,
  chopped
1 tomato, peeled, seeded
  and chopped

½ teaspoon salt
⅛ teaspoon fresh ground
  pepper
2 tablespoons breadcrumbs
  crumbs
Juice of 1 lemon
1½ ounce Dry Cooking
  Sherry

Melt the butter in sauté pan, over moderate heat. Add onion, garlic, chives, salt and pepper. Sauté until onion is tender. Add the scallops and cook until they are opaque and white. Add tomato, lemon juice and Sherry; cook a few minutes longer sprinkle with breadcrumbs and serve.

Shrimp Stephan

Serves four

¼ pound butter
4 garlic cloves, pressed
3 tablespoons chives
8 drops Worchestershire
  sauce
16 shrimp, boiled, peeled
  and deveined

½ cup croutons
1 lemon
4 tablespoons Parmesan
  cheese
3 ounces dry white wine
Salt and fresh ground
  pepper to taste

Place butter in a chafing dish or skillet. Add chives, garlic and Worchestershire sauce. Add shrimp and cook for 4 minutes, stirring constantly. Add croutons, squeeze lemon juice onto the mixture and stir. Add the cheese and wine and stir again. Season with salt and fresh ground pepper to taste. Serve at once.

Be sure to have lots of French bread for dunking.

Champagne Sole Flambé

Serves four

1 cup Champagne	¼ cup whipping cream
6 tablespoons butter	8 sole fillets
1 bay leaf	¼ cup flour
2 tablespoons chopped parsley	1 cup shredded Swiss cheese
1 small onion, peeled and minced	1½ ounces 151 Proof Rum
¼ pound fresh sliced mushrooms	Salt and fresh ground pepper to taste

In a saucepan over moderate heat combine: Champagne, 2 tablespoons butter, bay leaf, parsley, onion and mushrooms. Bring mixture to a boil; then reduce heat and simmer uncovered until mixture is reduced by half. Remove bay leaf and whisk in whipping cream.

Season sole fillets with salt and fresh ground pepper to taste and dredge in flour. Melt remaining butter in a sauté pan over moderate heat and cook sole fillets until golden brown, turning only once. Sprinkle shredded cheese on top of sole fillets and pour 151 Rum around perimeter of pan. Ignite allowing the cheese to melt. Transfer sole fillets to a heated serving platter and top with Champagne sauce.

Sweet and Sour Fish

Serves four

4 small sea bass, ½ pound each	1 green onion, sliced thin
1 cup dry breadcrumbs	1 cup pineapple chunks, drained
6 tablespoon cornstarch	1 teaspoon grated ginger
3 egg yolks	½ cup honey
¼ cup white wine	½ teaspoon soy sauce
2 carrots sliced thin	½ cup cold water
¼ cup cocktail onions, drained	1 cup vegetable shortening
1 green pepper, seeded and cut in julienne strips	¼ cup vegetable oil
¼ cup red wine vinegar	Salt and fresh ground pepper to taste

Wash and dry fish, and season with salt and pepper to taste. Beat egg yolks with 4 tablespoons of cornstarch and wine. Dip fish into egg mixture coating well. Dredge fish in breadcrumbs.

Heat vegetable shortening over high heat and fry fish for 6 minutes on each side. Remove fish from pan and transfer to a heated platter. Keep fish warm.

Heat oil over moderate heat in a sauté pan and cook green onion, carrot and green pepper until crispy-tender. Add pineapple chunks, cocktail onions, soy sauce, honey, vinegar and ginger, mixing well. Mix remaining cornstarch with water. Add to pan and cook stirring constantly, until sauce thickens and is glazed. Pour sauce over fish and serve.

Fillet of Sole Marsala

Serves four

8 sole fillets dusted with 3 tablespoons flour	1 tablespoon minced parsley
4 tablespoons butter	Salt and white pepper to taste
2 tablespoons olive oil	4 tablespoons whipping cream
1 ounce Marsala wine	

Season sole fillets with salt and pepper to taste. Melt butter with oil over moderate heat and sauté sole fillets until golden brown, turning only once. Transfer fillets to a warmed serving platter and keep warm. Add Marsala, cream and parsley to pan in which sole was sautéed and whisk until sauce is well blended and hot. Pour sauce over sole fillets and serve.

Scampi Spumanté

Serves four

24 large scampi, peeled and deveined	½ bottle Spumanti wine
6 tablespoons butter	1½ cups whipping cream
2 tablespoons chopped onion	3 egg yolks
½ pound fresh mushrooms, sliced	1 tablespoon dill weed
	Salt and fresh ground pepper to taste

Melt 4 tablespoons butter in a large sauté pan over moderate heat. Add onion and sauté until tender. Add scampi and mushrooms; season with salt and pepper to taste and cook until scampi are opaque. Add Spumanti wine and dill. Bring mixture to a boil then reduce heat and simmer for 10 minutes.

Transfer scampi and mushrooms to be a heated serving platter with a slotted spoon. Reduce sauce remaining by ¼ and then whisk in whipping cream. Beat eggs in a small mixing bowl. Add ¼ cup cream mixture to eggs and beat vigorously. Add egg mixture to cream mixture stirring constantly until thickened.

Swirl in remaining butter bit by bit. Pour sauce over scampi. Place dish under broiler for 3 minutes until top is glazed.

Red Snapper Paul

Serves four

1 cup olive oil
⅓ cup dry white wine
Juice of 2 lemons
4–8 ounce fillets of
  snapper
½ cup butter
4 green onions, chopped
  fine
12 garlic cloves, pressed
2 tablespoons chives,
  chopped

½ cup whipping cream
1 tablespoon flour
1 tablespoon Worchester-
  shire sauce
16 shrimp, boiled, peeled,
  and deveined
½ cup grated Parmesan
  cheese
Salt and pepper to
  taste

Heat ½ cup oil in a sauté pan over moderate heat. Season the snapper with salt and pepper and sauté until done. Add the wine and lemon juice and cook 2 minutes longer. Place the snapper on a heated platter and keep warm. Add the butter and remaining oil to the pan, along with the onions, garlic, chives and sauté until the onions are tender. Add the cream mixed with flour, Worcestershire, shrimp and salt and pepper to taste, stirring constantly until the mixture is thickened and reduced to ½ the original amount. Pour the sauce over the snapper and top with Parmesan cheese.

Lobster Curry

Serves two

1 pound cubed lobster
2½ cups half and half
½ cup sour cream
1½ cups sweetened,
  packaged, shredded
  coconut
2 cups chopped green
  onion
¼ pound butter
2 cloves garlic, pressed

2 teaspoons curry powder
1½ teaspoons salt
2 teaspoons powdered
  ginger
⅛ teaspoon cayenne
2 tomatoes, peeled,
  seeded and chopped
2 tablespoons flour
2 tablespoons lemon juice
½ ounce Brandy

Combine half and half with coconut in a saucepan and bring to a boil. Remove from heat and allow to cool. Drain well, pressing half and half from coconut. Discard coconut and set half and half aside.

Melt butter in a sauté pan over moderate heat and sauté onion and garlic until tender and transparent. Add ginger, salt, cayenne, curry powder, and tomatoes. Cook, stirring constantly, until tomatoes are thoroughly heated and tender. Sprinkle in flour and stir until flour is lightly browned. Add half and half in a slow stream, stirring constantly, until mixture reaches a simmering point. Add lobster and sour cream and cook over low heat for 10 minutes. Mix lemon juice and Brandy together and stir into the lobster mixture before serving.

Octopus Burgundy

Serves four

1 pound pre-cooked
  octopus, cut in 1″ cubes
4 green onions, chopped
  fine
½ cup olive oil
2 tablespoons capers

½ cup Burgundy wine
1 teaspoon salt
¼ teaspoon white pepper
8 toast points
½ teaspoon oregano′
Juice of ½ lemon

Place olive oil and onions in a sauté pan over moderate heat and sauté onions until tender. Add capers, oregano, lemon juice and wine. Season octopus with salt and pepper and cook for 10 minutes. Serve on toast points.

Sea Bass with Egg Lemon Sauce

Serves four

4 1-pound sea bass
4 stalks celery, chopped
  coarse
1 medium onion, chopped
  fine

1 cup olive oil
2 eggs
2 lemons
Salt and pepper to taste

Heat olive oil over moderate heat in a sauté pan. Add onion and sauté until tender and transparent. Add celery and 1 cup of water. Simmer until celery is tender.

Season bass with salt and pepper to taste and add to sauté pan. Cover pan and simmer for 20 minutes.

Meanwhile, beat eggs well and add lemon juice slowly, beating continuously. Remove ¼ cup of stock from sauté pan and gradually whisk into eggs.

Transfer bass to heated serving platter and immediately whisk egg mixture into remaining stock in pan. Pour egg lemon sauce over sea bass.

Scallops Nectarine

Serves two

8 ounces raw sea scallops
1 tablespoon flour
1 tablespoon oil
6 thin nectarine wedges
¼ cup butter
Juice of ½ lemon

1 ounce dry white wine
1 garlic clove, pressed
1 tablespoon minced
   parsley
Salt and pepper to taste

Season scallops with salt and pepper and dredge with flour. Heat oil over high heat in a sauté pan and sauté scallops until golden brown. Do not overcook or scallops will become tough. Place scallops attractively on a serving plate. Add nectarine wedges to pan and sauté until thoroughly heated. Place decoratively on scallops. Melt butter in a clean pan, add lemon juice, wine, garlic and parsley. When all ingredients are heated thoroughly, pour over scallops and nectarines. Serve immediately.

Scampi Caruso

Serves four

20 large scampi, shelled
   with tail on
4 garlic cloves, pressed
2 tablespoons fresh
   chopped parsley
2 tablespoons olive oil
6 tablespoons butter

½ cup dry white wine
½ cup breadcrumbs
¼ cup grated Parmesan
   cheese
Juice of 1 lemon
Salt and fresh ground
   pepper to taste

Season scampi with salt and pepper to taste. Melt butter with olive oil over moderate heat and sauté garlic until golden. Add scampi to pan and cook until tender and opaque. Transfer scampi to individual oven-proof casseroles. Add white wine, lemon juice and parsley to pan and cook until reduced by ⅓ amount. Pour sauce over scampi. Sprinkle scampi with bread-crumbs and Parmesan cheese. Place casseroles until preheated broiler until breadcrumbs turn golden brown.

Chicken & Game

Rock Cornish Hens Flambé with Stuffing

Serves four

4 tart baking apples, peeled and sliced and cored
4 Rock cornish hens
½ cup butter
4 tablespoons shallots, chopped fine
1 tablespoon chopped parsley
¼ teaspoon thyme
2 ounces white wine
2 ounces Applejack
Salt and pepper to taste

Place apples in cavities of cornish hens. Truss birds loosely and season with salt and pepper to taste. In a skillet melt butter over moderate heat and sauté shallots until tender; add parsley, thyme and white wine. Place hens in a greased, baking casserole and pour shallot mixture over the hens. Bake in a preheated 350° F. oven for 40 minutes.

Arrange hens on a heated platter and warm. Pour Applejack over hens and ignite. Serve hens flaming.

Chicken Tamara

Serves six

6 boneless breasts of chicken
½ teaspoon salt
3 tablespoons unsalted butter
3 tablespoons vegetable oil
5 garlic cloves, pressed
1 cup tomato pureé
½ cup tarragon vinegar
½ cup dry red wine
1 bunch parsley, minced
½ teaspoon fresh ground pepper

Rinse chicken, pat dry with paper towels and sprinkle with ½ teaspoon salt. Heat butter and oil over moderate heat in a large sauté pan. Add garlic and cook chicken until lightly browned on both sides. Remove chicken and place on a heated platter. Pour out all but 1 tablespoon drippings from the sauté pan. Stir in tomato pureé, vinegar and wine. Boil rapidly until reduced to 1 cup liquid. Add parsley, pepper, and stir. Add chicken and simmer covered for 20 minutes or until chicken is tender.

Chicken Antonio

Serves four

1 chicken cut in pieces
4 tablespoons olive oil
2 cloves garlic, pressed
1 tablespoon minced shallots
8 ounces white wine
2 teaspoons marjoram
24 shrimp, peeled and deveined
Juice of ½ lemon
1 teaspoon cornstarch mixed with 2 tablespoons water
Salt and pepper to taste

Season chicken with salt and pepper. In a large skillet heat oil over moderate heat. Add chicken and cook until each piece is browned. Transfer chicken to a heated platter and set aside. Add garlic, shallots and marjoram. Pour in wine and bring to a boil. Reduce heat to low and return chicken to skillet. Cover skillet and simmer for 45 minutes or until chicken is tender. Add shrimp and cook 5 minutes longer. r.

Transfer chicken to a heated serving platter and arrange shrimp around chicken.

Bring liquid in skillet to a boil. Squeeze juice of lemon into skillet and stir in cornstarch mixture. Cook, stirring constantly until sauce thickens. Pour sauce over chicken and serve.

Chicken Créole

Serves four

2 chickens (2½ pounds) disjointed
Salt and white pepper to taste
1 cup olive oil
2 tablespoons butter
2 green peppers sliced julienne
2 onions, sliced
3 cups chopped skinned, seeded tomatoes
¼ teaspoon dried thyme
2 bay leaves
4 cloves minced garlic
2 tablespoons minced parsley
1 teaspoon paprika
⅛ teaspoon cayenne

Melt butter over moderate heat in a Dutch oven or large saucepan and sauté onions and green pepper until tender. Add all ingredients except chicken and olive oil and blend well.

In a large skillet heat olive oil over moderate heat. Season chicken with salt and pepper and brown in olive oil. Transfer chicken to Creole sauce and simmer until tender.

Sesame Chicken with Sauce Exotica

Serves four

2 cups flour	½ teaspoon sugar
12 ounces beer	1 teaspoon sesame oil
1 teaspoon salt	1 teaspoon cooking Sherry
1 tablespoon soy sauce	4 chicken breasts,
4 tablespoons sesame	deboned and skinned
seed, toasted	Oil for deep frying

Combine all ingredients, except chicken and oil in a mixing bowl. Beat the ingredients until smooth and creamy. Allow mixture to set for ½ hour. Heat 2 inches oil in a large skillet and dip chicken into batter and fry in oil until golden brown on both sides. Drain on paper towels. Serve with sauce below.

Sauce Exotica

¼ cup soy sauce	1 teaspoon lemon juice
2 tablespoons honey	1 teaspoon cornstarch
2 tablespoons cooking Sherry	Salt and white pepper to taste.
1-8 ounce can crushed pineapple	

Combine above ingredients in a saucepan over moderate heat and simmer for 10 minutes, stirring occasionally.

Apricot Chicken Flambé

Serves four

4 chicken breasts, boned	¼ cup honey
½ cup flour	1 tablespoon butter
¼ cup cooking oil	2 ounces Apricot Brandy
8 slices cooked ham	Salt and fresh ground
20 apricot halves	pepper to taste
½ cup apricot juice	

Season chicken breasts with salt and pepper and dredge with flour. Heat oil in a large heavy skillet over moderate heat and sauté chicken turning frequently, until cooked through. Warm ham and place in a warmed serving platter. Lay the chicken breasts on top of the ham. In the same pan heat apricots, honey and apricot juice. Swirl in butter and pour sauce over chicken. Heat Brandy and pour over chicken. Ignite and serve when flames have extinguished.

Chicken Kiev

Serves four

½ cup butter, room temperature	8 chicken breasts, skinned, boned and pounded ½ " thick
Grated rind and juice of one lemon	½ cup all-purpose flour
1 tablespoon chopped parsley	2 eggs, well beaten
1 tablespoon chopped chives	1 cup dry breadcrumbs
2 garlic cloves, pressed	Salt and fresh ground pepper to taste
Vegetable oil for deep frying	8 wooden tooth picks

Beat butter, lemon rind and juice, parsley, chives, garlic, salt and pepper together and shape into 8 cylinders. Freeze for 40 minutes.

Place a butter cylinder on the small end of each chicken breast and roll from the smallest end to the largest. Secure with wooden toothpicks. Mix flour with salt and pepper to taste and coat chicken rolls. Dip rolls in beaten eggs, then in breadcrumbs. Half fill a deep fat fryer with oil and heat until it is 375° F. Grasp chicken rolls with tongs and lower into oil. Fry for 10 minutes or until crisp and golden brown. Drain on absorbent paper towels. Serve hot.

Chicken Tarragon

Serves four

4 chicken breasts, boned and skinned	¼ cup dry white wine
½ cup all-purpose flour	¼ teaspoon tarragon leaves
¼ cup butter	¼ cup chicken broth
2 tablespoons chopped shallots	¼ cup whipping cream
1 teaspoon Worchestershire sauce	Salt and fresh ground pepper to taste

Season chicken breasts with salt and pepper and dredge in flour. Heat butter over moderate heat in a large skillet and brown chicken on both sides. Transfer chicken to a heated platter. Add shallots and Worchestershire to skillet and sauté shallots until tender. Add wine and cook uncovered for 10 minutes. Sprinkle one tablespoon flour over skillet and stir until well blended. Sprinkle with tarragon and add chicken broth. Return chicken to skillet and simmer covered for 25 minutes. Place chicken on a serving platter and add cream to sauce in pan. Whisk until well blended and pour over chicken.

Chicken with Green Peppercorn Sauce

Serves four

4 boneless breasts of chicken cut in 2″ strips	1½ cups fresh sliced mushrooms
1 cup flour	1 green pepper, seeded and cut in julienne strips
1 teaspoon paprika	
½ teaspoon salt	1 tablespoon green peppercorns, slightly crushed
½ teaspoon fresh ground white pepper	
6 tablespoons butter	½ cup whipping cream
3 tablespoons olive oil	1 tablespoon chopped parsley

Mix flour, paprika, salt and white pepper together and dredge chicken in flour mixture. Melt butter over moderate heat in a large skillet and cook chicken until golden brown and opaque. Place cooked chicken on a heated serving platter and keep warm.

Add oil to skillet and sauté green pepper and garlic until tender. Add mushrooms and sauté until tender. Add green peppercorns and whipping cream. Bring mixture to a simmer and cook 5 minutes, stirring constantly. Pour sauce over chicken; sprinkle with parsley and serve.

Chicken Marsala

Serves four

4 chicken breasts, deboned and skinned	½ cup whipping cream
	2 tablespoons minced parsley
5 tablespoons butter	
⅓ cup Marsala wine	Salt and fresh ground pepper to taste
½ cup chicken broth	
¼ cup flour	¼ cup fresh sliced mushrooms

Butterfly the chicken breasts by slitting the chicken horizontally without cutting all the way through and flatten them. Season chicken with salt and pepper and dust with flour. Place chicken between two pieces of wax paper and pound with a mallet until ⅜-inch thick.

In a large skillet, melt butter over moderate heat and cook chicken until lightly browned. Transfer chicken to a heated serving platter. Add Marsala wine to the skillet and stir, scraping. Add the mushrooms, broth, whipping cream, salt and pepper to taste and cook mixture until thickened. Pour the sauce over the chicken and sprinkle with parsley.

Almond Chicken Flambé

Serves four

4 chicken breasts	½ cup cubed ham
6 tablespoons oil	1½ ounce Vodka
1 medium onion minced	¼ cup chicken broth
1 clove garlic, pressed	¾ cup ground almonds
1½ ounce Creme de Almond liqueur	Juice of one lemon
	Salt and pepper to taste

Heat oil in a skillet over moderate heat. Season chicken with salt and pepper to taste and cook until browned. Add onion, garlic and ham and cook until onion is transparent. Pour Vodka towards the front of the pan and ignite. Add Creme de Almond and chicken broth. Squeeze lemon juice over chicken breasts then spread ground almonds over breasts. Cook until breasts are tender.

Cornish Hens in Wine Sauce

Serves six

6 cornish hens	2 medium onions, peeled and minced
3 tablespoons butter	
2 tablespoons vegetable oil	2 cloves garlic pressed
	2 bay leaves
⅓ cup seedless white raisins	6 whole black peppercorns
	2 cups white wine
4 tablespoons pine nuts	½ cup whipping cream
3 cups breadcrumbs	Salt and pepper to taste

Clean hens and pat dry with paper towels. Sprinkle inside and out with salt and pepper. Heat oil over moderate heat in a saute pan; add onions and sauté until tender and transparent. Add raisins, pine nuts and breadcrumbs. Toss until well blended. Place inside hens and truss hens.

Melt butter over moderate heat in a Dutch oven and brown hens lightly on all sides. Add remaining ingredients, except cream; cover and simmer for 30 minutes or until hens are tender. Transfer hens to a warmed serving platter. Remove bay leaves. Whisk in whipping cream and pour sauce over hens.

Chicken Moutard Flambé

Serves four

4 boned chicken breasts	⅛ teaspoon paprika
3 tablespoons butter	¼ teaspoon oregano
2 tablespoons cooking oil	Curry powder to taste
2 teaspoons Dijon-style mustard	1½ ounce Whiskey or Cognac
2 ounces dry white wine	2 tablespoons semi-whipped cream
¼ cup chicken broth	
⅛ teaspoon black pepper	

Fry the chicken in the oil until done and keep warm. Melt the butter in a sauté pan or chafing dish over a moderate flame. Add the mustard, white wine, and chicken broth; stir well and simmer for 5 minutes. Add the seasoning and when the sauce begins to thicken, blend in the cream and stir well. Replace the chicken breasts in the pan, pour in the liquor and ignite. Serve immediately.

Chicken Applejack Flambé

Serves four

2 pound chicken, cut in serving pieces	1 tablespoon chopped parsley
½ cup vegetable oil	¼ teaspoon thyme
½ cup Applejack	½ cup white wine
½ cup chopped, peeled and cored apple	½ cup whipping cream
½ cup onion finely chopped	Salt and fresh ground pepper to taste

Season chicken with salt and pepper. Heat oil in a large sauté pan over moderate heat. Saute chicken until completely cooked and browned on both sides. Meanwhile warm the Applejack and add it to the chicken. Ignite and shake the pan until the flame has extinguished. Transfer chicken to a warmed serving platter. Sauté apples and onion in remaining oil in the same pan until tender; add parsley, thyme and white wine. Blend ingredients and add cream. Cook, stirring constantly with a wire whisk, until cream is heated. Do not allow the sauce to boil. Pour sauce over chicken before serving.

Chicken Molé

Serves four

⅓ cup all-purpose flour	3 tablespoons vegetable oil
3 tablespoons chili powder	1 cup chopped onion
2 teaspoons salt	3 cloves garlic, minced
½ teaspoon fresh ground pepper	¼ cup water
3 pounds fryer chicken pieces	1 cup chopped peanuts
	2 tablespoons sesame seeds

Molé Sauce

1 10-ounce can tomatoes	6 ounces semisweet chocolate, melted
2 green chilies, minced	1 cup chicken stock
1 cup tomato pureé	

In a large mixing bowl, combine flour, one tablespoon chili powder, salt and pepper. Add chicken a couple pieces at a time and dredge well. Heat oil in a large skillet over moderate heat and brown chicken on all sides until lightly browned and opaque. Transfer chicken to a heated serving platter lined with paper towels. In the same skillet, sauté onions and garlic until tender and transparent. Return chicken to skillet and add the water. Simmer, covered for 30 minutes.

Meanwhile in a small saucepan over low heat, combine tomatoes, chilies, tomato pureé, chocolate and remaining chili powder. Stir in chicken stock. Cook over low heat, stirring constantly until all ingredients are thoroughly heated and well blended.

Place cooked chicken on a serving platter, and top with Molé sauce. Garnish with chopped peanuts and sesame seeds and serve.

Chicken Caruso

Serves four

3 chicken breasts, deboned, skinned and cut into thin strips	12 black olives, cut in halves
2 cloves garlic, pressed	¼ cup dry red wine
4 tablespoons butter	¼ cup cooking rice, cooked and warmed
1 cup spaghetti sauce	Salt and fresh ground pepper to taste
¼ teaspoon oregano	
1 cup sliced celery	

Season the chicken with salt and pepper, and sauté in butter along with garlic, 3 minutes over moderate heat. Stir in spaghetti sauce and oregano; cover and simmer for 10 minutes. Add celery, olives and wine and cook until celery is tender. Serve over white rice. Sprinkle with Parmesan cheese if desired.

Chicken Manaté Flambé

Serves two

1 ripe pineapple
3 tablespoons butter
2 tablespoons brown sugar
¼ cup green pepper,
  julienne sliced
¼ cup minced onions
12 maraschino cherries

½ cup cubed cooked
  chicken meat
1½ ounces 151 Proof
  Rum
1½ ounces Anisette
  liqueur
¼ cup pineapple juice

Cut pineapple in half lengthwise leaving leaves on. Scoop out the middle discarding the tough pulp; cut pineapple into 1-inch cubes. Melt butter in a sauté pan over moderate heat and sauté green pepper and onion until tender. Add cherries, brown sugar, pineapple, chicken and pineapple juice. Stir until all ingredients are heated thoroughly. Pour 151 Rum towards the front of pan and ignite. Add Anisette. Spoon pineapple mixture into carved pineapple halves and serve.

Coq Au Vin

Serves four

6 slices bacon
3½ pound fryer, cut in
  serving pieces
16 small pearl onions
1½ cup fresh sliced
  mushrooms
4 potatoes, quartered
2 cups dry red wine
2 cloves garlic, pressed
⅛ teaspoon fresh ground
  pepper

Bouuet garni (in cheese
  cloth): 2 sprigs of
  parsley, 1 bay leaf, ¼
  teaspoon dried thyme
  leaves
⅓ cup water
2 tablespoons flour
Parsley for garnish
1 teaspoon salt

Fry bacon in a large skillet over moderate heat until crisp. Remove bacon and drain on paper towels. Brown chicken in hot bacon fat, about 10 minutes on each side. Remove chicken from pan and set aside. Cook onions and mushrooms in remaining bacon fat until tender. Return chicken to skillet, crumble bacon over chicken. Add potatoes, wine, garlic, salt and pepper and bouquet garni. Heat mixture to boiling then reduce to a covered simmer for 1 hour. Remove bouquet garni and discard. Remove chicken and vegetables to a warm serving platter and keep warm.

To prepare sauce: Skim off excess fat. Mix water and flour in a cup. Stir flour mixture slowly into liquid. Stir constantly until slightly thickened. Pour sauce over chicken and garnish with parsley.

Breast of Chicken in Puffed Pastry Flambé

Serves four

4 chicken breasts, deboned and skin removed	½ cup pineapple juice
2 tablespoons oil	½ cup brown sugar
4 canned pineapple rings, drained	¼ teaspoon cinnamon
2 sheets puffed pastry dough, 5"×5"	4 peach halves
2 tablespoons butter	1 ounce Grand Marnier
	1 ounce 151 Proof Rum
	Salt and pepper to taste

Season the chicken with salt and pepper. Heat oil over moderate heat in a sauté pan and cook the chicken breasts until lightly browned. Remove the chicken from the pan and allow it to cool. Top each breast with a pineapple ring and envelope with puffed dough. Place on a greased baking pan in a preheated 375° F. oven for 8–10 minutes or until the dough is puffy and lightly browned.

Meanwhile place butter, pineapple juice, brown sugar, and cinnamon in a heavy sauce pan over moderate heat, stirring constantly, until the sauce is hot and slightly thickened. Add the peaches and cook until heated thoroughly.

When ready to serve, place the chicken in puffed dough on serving plates, topping each with a peach half. Pour 151 Rum and Grand Marnier in the sauce and ignite. Pour the flaming sauce over the chicken and serve.

Chicken Cacciatore

Serves four

1 medium-sized roasting chicken, disjointed	1 large onion, chopped fine
6 tablespoons flour	1 teaspoon sugar
¼ cup butter	¾ cup chicken stock
1 tablespoon olive oil	2½ cups sliced fresh mushrooms
2 cloves garlic, pressed	1½ ounces Marsala wine
8 medium tomatoes, skinned and chopped	Salt and fresh ground pepper to taste
3 tablespoons tomato paste	

Coat chicken pieces with flour and season with salt and pepper to taste. Heat butter and oil in a large pan over high heat. Place chicken pieces in pan and fry until crisp and golden brown. Transfer to a heated platter. Add garlic and onion to pan and sauté until transparent. Stir in tomato paste, sugar, chicken stock and tomatoes. Season with salt and pepper to taste. Bring mixture to a boil and replace chicken. Cover pan and simmer for 30 minutes. Add mushrooms and Marsala wine and simmer 20 minutes longer. Serve with pasta cooked al dente.

Chicken Bonne Femme

Serves four

½ pound bacon, cut in julienne strips	¾ cup butter
2 large potatoes, peeled and cut in ⅛" slices	1 cup chopped onion
2 chickens, 1½ pounds each, disjointed	2 cloves garlic, pressed
	Salt and fresh ground pepper to taste

Heat skillet over moderate heat and sauté bacon until crisp. Remove bacon and set it aside. Sauté potatoes in bacon drippings until done.

Season chicken with salt and pepper to taste. Melt butter in a separate skillet over moderate heat and sauté chicken until golden brown and tender. Add onions and garlic, cook until transparent. Combine bacon, potatoes and chicken and cook for 10 minutes longer.

Chicken Wellington

Serves two

2 ounces boneless breast of chicken	2 ounces thin sliced ham
2 squares puffed pastry dough, 5"×5" each	2 slices Mozzarella cheese ¼" thick
	Salt and fresh ground pepper to taste

Season chicken with salt and pepper to taste and enclose in foil. Bake at 350° F. until tender. Place the baked breast of chicken in the middle of the puffed pastry dough and top with a slice of ham and Mozzarella cheese. Pull the edges of the puffed pastry to the top and twist to form a decorative top-knot. Make sure all edges are sealed to insure moistness. Bake at 350° F. for 10 minutes or until puffed and golden brown.

Chicken Papaya Flambé

Serves eight

8 chicken breasts or 2
  fryers, cut up
½ teaspoon salt
¼ teaspoon white pepper
¼ cup flour
¼ cup vegetable oil
½ cup minced celery
¼ cup minced onions
2 apples, peeled, cored
  and diced
½ cup white raisins

1½ tablespoons curry
  powder
½ cup flaked coconut
½ cup pineapple chunks,
  drained
2 tablespoons Worchester-
  shire sauce
½ cup whipping cream
2 ounces Sauterne wine
1 banana, sliced
2 papayas, sliced
1½ ounces Jamaican Rum

Season chicken with salt and pepper and dredge in
flour. Heat oil over moderate heat in a large skillet and
fry chicken until browned on both sides. Drain chicken
on paper towels.

In remaining drippings in skillet, saute celery and
onion until tender. Add apples, raisins, curry powder,
coconut, pineapple, Worchestershire and Sauterne and
cook for 4 minutes. Add ½ cup water and return
chicken to skillet. Cover, reduce heat and simmer for
45 minutes stirring occasionally.

Stir in whipping cream and arrange banana and
papaya slices on chicken. Meanwhile heat Jamaican
Rum in a small saucepan. Ignite Rum and pour over
chicken and fruit before serving.

Chicken Chausseur

Serves four

4 boneless breasts of
  chicken
4 tablespoons butter
¼ cup shallots, minced
2 tomatoes; peeled,
  seeded and chopped
1 clove garlic, pressed
½ cup fresh sliced
  mushrooms

½ teaspoon basil
⅓ cup dry white wine
½ cup Brown sauce
1 tablespoon minced
  parsley
Salt and fresh ground
  pepper to taste

Season chicken with salt and pepper to taste. Melt
butter over moderate heat in a sauté pan and cook
chicken until golden brown and opaque. Transfer
chicken to a heated serving platter and keep warm.
Add shallots to pan and sauté until tender and
transparent. Add tomatoes, garlic, mushrooms and
basil. Cover pan and simmer for 5 minutes. Add
wine and Brown sauce. Cook uncovered over high heat
for 5 minutes, stirring constantly. Pour sauce over
chicken; sprinkle with parsley and serve.

Squabs with Grape Stuffing

Serves four

4 plump squabs
1½ pound red grapes
½ cup dry breadcrumbs
1 tablespoon Brandy

⅔ cup Port wine
½ teaspoon flour mixed
  with 1 tablespoon butter
Salt and pepper to taste

Clean squabs and season with salt and pepper. Peel
and seed grapes. Mix ½ of the grapes with the breadcrumbs, Brandy, and salt and pepper to taste. Divide
mixture and stuff cavities of birds. Arrange squabs in a
greased baking casserole. Mix ¼ cup water with Port
and remaining grapes; add to the pan. Bake in a
preheated 425°F. oven for 30 minutes, basting
frequently. Remove squabs on a heated serving platter
and add flour mixture to remaining juices in pan. Bring
mixture to a boil stirring constantly. When sauce has
thickened, pour over squabs. Flame squabs with
additional heated Brandy if desired.

Breast of Turkey Flambé

Serves four

2 small turkey breasts,
  boned and skinned
Flour
2 eggs beaten
2 cups fresh breadcrumbs
½ teaspoon marjoram

3 tablespoons butter
3 tablespoons oil
1½ ounces Brandy
Salt and fresh ground
  pepper to taste

Season turkey breasts lightly with salt, pepper and
marjoram; dust with flour, dip in beaten egg and roll in
breadcrumbs. Heat butter and oil in a fry pan over
moderate heat and cook turkey breasts until golden
brown and springy to the touch. Pour Brandy towards
the front of the pan and ignite. Serve when flames
have extinguished.

Roast Pheasant Flambé

Serves four

2 young pheasants, 2½ pounds each	¼ cup all-purpose flour
4 bacon slices	4 tablespoons whipping cream
¼ cup butter	1½ ounce Cognac
1¼ cup Burgundy wine	Salt and fresh ground pepper to taste
1 bouquet garni	

Rub pheasants with salt and pepper. Tie bacon slices over the breasts. Melt 2 tablespoons butter in an oven-proof Dutch oven. Add pheasants and brown on all 4 sides. Pour in wine and bring to a boil. Add bouquet garni, cover and place in a preheated 400°F. oven. Roast for 1 hour or until pheasants are tender.

Transfer pheasants to a warm serving platter and keep hot. Discard the bouquet garni and skim off surface fat. Reserve fat.

Melt remaining butter in a saucepan over moderate heat. Add flour and cook, stirring until lightly browned. Stir in remaining juices a small amount at a time and bring mixture to a boil, stirring constantly. Simmer until thickened and smooth. Lower heat. Whisk in cream and salt and pepper to taste. Heat sauce, flame with Cognac. When flames have extinguished, serve sauce over pheasants.

Roast Pheasant with Chestnut Stuffing

Serves two

1 four-pound pheasant	¼ cup white raisins
1 teaspoon salt	12 slices day-old bread, cubed
½ teaspoon white pepper	½ teaspoon tarragon
3 tablespoons butter	¼ teaspoon sugar
2 onions, chopped fine	⅛ teaspoon cinnamon
2 cups roasted, shelled chestnuts	1 cup Champagne
	¼ pound chicken livers

Wash and dry pheasant. Season inside and out with salt and pepper. Melt butter in a skillet over moderate heat and sauté onion and chicken livers until golden brown. Add chestnuts, raisins, bread cubes, tarragon, sugar and cinnamon and saute for 5 minutes longer Place ingredients inside pheasant—truss pheasant and place in a roasting pan. Pour champagne over pheasant. Preheat over to 350°F. and roast pheasant for 2 hours basting frequently. Remove from oven and allow to cool for 5 minutes before carving.

Rock Cornish Hens Cherise Flambé

Serves four

4 Rock cornish hens	½ cup Kirsch
1 cup butter, melted	1½ ounces Cognac
2 cups pitted black cherries	⅓ cup brown sugar
	Salt and pepper to taste

Clean cornish hens and season with salt and pepper inside and out. Place ½ cup of the melted butter in the bottom of a roasting pan and arrange hens in pan. Pour remaining butter on hens and bake at 350°F. for 30 minutes. Meanwhile place cherries, Kirsch and brown sugar in a saucepan and bring to a boil.

Arrange hens on a serving platter and pour cherry mixture into the juice in which the hens were baked. Bring to a boil and pour over hens. Heat Cognac and pour over hens. Ignite and serve flaming hens.

Chicken Breasts Tarragon Flambé

Serves four

4 chicken breasts, boned and slightly flattened	2 green onions chopped
4 tablespoons butter	1½ ounces white wine
1 clove garlic, pressed	1½ ounces Brandy
½ pound fresh sliced mushrooms	1 cup whipping cream
1½ tablespoons finely chopped tarragon leaves	½ teaspoon Dijon-style mustard
	Salt and fresh pepper to taste

Season chicken with salt and pepper to taste. Melt butter over moderate heat in a skillet and cook chicken until tender and browned. Pour Brandy towards front of skillet and ignite. When flames have extinguished transfer chicken to a heated serving platter and keep warm.

Add mushrooms, green onion and tarragon garlic and sauté until tender. Add cream and white wine with a whisk. Blend in Dijon mustard and cook, stirring occasionally until mixture is reduced by one-fourth. Pour sauce over chicken and serve.

Lapin en Vin Blanc

Serves six

1-5 pound rabbit, disjoined	Juice of one lemon
2 cups flour seasoned with salt and fresh ground pepper to taste	2½ cups fresh sliced mushrooms
¼ cup butter	1½ cup dry white wine
2 tablespoons olive oil	¾ cup chicken stock
1 garlic clove, pressed	½ teaspoon dried rosemary
1 medium onion, minced	⅛ teaspoon thyme
2 carrots, grated	Salt and fresh ground pepper to taste
2 slices bacon	

Dredge rabbit with seasoned flour. Melt butter with olive oil over high heat in a large pan. Add rabbit and fry until golden brown on all sides. Transfer to a plate. Add onion, garlic, carrots, and bacon and sauté over low heat until onions are transparent. Add lemon juice, mushrooms, wine, chicken stock, rosemary, thyme, and salt and pepper to taste. Bring mixture to a boil, add rabbit, cover pan and simmer for 45 minutes or until rabbit is tender.

Braised Venison Steaks

Serves four

4 venison steaks, 8 ounces each	1 teaspoon caraway seeds
½ cup Burgundy wine	1 tablespoon horseradish
2 tablespoons sugar	2 cloves garlic, pressed
1 teaspoon Dijon-style mustard	1 cup sauerkraut
½ cup olive oil	⅔ cup sour cream
2 onions peeled and sliced thin	2 teaspoons paprika
	Salt and fresh ground pepper to taste
	2 tablespoons chopped green pepper

In a shallow mixing bowl mix: ¼ cup olive oil, mustard, wine, sugar and horseradish. Rub venison steaks with garlic and season with salt and pepper. Marinate steaks for ½ hour.

Heat remaining oil over moderate heat in a skillet and cook venison until browned. Add onion and green pepper and sauté until tender. Add sauerkraut and caraway seeds and sauté 3 minutes longer. Blend in in sour cream and paprika and cover skillet. Simmer for 30 minutes.

Venison Rolls Flambé

Serves four

8 thin slices venison steak	2 teaspoons paprika
1½ ounces Madeira wine	2 tablespoons olive oil
8 slices proscuitto	Salt and fresh ground pepper to taste
5 tablespoons apricot jam	1½ ounces Cognac
2 teaspoons Dijon-style mustard	

Pound venison steaks to ⅜-inch thick and marinate in Madeira for 15 minutes. Season with salt and pepper to taste. Place a slice of proscuitto on each piece of venison, roll up and secure with a wooden toothpick. Place venison rolls on a broiler pan and brush with oil. Broil until browned on all sides. Transfer to serving platter.

Meanwhile in a saucepan over moderate heat, blend apricot jam with paprika, mustard, and remaining marinade. Simmer until slightly thickened and place in sauce boat. Sprinkle Cognac over venison rolls and ignite. Serve with sauce.

Duck Baggarrate

Serves four

1-5 pound duck	½ cup red wine
Grated rind of four oranges	1½ ounce Grand Marnier
1 tablespoon butter	1 cup brown sauce
1 medium onion, minced	2 teaspoons salt
Juice of two oranges	½ teaspoon white pepper
	1 orange sliced thin

Preheat oven to 375 °F. Wash and dry duck. Season inside and out with salt and pepper. Place duck in roasting pan and bake for 2½ hours. While duck is roasting, boil orange rind for 20 minutes. Drain water and place orange rind aside. Melt butter in a skillet and sauté onion until lightly browned. Add wine and simmer uncovered for 15 minutes. Add remaining ingredients, except sliced orange, and simmer for 15 minutes longer. Remove duck from oven and quarter. Pour sauce over duck and decorate with orange slices.

Beef

Tournedos with Crabmeat and Mushrooms Flambé

Serves four

5 tablespoons butter	½ pound Alaskan crabmeat
¼ cup chopped onions	4 tournedos of beef
1 tablespoon chives	1½ ounce Burgundy wine
3 cloves garlic, pressed	1½ ounce 151 Proof Rum
Salt and fresh ground pepper to taste	½ cup sliced fresh mushrooms
1 teaspoon Worchestershire sauce	

Heat butter in a sauté pan over moderate heat and add onions, chives, garlic, Worchestershire, mushrooms and salt and pepper to taste. When onion is tender and transparent, push the mixture to the side of the pan and add beef. Cook for about 3–4 minutes on each side. While steaks are cooking, add crabmeat and wine to pan and heat thoroughly. Place even amounts of mushroom mixture on steaks and top with crabmeat. Pour 151 Rum towards the front of the pan and ignite. When the flames have extinguished, transfer to dinner plates. Garnish with Bordelaise or Bearnaise sauce if desired.

Tournedos Espagnole

Serves four

4 tournedos, 1½″ thick, 6 ounces each	⅓ cup minced shallots
2 tablespoons freshly ground pepper	2 cups dry white wine
	⅓ cup Espagnole sauce
5 tablespoons clarified butter	1 teaspoon minced parsley
	1 tablespoon lemon juice
4 toast rounds, same size as beef	3 tablespoons butter, cut into small bits

Dry tournedos with a paper towel and sprinkle ground pepper generously on both sides of the meat. Heat clarified butter in a heavy skillet over high heat. Add tournedos and sear for 3½ minutes on each side. Transfer the meat to a heated platter with a slotted spatula, placing each steak on a toast round. Keep warm.

Add the shallots to the skillet and cook over moderate heat until tender. Stir in the dry wine and cook until reduced to 1 cup. Stir in ⅓ cup Espagnole sauce. Add parsley and simmer for 2 minutes, or until slightly thickened. Remove skillet from heat and stir in lemon juice. Swirl in softened butter and pour over tournedos.

Tournedos Rossini

Serves four

4 tournedos of beef, 6 ounces each, 1″ thick	1 bay leaf
	1 clove
4 tablespoons butter	½ ounce Brandy
1½ tablespoons flour	½ ounce Burgundy wine
1 cup strong beef stock	2 tablespoons olive oil
¼ teaspoon fresh ground black pepper	4 slices pate de fois gras
	4 toast rounds

Melt butter over moderate heat in a small saucepan and blend in flour, stirring until browned. Stir in beef stock, blending until smooth. Add crushed pepper, bay leaf, clove, Brandy and Burgundy and simmer for 5 minutes.

Meanwhile heat olive oil over moderate heat in a skillet and cook tournedos until medium-rare. Place toast rounds on a serving platter and top with tournedos. Top tournedos with a slice of pate and spoon sauce over all.

Filet with Scallion Mustard Sauce

Serves four

1 tablespoon vegetable oil	1 cup chopped green onion, including tops
8 medallions, filet mignon, ½″ thick	1 tablespoon Dijon-style mustard
1 tablespoon unsalted butter	1 tablespoon beef broth

Heat oil over high heat in a sauté pan until oil begins to smoke. Add filets and sear 2 minutes on each side. Reduce heat to moderate and cook until meat is medium-rare. Transfer to a serving platter. Add butter to skillet and sauté onion, stirring constantly, until tender. Stir in mustard and beef broth, blending well. Pour scallion-mustard sauce over cooked filets.

Filet Fromage

Serves six

3 pounds beef tenderloin, trimmed	½ cup butter softened
3 tablespoons fresh ground black pepper	¼ pound Bleu cheese, crumbled
1 cup half-and-half	1 cup dry white wine
	¼ teaspoon white pepper

Sprinkle tenderloin generously with freshly ground pepper, pressing the pepper into all sides of the beef. Preheat oven to broil. Spread the beef with ¼ cup of softened butter, reserving the remaining ¼ cup for later use. Place beef on a baking sheet and broil for 20–25 minutes or until rare.

Transfer beef to a cutting board and let it cool for 10 minutes. Meanwhile in a small bowl, cream together cheese and remaining butter. Add the white wine to the drippings from the baking sheet in which the filet was broiled, scraping up any bits clinging to the bottom. Pour the sauce in a heavy saucepan and cook over moderate heat until reduced to 2 tablespoons. Add the half and half and cheese mixture, stirring for 4 minutes. Strain the sauce through a fine sieve into a heated sauce boat. Sprinkle with white pepper.

Cut the beef into ½-inch slices and arrange overlapping on a heated platter. Serve the beef with the sauce.

Steak Joseph Flambé

Serves four

4 tablespoons butter	1-8 ounce can artichoke hearts, drained and quartered
2 tablespoons finely chopped shallots	
¼ teaspoon oregano	1 cup heavy cream–blended with 1 tablespoon flour
4 lean rib eye steaks, about 8 ounces each	¼ teaspoon salt
1 ounce Cognac	1 teaspoon fresh ground pepper
2 ounces Burgundy wine	
½ cup thinly sliced fresh mushrooms	

Melt butter in a sauté pan over moderate heat and add shallots, oregano, salt and pepper. Sauté until shallots are tender and transparent. Push mixture to the side of the pan and add steaks. Cook steaks until medium-rare. Pour Cognac towards the front of the pan and ignite. When the flame has extinguished, add the wine. Transfer steaks to a warmed serving platter and add the mushrooms and artichoke hearts. Cook, stirring constantly, until the mushrooms are tender. Add cream mixture and cook until slightly thickened. Pour the artichoke-mushroom sauce over the steaks and serve.

Filet Royale

Serves four

4 filet mignons, 10 ounces each	⅛ teaspoon thyme
8 tablespoons butter	¼ pound sweetbreads, parboiled and chopped
½ cup chopped green onion	4 artichoke hearts
¼ cup breadcrumbs	½ cup Bearnise sauce
4 tablespoons olive oil	Salt and fresh ground pepper to taste
1 teaspoon paprika	
1 teaspoon capers	

Melt butter over moderate heat in a skillet and sauté onion until tender. Add sweetbreads, breadcrumbs, paprika, capers, thyme and salt and pepper to taste. Divide this mixture into 4 equal portions when all ingredients are thoroughly heated and place in middle of artichoke heart.

In another skillet heat olive oil over moderate heat and cook filets until medium-rare. Place filets on serving plates and top with an artichoke heart. Spoon Bearnaise sauce over artichokes.

Filet Italiano Flambé

Serves four

4 slices filet mignon, 1½" thick	4 thin slices Mozzarella cheese
2 tablespoons butter	1½ ounces 151 Proof Rum
2 tablespoons chopped chives	1 ounce Sweet Vermouth
½ teaspoon Worchestershire sauce	Salt and fresh ground pepper to taste
4 paper thin slices proscuitto	2 tablespoons olive oil

Melt butter and olive oil in a sauté pan over moderate heat. Add chives and Worchestershire sauce. Season the filets with salt and fresh ground pepper and cook until medium-rare. Heat the proscuitto in butter and place on top of filets. Top proscuitto with Mozzarella. Pour 151 Rum around the perimeter of the pan and ignite. When the flame has extinguished, add the Vermouth and spoon the juices over the cheese until it is melted. Transfer to dinner plates.

Beef Wellington

Serves four

4 tournedos, 6 ounces each	Salt and fresh ground pepper to taste
4 tablespoons unsalted butter	1½ pounds puff-pastry dough
4 thin slices paté de fois gras	1 egg, lightly beaten
	1½ cups Bordelaise Sauce

Preheat oven to 450° F. Melt butter in a sauté pan over moderate heat and sauté tournedos until rare. Season with salt and pepper and set aside. Divide puff pastry into 4 portions and roll into a square ¼-inch thick. Place each tournedo on one side of pastry leaving room to fold over. Top with a slice of paté and fold dough around tournedo sealing edges well with egg wash. Brush the tops of the tournedos with egg wash. Place on an ungreased baking sheet and bake for 15–20 minutes or until pastry is flaky and golden brown.

Warm Bordelaise sauce and spoon on heated serving plates. Place tournedos on sauce and serve.

Stefatho (Greek Beef Stew)

Serves six

3 pounds top round of beef cut in 1″ cubes	1 ounce dry red wine
2 pounds small white onions	½ cup tomato paste
2 bay leaves	⅛ teaspoon cinnamon
2 cloves garlic, pressed	1½ cups water
2 tablespoons wine vinegar	3 tablespoons butter
	2 tablespoons olive oil
	Salt and fresh ground pepper to taste

Heat butter and oil over high heat in a sauté pan and brown beef cubes. Add onions and sauté until tender and transparent. Transfer beef and onions to a casserole. Dilute tomato paste in water and add cinnamon, garlic, bay leaves, wine vinegar, wine and salt and pepper to taste. Pour over beef and onions in casserole and bring mixture to a boil. Cover casserole tightly and simmer for 2 hours or until meat is tender. Garnish with chopped walnuts or pecans if desired.

Beef Stroganoff

Serves four

2 pounds tenderloin	1 cup sour cream
1 pound fresh sliced mushrooms	1 tablespoon Worchestershire sauce
1 cup butter	1½ ounces Brandy
3 Bermuda onions, chopped	Salt and fresh ground pepper to taste
1 can tomato soup	1 pound cooked buttered noodles
1 can tomato paste	

Slice tenderloin in very thin slices. In a large skillet brown steak and mushrooms in butter over moderate heat. Add onions, soup, tomato paste, sour cream, Worchestershire, salt and pepper. Cover and simmer for ½ hour. When ready to serve, heat Brandy in a small pot, and ignite with a match. Pour flaming Brandy over stroganoff. Serve over buttered noodles.

Glazed Sweetbreads Flambé

Serves two

1 pair calf sweetbreads	½ cup dry white wine
6 tablespoons butter	½ cup fresh sliced
2 tablespoons finely	mushrooms
chopped carrots	1 tablespoon minced
2 tablespoons chopped	parsley
shallots	1½ ounces Brandy
1½ cup veal stock	Salt and pepper to taste

Rinse sweetbreads with cold water and place in a saucepan. Cover with cold water. Place cover on saucepan and bring to boil, reduce heat and simmer 20 minutes. Drain sweetbreads and cover with cold water.

Melt 4 tablespoons butter in a large sauté pan over moderate heat and sauté carrots and shallots until tender. Add sweetbreads and sauté lightly. Add veal stock and cover pan. Simmer for 20 minutes. Pour Brandy towards front of pan and flame. Transfer sweetbreads to a heated platter and keep warm.

Deglaze pan by adding wine and season with salt and pepper to taste. Cook uncovered until liquid is reduced by one-half.

Meanwhile in another skillet melt remaining butter over moderate heat and sauté mushrooms until tender. Top sweetbreads with glaze and mushrooms. Sprinkle with parsley and serve.

Boeuf Au Fois Gras Flambé

Serves four

4 slices filet mignon,	1½ ounce 151 Proof Rum
1¾ " thick	1½ ounce Burgundy wine
4 tablespoons clarified	4 canned artichoke hearts
butter	½ cup heavy cream
1 teaspoon	1 teaspoon flour dissolved
Worcestershire sauce	in 2 tablespoons water
1 cup fresh sliced	Salt and fresh ground
mushrooms	pepper to taste
4 thin slices paté de fois	
gras or chicken liver paté	

Season filets with salt and fresh ground pepper. Melt butter with Worcestershire in a sauté pan over moderate heat. Sauté mushrooms until tender, add filet and cook until medium-rare. Top with a slice of paté. Pour the 151 Rum towards the front of the pan and ignite. When the flame has extinguished, add the Burgundy and transfer the filets to a serving platter. Add the artichoke hearts, cream, and flour dissolved in water and cook stirring constantly until slightly thickened. Place an artichoke heart on each filet and pour the sauce over the filets.

London Broil

Serves four

2 flank steaks (1½ pound)	6 drops red hot pepper
½ cup oil	sauce
½ cup Burgundy wine	½ teaspoon Worcestershire
2 tablespoons minced onion	sauce
2 cloves garlic, pressed	½ teaspoon ground pepper
1½ teaspoon salt	

Score both sides of the steaks in diamond patterns ⅛-inch deep. Combine all ingredients for marinade in a shallow dish or casserole. marinate the steaks for 2 hours turning steaks over every half hour. Broil steaks until medium-rare and slice diagonally into thin slices before serving.

Beef Casino

Serves four

4 club steaks, 8 ounces	1 tablespoon chopped
each	parsley
6 tablespoons butter	½ cup Diablo sauce
¼ pound fresh sliced	½ cup white wine
mushrooms	Juice of ½ lemon
¼ pound ham, cut in	Salt and fresh ground
julienne slices	pepper to taste

Melt 4 tablespoons butter in a skillet over high heat add club steaks cooking until medium-rare. Season steaks with salt and pepper to taste and transfer to a heated serving platter. Add mushrooms, ham and parsley, and sauté until mushrooms are tender. Add white wine and lemon juice and cook until almost all liquid has evaporated. Add Diablo sauce and swirl remaining butter. Spoon sauce over steaks and serve.

Beef à la Greco

Serves four

2½ pound beef pot roast	1 8-ounce can tomato
½ cup butter	sauce
2 onions, quartered	½ cup water
3 garlic cloves, pressed	½ cup Burgundy wine
2 celery stalks, coarsely	2 ounces Metaxa Brandy
chopped	1 zucchini, sliced ½″
½ teaspoon cinnamon	thick
½ teaspoon allspice	4 potatoes, peeled and
3 bay leaves	quartered
1 8-ounce can stewed	Salt and fresh ground
tomatoes	pepper to taste

Season beef with salt and fresh ground pepper. Melt butter in a Dutch oven and brown beef on all sides. Add onions, garlic, bay leaves, celery, cinnamon, allspice, tomatoes, tomato sauce, ½ cup water and wine. Cover and simmer 1 hour. Place the zucchini slices on beef and potatoes in juices around beef. Simmer 1 hour longer. Arrange on a platter with potatoes surrounding roast. To flame, heat Metaxa Brandy, ignite, and pour flaming Brandy over beef.

Shepherd's Pie

Serves six

6 tablespoons butter	½ teaspoon thyme
2 onions, chopped fine	½ teaspoon rosemary
2 pounds ground lamb or	2 teaspoons Worchester-
ground chuck	shire sauce
2 teaspoons salt	¼ cup beef stock
1 teaspoon fresh ground	3 pounds warm, whipped
pepper	potatoes
½ teaspoon oregano	¼ cup warm milk
flakes	

Preheat oven to 400°F. Melt half of the butter in a large sauce pan over moderate heat. Add onion and sauté until onion is tender. Stir in meat, half of salt, half of pepper, herbs and Worchestershire sauce. Cook, stirring constantly, for 5 minutes. Add stock and remove pan from heat. Place mixture in a shallow baking casserole. Place mashed potatoes in a mixing bowl and beat in remaining butter, salt and pepper and hot milk. Spoon potatoes over meat and bake pie in oven for 30 minutes or until potatoes have lightly browned.

Steak Morateur

Serves two

2 anchovies	1 tablespoon butter
2 tablespoons unsalted	4 medallions, filet mignon,
butter	each 1½″ thick
1 teaspoon anchovy paste	1 shallot, minced
½ teaspoon fresh ground	½ dry white wine
pepper	1½ ounces Cognac

In a small mixing bowl, blend anchovy filets with unsalted butter to form a paste. Blend in anchovy paste and fresh ground pepper.

Heat butter in a sauté pan over moderate heat. Cook filet for about 3 minutes on each side, or until done medium-rare. Pour Cognac towards front of pan and ignite. Remove filets from pan and transfer to a warmed platter. Stir shallot into pan and cook until tender. Pour in wine and simmer until mixture is reduced by half. Stir in anchovy mixture and simmer 3 minutes longer. Pour sauce over steaks and serve.

Marinated Filet Flambé

Serves four

4–8 ounce filets,	3 tablespoons vegetable
1½″ thick	oil
Zest of 1 lemon grated	2 tablespoons butter
Zest of 1 orange grated	½ cup whipping cream
1 onion grated	2 ounces Cognac
2 tablespoons minced	Salt and fresh ground
parsley	pepper to taste

Mix vegetable oil, lemon and orange zest, parsley and grated onion in a shallow baking dish. Season filets with salt and pepper to taste and marinate in mixture for at least 4 hours, turning occasionally.

Melt butter in a skillet over moderate heat and cook filets until done medium-rare. Pour Cognac towards the front of the pan and ignite. When flames have extinguished, transfer filets to a heated serving platter and keep warm. Whisk in cream and stir until slightly thickened. Pour over filets and serve.

Beef Oriental

Serves four

¾ pound tenderloin of
  beef, sliced into 1½ ″
  julienne strips
1 ounce red Burgundy wine
2 tablespoons soy sauce
½ teaspoon fresh ground
  pepper
⅛ teaspoon celery salt

⅛ teaspoon onion salt
1 teaspoon cornstarch
2 tablespoons cooking oil
2 cups frozen or fresh
  Chinese sweet snow peas
½ cup sliced fresh
  mushrooms

Marinate beef in wine, soy sauce and cornstarch for
15 minutes. Heat oil in a skillet or wok over high heat.
Add beef, including the marinade and sauté for 3½
minutes stirring constantly. Add snow peas and
mushrooms, salts and pepper. Cook 2 minutes more,
stirring frequently. Serve with white steamed rice.

Steak Au Poivre Flambé

Serves four

4 strips sirloin steaks,
  8 ounces each
3 tablespoons fresh
  ground pepper
½ teaspoon dried thyme
½ teaspoon dried tarragon
1 teaspoon salt
3 tablespoons unsalted
  butter

1 tablespoon olive oil
2 tablespoons finely
  chopped shallots
1 tablespoon chopped
  parsley
2 ounces Cognac

Rub the steak on both sides with pepper, thyme and
tarragon. Allow the steaks to stand at room temperature
for 30 minutes. Sprinkle steaks with salt. Heat butter
and oil over moderate heat in a large sauté pan. Add
the steaks and sauté for 2 minutes on each side. Add
the shallot and continue to cook the steaks until they
are done medium-rare. Place steaks on a heated platter
and sprinkle with parsley. Add Cognac to the pan and
ignite. Pour sauce over the steaks.

Hamburg Shisk-Kabob Flambé

Serves four

⅓ cup fine dry bread-
  crumbs
½ cup milk
4 green onions, finely
  chopped
½ cup chopped parsley
2 tablespoons butter
2 pounds ground beef
2 egg yolks
2 whole eggs
4 cloves garlic, pressed
2 teaspoons salt
3 tablespoons lemon juice
¼ teaspoon oregano

3 tablespoons olive oil
2 tomatoes, cut in 8
  wedges
2 green peppers, cut in
  1½″ cubes
2 medium onions,
  quartered
16 large pitted black
  olives
16 mushroom caps
1½ ounces Cognac
Salt and fresh ground
  pepper, to taste
1 ounce Burgundy wine

Soak the breadcrumbs in milk until soft. Sauté the onion and parsley in butter until tender and mix thoroughly with the ground beef, egg yolks, whole eggs, garlic salt and pepper and milk-crumb mixture. Shape into ½-inch balls. Heat butter in a large frying pan and add the balls. Cook until very lightly browned. Remove from the pan and reserve.

Mix the wine, lemon juice, olive oil, salt and pepper to taste and oregano in a small bowl.

Skewer the vegetables and meat-balls on 4 large skewers, alternating for a colorful effect. Preheat oven to broil. Brush the skewered shish-kabobs generously with the wine mixture. Place on a broiling pan and cook until vegetables are tender, basting with wine mixture frequently. Turn meat once during broiling. Heat Cognac in a small saucepan. Ignite Cognac and pour over shish-kabobs. Serve flaming with rice pilaf.

Moussaka

Serves six to eight

2 pounds eggplant
Salt to season
1½ pounds ground beef
5 tablespoons butter
1 onion, grated
½ cup tomato pureé
  (or 3 ripe tomatoes
  peeled, seeded and
  chopped)
3 tablespoons chopped
  parsley

Freshly ground black
  pepper
⅛ teaspoon ground
  cinnamon
Oil, enough for frying
3 eggs
2 cups unflavored yogurt,
  beaten until smooth
¾ cup grated cheese
  (Kefalotiri, Parmesan,
  or Gruyere)
Grated nutmeg

Peel the eggplants and cut into ½-inch rounds. Salt them and leave to drain in the colander for 30 minutes.

Brown the meat in 4 tablespoons of butter with the onion. Add the tomato pureé, parsley, salt and pepper to taste, and the cinnamon. Simmer gently until all the liquid evaporates. Allow to cool.

Rinse the eggplant slices, and pat dry with paper towels. Heat the oil in the skillet and fry the eggplant slices until brown on both sides. Drain and set aside.

Thoroughly beat the 3 eggs. Slowly stir in the yogurt. Mix in the cheese. Season with salt, pepper and grated nutmeg.

Preheat oven to 375°F.

Arrange half the eggplant slices in one layer on the bottom of a buttered oven dish. Cover with a layer of cooked meat and a final layer of eggplant. Pour the sauce over the top and dot with butter. Set in the oven to bake for 45 minutes or until the top is golden brown.

Tournedos á la Bearnaise

Serves four

8 tournedos of beef, ¾″
  thick, 4 ounces each
4 tablespoons butter
¾ cup Bearnaise sauce

Melt butter over moderate heat in a skillet and sauté tournedos until medium-rare. Place tournedos on serving dishes and top with Bearnaise sauce before serving.

Baby Beef Liver Oreganato

Serves four

2 pounds baby beef liver
2 tablespoons butter
2 tablespoons olive oil
1 cup flour

1½ teaspoon oregano
Juice of one lemon
Salt and fresh ground
  pepper to taste

Season liver with salt and pepper and dredge in flour. In a large skillet, heat butter and olive oil over moderate heat. Sauté liver until golden brown on both sides. Sprinkle cooked liver with oregano and lemon juice. Add more olive oil and butter, as needed, to sauté remaining liver.

Steak Diane Flambé

Serves two

1 tablespoon olive oil	1 teaspoon dry mustard
3 tablespoons chopped shallots	¼ teaspoon oregano
1 cup fresh sliced mushrooms	1 pound filet mignon, cut into ½" slices
2 cloves garlic, pressed	1½ ounce 151 Proof Rum
2 teaspoons Worchestershire sauce	1 ounce Burgundy Wine
2 tablespoons chopped chives	½ cup Bordelaise sauce
	Salt and fresh ground pepper to taste

Heat olive oil in a sauté pan, and sauté shallots and mushrooms with garlic, Worchestershire sauce, chives, dry mustard, oregano and salt and pepper to taste. Push mixture to side of the pan. Add meat and sauté until medium-rare and cooked on both sides. Add 151 Rum and ignite. When flames have extinguished, add wine and Bordelaise sauce. Cook until sauce is heated and serve.

Herbed Rib Eye Flambé

Serves four

4 rib eye steaks, ¾" thick, 8 ounces each	Salt and fresh ground pepper to taste
4 tablespoons olive oil	4 chopped anchovies
½ teaspoon oregano	2 ounces Cognac
½ teaspoon rosemary	

Season rib eyes with salt, pepper, rosemary and oregano. Heat oil in a skillet over moderate heat and cook steaks until medium-rare. Place portion of chopped anchovy on each steak. Pour Cognac towards front of pan and ignite. Serve when flames have extinguished.

Minced Beef Provençal

Serves six

6 medium tomatoes	1 tablespoon chopped parsley
⅓ cup oil	Salt and pepper to taste

Halve the tomatoes. Heat the oil in a large skillet and place the tomatoes cut side down, in the skillet. Pierce each tomato with a fork, cook for 5 minutes and turn. Sprinkle with the parsley, salt and pepper. Lower the flame and cook the tomatoes until tender.

⅓ cup olive oil	4 teaspoons flour
4 onions, chopped	1½ cups bouillon
2 pounds fresh ground beef	Salt and pepper to taste

In a skillet heat the olive oil and sauté the onions until they are golden. Add the ground beef, stir, and sprinkle with the flour. Stir until the flour disappears and stir in the bouillon. Add the salt and pepper and cook for 15 minutes. Put the beef in a shallow platter that is heatproof and arrange the tomatoes over top. Pour the cooking juices from the tomatoes over all, and heat for 15 minutes in a hot oven.

Veal

Veal Oscar

Serves four

4 veal scallops, 4 ounces each, ⅜" thick
5 tablespoons butter
½ pound Alaskan king crabmeat
8 asparagus spears, cooked al dente'
¾ cup Bearnaise or Hollandaise sauce
Salt and fresh ground pepper to taste

Season veal with salt and fresh ground pepper. Heat butter over moderate heat in a skillet and cook veal until lightly browned. Heat crabmeat and asparagus in butter and distribute evenly on veal beginning with asparagus and topping with crabmeat. Top with Bearnaise sauce. Place under a broiler for a few seconds to glaze the top and serve.

Veal Proscuitto Flambe'

Serves four

8 veal scallops, 2 ounces each, pounded ⅜" thick
3 tablespoons flour
5 tablespoons butter
8 thin slices firm, ripe honeydew melon
8 paper thin slices proscuitto
Juice of ½ lime
¼ cup cocktail onions
1½ ounce 151 Proof Rum
1½ ounce Sauterne wine
2 tablespoons capers, drained
Salt and fresh ground pepper to taste

Season veal with salt and pepper and dredge in flour. Heat butter in a saute' pan over moderate heat. Saute' veal until golden brown on both sides. Heat the melon, proscuitto and cocktail onions in the butter. Place a piece of proscuitto on each veal slice and top with a slice of melon. Pour the 151 Rum towards the front of the pan and ignite. Squeeze the lime over the melon slices. When the flame has extinguished, add Sauterne and simmer for 3 minutes. Transfer veal to a serving platter, top with cocktail onions and sprinkle with capers.

Veal Scallopine à la Moutard Flambe'

Serves four

8 veal scallops, 2 ounces each, pounded ⅜" thick
3 tablespoons flour
4 tablespoons butter
1 teaspoon Worchestershire sauce
2 tablespoons minced shallots
1 ounce 151 Proof Rum
1½ ounce Dry Vermouth
½ teaspoon dry mustard
1 cup heavy cream
½ teaspoon minced parsley
Salt and fresh ground pepper to taste

Season the veal with salt and pepper and dredge in flour. Heat the butter in a saute' pan or chafing dish over moderate heat. Add the Worchestershire and shallots, and saute' until shallots are tender. Add veal slices and saute' until they are golden on both sides. Pour the 151 Rum and Vermouth towards the front of the pan and ignite to flame. When the flame is extinguished, transfer veal to a serving platter. Add the mustard and cream to the drippings in the pan, stirring until the sauce begins to boil. Pour over the veal scallopine and sprinkle with parsley.

Veal Royale Flambe'

Serves four

8 veal scallops, pounded ⅜" thick
5 tablespoons butter
2 garlic cloves, pressed
½ cup chopped green pepper
1 small onion, finely minced
¼ teaspoon thyme
1 cup pitted black olives, sliced
1 tablespoon minced parsley
1 ounce Cognac
1 ounce Burgundy wine
Juice of ½ lemon
Salt and fresh ground pepper to taste

Place butter, garlic, green pepper and onion in a saute' pan over moderate heat and saute' until onion is transparent and tender. Season veal with thyme, salt and pepper and saute' until lightly browned on both sides. Add olives and parsley, stirring until olives are thoroughly heated. Spoon olive-onion mixture evenly over veal and squeeze lemon juice over the entire mixture. Pour Cognac towards the front of the pan and ignite. Add wine when the flame is extinguished. Saute' for 3 minutes. Place on serving plate, spooning the juices over the veal scallops.

Veal Tarragon

Serves four

8 veal scallops, 4 ounces each, pounded ⅜″ thick
Salt and fresh ground pepper to taste
1 cup flour
4 tablespoons butter
1 clove garlic, pressed
1 medium onion, chopped
1 cup sour cream
½ pound fresh sliced mushrooms
1 tablespoon finely chopped tarragon
½ teaspoon Worchestershire sauce
1½ ounces white wine
1½ ounces Brandy

Season veal with salt and pepper to taste and dredge in flour. Heat butter over moderate heat in a skillet and sauté onions and garlic until golden. Add mushrooms, tarragon and Worchestershire and sauté until mushrooms are tender. Push onion and mushrooms mixture to the side of the pan and cook veal until lightly browned. Pour Brandy towards the front of the pan and ignite. Transfer veal to a heated serving platter.

Add sour cream and white wine to skillet and blend well. Cook, stirring occasionally until mixture is reduced by one quarter. Pour sauce over veal and serve.

Veal Saltimbocco Flambé

Serves Four

8 veal scallops, 2 ounces each, pounded ⅜″ thick
2 tablespoons flour
2 tablespoons butter
½ teaspoon Worchestershire sauce
1 tablespoon chopped chives
2 tablespoons olive oil
¼ cup sliced fresh mushrooms
4 thin slices proscuitto
4 thin slices Grueyere cheese
1½ ounce Marsala wine
Juice of ½ lemon
1½ ounce 151 Proof Rum
Salt and fresh ground pepper to taste

Sprinkle the veal with salt and pepper and then dredge with flour. Melt butter in a sauté pan or skillet over moderate heat, add the Worchestershire, chives and oil. Add the mushrooms and veal; sauté until the veal is lightly browned on both sides. Place 1 slice of proscuitto on each veal slice. Top with even amounts of mushrooms and a slice of cheese. Pour the 151 Rum around the perimeter of the pan and ignite. When the flame has extinguished, sprinkle the Marsala over the veal and then squeeze the lemon juice over the pan. Spoon the juices over the Saltimbocco, until the cheese has melted.

Veal Marsala

Serves four

16 veal scallops, 1½ ounces each, pounded ⅜″ thick
Salt and fresh ground pepper
1 cup flour
4 tablespoons oil
6 tablespoons butter
2 ounces Marsala wine
3 tablespoons chicken broth
1 tablespoon chopped parsley

Season veal with salt and pepper and dredge in flour. Heat butter and oil over moderate heat in a skillet and cook veal until lightly browned. Transfer to a heated serving platter. Add Marsala to skillet and stir for 1 minute. Add chicken broth and cook 2 minutes longer over high heat. Sprinkle parsley into sauce and spoon sauce over veal scallops.

Veal with Shrimp Flambé

Serves four

8 veal scallops, 2 ounces each, pounded ⅜″ thick
2 tablespoons butter
1½ ounce 151 Proof Rum
1 ounce Sherry
Salt and fresh ground pepper to taste
12 shrimp, boiled, peeled and deveined, kept warm
4 broccoli spears, cooked al denté, kept warm
¾ cup Hollandaise sauce

Season veal scallops with salt and pepper to taste. Melt butter over moderate heat in a skillet and cook veal until lightly browned. Place scallops in overlapping pairs and pour 151 Rum towards the front of the pan and ignite. When flames have extinguished, sprinkle veal with Sherry. Decorate each scallop pair with a broccoli spear and 3 shrimp. Top with Hollandaise sauce.

Veal Caraway Flambé

Serves four

8 veal scallops, 2 ounces
  each, pounded ⅜″ thick
3 tablespoons butter
½ cup flour
1 medium onion finely
  chopped
¼ cup dry white wine
½ teaspoon caraway seeds

½ cup heavy cream
½ teaspoon Worchestershire
  sauce
Juice of ½ lemon
1½ ounces Brandy
Salt and fresh ground
  pepper to taste

Season veal with salt and pepper to taste and dredge
in flour. Heat butter over moderate heat in a skillet and
cook veal until golden. Transfer veal to a heated
platter.

Add onion, caraway and Worchestershire to skillet
and cook, stirring constantly until onions are
transparent. Add wine and whisk in cream. Reduce
mixture by ½ and then return veal to skillet to reheat.
Pour Brandy towards front of skillet and ignite.
Squeeze lemon juice over all and serve.

Veal Papillots

Serves four

4 veal chops, 1½″ thick,
  boned
2 tablespoons butter
1 teaspoon fresh chopped
  chives
½ cup sliced fresh
  mushrooms
¼ teaspoon oregano
  flakes

¼ cup minced onions
¼ cup feta cheese OR 4
  thin slices Mozzarella
  cheese
1½ ounce Chablis or a
  dry white wine
Salt and fresh ground
  pepper to taste

Over low heat in a sauté pan, melt the butter and
brown the veal very lightly on both sides. Remove the
veal and in the same skillet, over moderate heat, add
the onions, mushrooms, chives, oregano and salt and
pepper to taste. Sauté until the onions are tender and
add the wine. Place each piece of veal on a large piece
of aluminum foil and top with the onion-mushroom
mixture. Sprinkle with feta cheese or top with a slice
of Mozzarella. Fold foil to resemble a swan and place
the papillots on a cookie sheet in a 350°F. oven for
15–20 minutes. Remove from oven and slit center.
Serve immediately.

Veal Français Flambé

Serves four

4 veal scallops, 2 ounces
  each, pounded ⅜″ thick
Salt and fresh ground
  pepper to taste
1 cup flour
2 eggs, beaten

6 tablespoons butter
2 tablespoons chopped
  chives
1 ounce 151 Proof Rum
Juice of ½ lemon
6 paper-thin slices lemon

Season veal with salt and pepper, dip into egg and
dredge with flour. Melt butter over moderate heat in a
skillet and lightly brown veal, sprinkle with chopped
chives. Push veal to side of pan and pour 151 Rum
towards the front of the pan and ignite. Squeeze lemon
juice over veal and top each scallop with a lemon slice
before serving.

Weinerschnitzel à la Holstein

Serves four

4 veal cutlets,
  pounded ⅜″ thick
½ cup dry breadcrumbs
½ teaspoons salt
1½ teaspoons fresh
  ground pepper
1 teaspoon paprika

½ cup milk
½ cup flour
4 tablespoons butter
8 paper-thin slices lemon
4 anchovy fillets
1 tablespoon capers
4 poached eggs

Combine egg with milk and set aside. Combine
flour, breadcrumbs, salt, pepper, paprika. Dredge veal
cutlets in flour mixture, then in egg mixture; then again
in flour mixture. Melt butter over moderate heat in a
skillet and sauté veal cutlets until golden brown on
both sides. Transfer cutlets to heated dinner plates and
garnish each with 2 lemon slices, and a poached egg,
topped with an anchovy fillet and a few capers.

Veal Scallopine Grand Marnier

Six servings

6 veal scallops, pounded
  to 3/8″ thick
2 tablespoons butter
2 tablespoons olive oil
½ cup Italian bread-
  crumbs
½ cup white, seedless
  grapes
1 cup thinly sliced, fresh
  mushrooms

1 teaspoon fresh, minced
  parsley
6 paper-thin slices orange
1 ounce Cognac
1½ ounces Grand Marnier
½ cup beef stock
Juice of ½ orange
Salt and fresh ground
  pepper to taste

In a sauté pan, melt the butter and olive oil over
moderate heat. Season veal with salt and fresh
ground pepper to taste, then dredge in breadcrumbs. Place
grapes, mushrooms, parsley and veal in pan and sauté
until veal is very lightly browned on both sides. Place
mushrooms and grapes on veal and top with orange
slices. Pour Cognac towards the front of the pan and
ignite. When flame has extinguished, add Grand
Marnier and orange juice. Transfer the veal with the
grapes, mushrooms, and orange slices to a serving
platter. Add the beef broth and stir to pick up bits from
bottom of pan. Pour over the veal and serve.

Veal Piccata Flambé

Serves four

8 veal scallops, 2
  ounces each, pounded
  3/8″ thick
1 cup flour
6 tablespoons olive oil
4 tablespoons butter
Salt and fresh ground
  pepper to taste

2½ ounces dry white wine
½ cup chicken broth
Juice of 1 lemon
2 tablespoons chopped
  parsley
1½ ounces 151 Proof Rum

Season veal with salt and pepper and dredge in flour.
Heat butter and oil over moderate heat in a skillet and
lightly brown veal. Transfer veal scallops to a heated
platter. Add wine, chicken broth and parsley to skillet
and cook, stirring for 3 minutes. Return veal scallops
to skillet and squeeze lemon juice over veal. Pour 151
Rum towards the front of the pan and ignite. Serve
immediately, spooning remaining juices in pan over
veal.

Veal Hungarian Flambé

Serves four

6 tablespoons butter
2 garlic cloves, pressed
2 tablespoons chopped
  fresh chives
1 medium onion, minced
½ teaspoon Worchester-
  shire sauce
6 chicken livers, chopped
1½ pound veal, cut in
  julienne strips

3 tablespoons flour
1 ounce Brandy
1 ounce Tokay or
  Madeira wine
1 cup sour cream
½ cup beef stock
1 tablespoon paprika
Juice of ½ lemon
Salt and fresh ground
  pepper to taste

Place butter, garlic, chives, onion, and Worchestershire sauce in a sauté pan over moderate heat and sauté
onions until transparent and tender. Season chicken
livers and veal with salt and pepper and dredge in
flour. Sauté veal and livers until lightly browned. Pour
Brandy towards the front of the pan and ignite. When
the flame has extinguished, add the wine and squeeze
the lemon juice over veal and chicken livers. Stir in
sour cream and beef stock. Sprinkle paprika over the
mixture and cook over low heat for 10 minutes or until
veal is tender.

Veal Medallions with Onion & Cointreau

Serves four

8 veal medallions, 2 ounces each
1 large bermuda onion, peeled and sliced thin
2 cups chicken stock
¾ cup whipping cream
2 tablespoons flour
1 tablespoon red wine vinegar
2 tablespoon butter
1 tablespoon vegetable oil
½ cup Cointreau
Salt
Fresh ground pepper to taste

Place onions, 1½ cups chicken stock, vinegar, in a medium saucepan and season with salt and pepper to taste. Cover pan and cook over moderate heat until liquid has evaporated. Add cream to onions and bring mixture to a boil. Remove from heat and set aside.

Season veal medallions with salt and pepper to taste and dust with flour. Heat oil and ½ teaspoon butter in a skillet over moderate heat and sauté veal until golden brown on both sides. Transfer veal to a platter and keep warm.

Add Cointreau and remaining chicken stock to a skillet, and cook until reduced to 3 tablespoons. Swirl in remaining butter. Arrange onion mixture on serving plates, top with 2 veal medallions and lace with sauce from skillet.

Veal Marengo

Serves four

2 pounds lean veal, in 2" cubes
4 tablespoons vegetable oil
¼ cup water
1 medium onion chopped
1 clove garlic, pressed
½ cup diced carrots
1 bay leaf
½ teaspoon thyme
4 tablespoons tomato paste
2½ ounces dry white wine
1 cup veal or chicken broth
1 tablespoon chopped parsley
1 teaspoon cornstarch
¼ pound sliced fresh mushrooms
Salt and fresh ground pepper to taste

Preheat oven to 350°F. Season veal cubes with salt and pepper to taste. Heat oil in a Dutch oven over high heat and brown veal cubes. After veal is browned add onion, garlic, carrots, bay leaf and thyme. Cook, stirring occasionally, for 4 minutes. Add mushrooms and cook until mushrooms are tender. Add wine, water, tomato paste and parsley. Stir to blend and cover. Bake in preheated oven for 1½ hours.

Transfer meat to another casserole with a slotted spoon and discard bay leaf.

Blend cornstarch with 1 tablespoon of water and stir into juices remaining in casserole. Cook, stirring constantly over moderate heat until thickened. Pour sauce over veal and serve.

Veal Curry Flambé

Serves four

4 thin veal steaks, 6 ounces each
2 tablespoons butter
½ cup chopped celery
2 large garlic cloves, pressed
1 cup finely chopped onion
½ cup diced apple
2 bananas, sliced into ½" rounds
1½ tablespoons curry powder
1 cup diced peeled tomatoes
½ cup chicken broth
1½ ounce 151 Proof Rum
½ cup heavy cream
Salt and fresh ground pepper to taste

Heat butter in a sauté pan over moderate heat; add celery, garlic, apple and onion. Sauté until the onion is tender and transparent. Season the veal with salt and pepper and sauté until browned on both sides and thoroughly cooked. Add the bananas, curry powder, tomatoes and chicken broth. Pour the 151 Rum towards the front of the pan and ignite. When the flame has extinguished, add the cream. Stir the mixture well until the sauce is blended and begins to thicken. Serve with rice.

Veal Medallions with Mustard Sauce

Serves four

8 veal medallions, 2-3 ounces each
4 tablespoons butter
2 shallots minced
1½ ounces Brandy
¾ cup whipping cream
2 tablespoons Dijon style mustard
½ teaspoon ground green peppercorns
1½ ounces unsalted butter cut into small bits

Melt 4 tablespoons butter over moderate heat in a pan and sauté veal until golden brown on both sides. Add green pepper and shallots to pan. Pour Brandy towards front of pan and ignite. When flame is extinguished whisk in mustard and cream and cook uncovered over low heat until slightly reduced. Remove pan from heat and whisk in butter one bit at a time. Place 2 veal medallions on each serving plate and lace with sauce.

Pork

Pork Chops Italianna Flambé

Serves four

4 pork chops, cut 1″ thick	½ pound fresh sliced
4 tablespoons oil	mushrooms
2 cloves garlic, pressed	1½ ounces Cognac
2 green peppers, seeded	Salt and fresh ground
and cut in thin strips	pepper to taste
½ pound ripe tomatoes	
peeled, seeded and	
chopped	

Place oil in large pan over moderate heat and cook pork chops until thoroughly browned and done. Transfer chops to a heated serving platter. Add garlic, pepper, tomato, mushrooms, salt and pepper to taste and cook until green peppers are tender. Return chops to pan and pour Cognac towards the front of pan and ignite. When flames have extinguished, serve chops topped with vegetable mixture.

Pork Chops Rosé

Serves four

4 pork chops, ¾″ thick	¼ teaspoon ground
2 green onions, seeded	allspice
and sliced	¼ teaspoon sage
½ cup Rosé wine	¼ cup olive oil
½ cup Mandarin orange	Salt and fresh ground
segments	pepper to taste
2 tablespoons brown sugar	

Heat oil over moderate heat in a skillet and brown pork chops. Season with salt and pepper, sage and allspice. Add onions to skillet and sauté until tender. Mix wine and brown sugar together and add to skillet. Place orange sections on top of pork chops and cover skillet. Reduce heat and simmer until pork chops are tender, about 20 minutes. Spoon wine mixture over chops before serving.

Pork with Mustard Sauce

Serves two

4 pork chops, ½″ thick,	½ cup beef stock
filleted	¼ cup Sherry
½ teaspoon salt	2 tablespoons Dijon-style
½ teaspoon fresh ground	mustard
pepper	½ teaspoon Worchester-
¼ cup flour	shire sauce
1 tablespoon vegetable oil	¼ cup whipping cream
1 tablespoon butter	

Sprinkle pork fillets with salt and pepper; dredge with flour. Heat oil and butter over moderate heat in a sauté pan. Sauté pork fillets until meat is golden brown on both sides, about 8 minutes.

Transfer pork to a warmed serving platter. Drain fat remaining in skillet. Add beef stock, Sherry, mustard and Worchestershire sauce. Boil until mixture is reduced by one-third. Stir in whipping cream and continue to simmer until sauce is well blended. Pour sauce over pork.

Neopolitan Pork Chops Flambé

Serves four

4 center cut pork chops	2 green peppers, seeded
¾″ thick	and cut in thin strips
2 tablespoons olive oil	½ pound fresh sliced
2 tablespoons butter	mushrooms
1 clove garlic, pressed	1½ ounces Brandy
¼ teaspoon basil	Salt and fresh ground
3 tablespoons tomato	pepper to taste
pureé	1½ ounces white wine

Heat butter and oil over moderate heat in a skillet and brown pork chops. Season pork chops with salt and pepper and transfer to a heated serving platter. Add garlic, basil and green pepper to skillet and sauté until green pepper is tender. Add mushrooms and sauté until tender. Blend in tomato pureé and white wine. Return pork chops to skillet. Pour Brandy towards front of pan and ignite. Continue cooking until pork chops are done.

Pork with Plum Sauce

Serves six

2 tablespoons butter	1½ ounces Madeira wine
6 center cut pork chops, ½″ thick	½ teaspoon ground ginger
Salt and fresh ground pepper to taste	⅛ teaspoon grated orange rind
1 medium onion, minced	½ teaspoon cinnamon
1 clove garlic, pressed	1 can plums (16 ounce), pitted
1 tablespoon oil	1 cup plum juice
4 drops hot red pepper sauce	1 teaspoon cornstarch
	2 tablespoons brown sugar

Melt butter over moderate heat in a sauté pan. Season pork chops with salt and pepper and cook until browned on both sides. Meanwhile prepare sauce.

Sauté onions and garlic in oil over moderate heat. Add hot pepper sauce, brown sugar, Madeira, ground ginger, orange rind, cinnamon, plums and juice. Blend thoroughly and add cornstarch. Stir sauce constantly until thickened. Serve sauce over pork chops.

Pork with Prunes

Serves two

20 pitted canned prunes	¼ teaspoon thyme
2 cups demi-sec white wine	2 tablespoons butter
6 pork loin fillets, each about 1½ inches thick	1½ teaspoons vegetable oil
¼ cup flour	1 cup chicken stock
¼ teaspoon salt	1 cup heavy cream
½ teaspoon fresh ground pepper	4 tablespoons red currant jelly

Steep prunes in wine for 1 hour in a non-aluminum pot, then simmer for 10 minutes until prunes are soft. Drain prunes and reserve wine for sauce.

Add salt, pepper and thyme to flour and dredge pork fillets on both sides in the seasoned flour. Heat butter and oil over medium-high heat and brown the pork lightly on both sides. Tie pork fillets together with string, set aside, and pour off drippings from the pan. Add the wine from prunes to the pan and boil until reduced to ½ cup. Add chicken stock and pork. Cover and simmer very gently for 1 hour. Turn pork fillets once during cooking.

Remove pork from pan and place on warmed serving platter. Remove string. Add cream to the juices in the pan and bring to a boil, stirring constantly. Cook until reduced by one-fourth. Stir in jelly and prunes. Pour over pork and garnish pork with prunes.

Apricot Pork Chops Flambé

Serves four

8 loin pork chops, ¾″ thick	¼ teaspoon cinnamon
3 tablespoons vegetable oil	2 green peppers, peeled, seeded and chopped
1–30 ounce can apricot halves (drain and save syrup)	3 onions, chopped
	1½ ounces Apricot Brandy
½ cup Sauterne wine	Salt and fresh ground pepper to taste
2 teaspoons cornstarch	

Sprinkle chops with salt and pepper. Heat oil in a large skillet over moderate heat. Brown pork chops on both sides. Place pork chops in a baking casserole. Place 1 cup syrup from apricots, wine, cornstarch, cinnamon and salt and pepper in a saucepan over moderate heat. Cook, stirring constantly, until mixture is thickened. Cover chops with onions, peppers and drained apricots. Pour sauce over chops and cover baking casserole with foil. Bake at 375°F. for 45 minutes. Place on serving platter. Heat brandy, pour over chops, ignite and serve.

Pork Chops with Cucumber and Onion

Serves four

¼ cup butter	8 pork chops, ¾″ thick
1½ cups chopped scallions	½ cup flour
1½ cucumber, peeled and cut in chunks	1 egg, well beaten
	1½ cup dry bread crumbs
Salt and fresh ground pepper to taste	¼ cup vegetable oil
1 teaspoon chopped parsley	1¼ cups Hollandaise sauce (See page 32)

Melt butter in a saucepan over moderate heat. Add scallions and cucumber, salt and pepper. Cover and simmer for 7 minutes. Remove from heat and stir in parsley.

Dredge pork chops in flour, dip in egg, then in bread crumbs. Heat oil in a large skillet over moderate heat, and fry chops for 15 minutes or until lightly browned.

Warm Hollandaise sauce over warm water. Place chops on a serving platter and top with vegetables. Cover vegetables with Hollandaise sauce.

Pork Chops Exotic Flambé

Serves four

8 center cut pork chops
 1″ thick
½ cup flour
1 tablespoon ground ginger
⅓ cup olive oil

4 pineapple slices cut
 in half
½ cup toasted coconut
Salt and pepper to taste

Sweet and Sour Sauce:
½ cup apricot halves
1 tablespoon apricot
 preserves
1¼ cup water
¼ cup cider vinegar
¼ cup barbeque sauce
1 tablespoon dry mustard

4 whole cloves
1 teaspoon chicken base
3 drops red hot pepper sauce
1 teaspoon ground ginger
1 clove garlic, pressed
1 cup Brown sauce
1 ounce 151 Proof Rum

Place apricot halves, preserves, water, vinegar, barbeque sauce, dry mustard, cloves, chicken base, red hot pepper sauce, ginger, and garlic in a heavy saucepan over moderate heat. Cook uncovered, stirring occasionally for 20 minutes. Add Brown sauce.

Dredge pork chops in flour mixed with ginger and salt and pepper. Heat olive oil in a large skillet over high heat and sauté pork chops until lightly browned on both sides. Place pork chops in a greased baking casserole, spoon sauce over chops and bake for 30 minutes. Before serving, top with a pineapple ring and sprinkle with toasted coconut; pour 151 Rum towards the front of casserole and ignite. Serve flaming.

City Chicken in Red Wine

Serves four

½ pound 1″ pork cubes
½ pound 1″ veal cubes
8 wooden skewers
2 eggs
½ cup breadcrumbs

½ teaspoon sage
¼ cup olive oil
½ cup Burgundy wine
Salt and pepper to taste

Thread pork and veal cubes alternating one of each on wooden skewers. Beat egg and dip city chicken in egg then in breadcrumbs. Season city chicken with sage and salt and pepper to taste.

Heat oil over moderate heat in a skillet and brown city chicken. Add wine and bring to a boil. Reduce heat; cover pan and simmer for 30 minutes.

Pork Normandy

Serves four

4 rib pork chops, boned
¼ cup flour
½ teaspoon salt
¼ teaspoon fresh ground
 pepper
2 tablespoons butter
2 tart cooking apples,
 cored and sliced ¼″ thin

1 tablespoon olive oil
3 shallots, minced
½ cup chicken stock
½ cup Sauterne wine
½ cup whipping cream
¼ ounce Brandy

Season flour with salt and pepper and dredge pork fillets in flour. Melt butter in a large sauté pan over moderate heat and sauté apples until tender. Place apple slices on a heated serving platter. Heat oil and remaining butter and sauté pork fillets on both sides until golden and cooked thoroughly. Place pork on serving platter with apples. Add shallots to pan and sauté until tender. Add chicken broth and wine. Boil until mixture is reduced by one-half. Add cream and Brandy and continue to cook until sauce is well blended. Pour over meat and apples.

Pork Chops with Radish Sauce

Serves four

4 loin chops, 1″ thick
2 eggs lightly beaten
Flour
1½ cups dry breadcrumbs
4 tablespoons butter
½ teaspoon minced onion

1 teaspoon chopped
 parsley
½ cup whipping cream
¾ grated radishes
Salt and fresh ground
 pepper to taste

Season pork with salt and fresh ground pepper, dust with flour, dip in beaten egg and dredge with breadcrumbs. Heat butter over moderately high heat in a heavy skillet and quickly brown pork chops on both sides. Reduce heat to low; cover pan and continue cooking pork chops until done. Transfer to a heated serving platter and keep warm.

Sauté grated radish and onion in juices in pan until crisp-tender. Whisk in cream and season with salt and pepper to taste. Spoon sauce over pork, sprinkle with parsley and serve.

Neapolitan Pork Chops Flambé

Serves four

4 center cut pork chops
2 tablespoons olive oil
2 tablespoons butter
1 clove garlic, pressed
¼ teaspoon basil
3 tablespoons tomato
  purée
1½ ounces white wine

2 green peppers, seeded
  and cut in thin strips
½ pound fresh sliced
  mushrooms
1½ ounces Brandy
Salt and fresh ground
  pepper to taste

Heat butter and oil over moderate heat in a skillet and brown pork chops. Season pork chops with salt and pepper and transfer to a heated serving platter. Add garlic, basil and green pepper to skillet and sauté until green pepper is tender. Add mushrooms and sauté until tender. Blend in tomato paste and white wine. Return pork chops to skillet, pour Brandy towards front of pan and ignite. Continue cooking until pork chops are done.

Pork with Caper Sauce

Serves four

8 slices pork loin,
  ½″ thick
Flour for dredging
2 eggs, beaten
2 cups dry breadcrumbs
6 tablespoons butter

¼ cup white wine
2 tablespoons capers
1 tablespoon chopped
  parsley
Salt and fresh ground
  pepper to taste

Place pork medallions between pieces of waxed paper and flatten to ¼″ thick with a mallet or flat side of a meat cleaver. Season pork with salt and pepper to taste, dust with flour, dip in beaten egg and dredge with breadcrumbs.

Heat butter over moderate to high heat in a large skillet and cook pork until golden brown on both sides. Transfer cooked pork to a heated serving platter and keep warm. Add onion to skillet and cook until tender and transparent. Deglaze skillet with wine and stir in capers. Reduce sauce by ¼ over high heat. Pour sauce over pork and sprinkle with parsley before serving.

Flambéed Ribs

Serves four

4 pounds small pork
  spareribs
2 cloves garlic, split in half
Grated zest of one orange
Juice of one orange

1 teaspoon sugar
¼ cup Grand Marnier
Salt and fresh ground
  pepper to taste

Preheat oven to 375° F. Rub ribs on both sides with garlic cloves. Line a large shallow baking pan with aluminum foil. Sprinkle ribs generously on both sides with salt and fresh ground pepper. Bake uncovered for 45 minutes. Drain fat and turn ribs over. Bake for 35 minutes. Drain fat and sprinkle ribs with orange zest, juice, and sprinkle with sugar. Bake for 15 minutes. Transfer ribs to a heated platter. Warm Grand Marnier in a small saucepan and pour over ribs. Ignite and serve.

Pork Loin Provençale

Serves four

2½ pounds pork
  tenderloin,
1 teaspoon rosemary
3 tablespoons chopped
  parsley
½ teaspoon thyme
1 teaspoon dry mustard

2 eggs, beaten
2 cups dry bread crumbs
¼ cup olive oil
½ cup Rose wine
Salt and fresh ground
  pepper to taste

In a small mixing bowl blend dry mustard, rosemary, chopped parsley, thyme, and salt and pepper to taste. Rub this mixture into the pork loin to form a crust. Dip meat into beaten egg, then roll in breadcrumbs. Press breadcrumbs onto pork.

Grease a roasting pan with the olive oil and place pork loin in pan. Pour in wine and roast in a preheated 400° F. oven for 1½ hours or until well done.

Lamb

Lamb Loin Provençale

Serves four

1 loin of lamb (8 chops)
2 eggplants, sliced ¾"
  thick
2 onions, peeled and
  quartered
2 cloves garlic, pressed
1 teaspoon rosemary
⅔ cup olive oil
2½ ounces Rosé wine
4 tomatoes
¼ cup breadcrumbs
¼ cup grated Romano
  cheese
¼ cup butter
Salt and fresh ground
  pepper to taste

Rub lamb with garlic and season with rosemary, salt and pepper to taste. Heat oil over moderate heat in a Dutch oven and add onion and lamb and Rose. Cook lamb until browned on all sides. Place eggplant slices around lamb. Cover Dutch oven and place in a preheated 375° F. oven for one hour.

Meanwhile, cut tops off tomatoes and scoop out pulp. Mix breadcrumbs with cheese and place on tomatoes. Dot tomatoes with butter and add to lamb during last 15 minutes. Serve lamb with tomatoes and eggplant.

Lamb Chops Artichoke Flambé

Serves four

8 loin lamb chops,
  one inch thick
8 artichoke hearts
4 tablespoons olive oil
3 tablespoons butter
1 clove garlic, pressed
½ cup chopped ham
½ cup dry white wine
2 tablespoons chopped
  marjoram
1½ ounces Metaxa
  Brandy
Salt and fresh ground
  pepper to taste

Heat olive oil in a large pan over moderate heat and brown lamb chops until medium. Season chops with salt and pepper to taste and transfer to a heated serving platter. Add butter, garlic and ham to pan and cook, stirring constantly until garlic is golden. Add wine, marjoram and artichokes. Simmer until artichokes are thoroughly heated. Garnish lamb chops with artichokes. Pour Metaxa Brandy towards front of pan and ignite. Pour flaming sauce on chops and serve.

Lamb Chops Mustard Flambé

Serves four

8 lamb chops, one inch
  thick
¼ cup Dijon-style
  mustard
2 tablespoons Worchester-
  shire sauce
2 garlic cloves, pressed
1 teaspoon ground ginger
1 teaspoon thyme
½ teaspoon fresh ground
  pepper
2 tablespoons oil
1 ounce Metaxa Brandy

Blend mustard, Worchestershire, garlic, ginger, thyme and pepper in a mixing bowl. Add oil and blend thoroughly. Brush lamb chops with sauce. Roast chops in a preheated 375° F. oven for 15 minutes. Pour Brandy over chops and ignite. Serve flaming.

Lamb Epinard

Serves four

1 breast of spring lamb (have butcher remove all bones)
½ cup green onions, chopped
2 tablespoons parsley, chopped
1 teaspoon dry mustard
1 tablespoon fresh dill weed
2 sticks or ½ pound butter
Juice of one lemon

1 pound chopped fresh spinach
½ pound ripe tomatoes, skinned then chopped
½ cup white wine
⅔ cup croutons
½ cup grated Romano cheese
⅔ pound ground beef
Salt and fresh ground pepper to taste

Wash breast of lamb and pat dry with paper towels. Season with salt and pepper and dry mustard. Melt one-third of butter in a sauté pan over moderate heat. Sauté onions and ground beef until beef is lightly browned. Season with salt and pepper to taste, parsley and dill. Add wine very slowly so it is absorbed by the ground beef. Add tomatoes to ground beef mashing with a fork. Cook mixture until all excess moisture evaporates. Reduce heat; add croutons, spinach and cheese and mix well. Spread ground beef, spinach mixture on breast of lamb and roll lamb to enclose the mixture and secure with string. Sprinkle lamb with dill and lemon juice.

Place remaining butter in roasting pan and roast lamb at 425° F. for ½ hour. Reduce oven temperature to 275° F. and roast for two hours longer. Remove string before serving and cut into 2 inch slices. Spoon juices remaining in roasting pan over lamb if desired.

Lamb Moutard

Serves four

8 lamb chops, 1½" thick, filleted
2 tablespoons Virgin olive oil
1½ cup fresh diced mushrooms
½ cup pitted black olives sliced
½ pound zucchini sliced ½" thick
2 tomatoes, peeled, seeded and chopped

2 cloves garlic, pressed
¼ teaspoon thyme
¼ teaspoon oregano
4 tablespoon butter
1 cup dry white wine
½ cup whipping cream
2 teaspoons Dijon style mustard
Salt and fresh ground pepper to taste

Heat olive oil in a large skillet over moderate heat and sauté mushrooms and zucchini until tender. Season with salt and pepper to taste, garlic and thyme. Add olives and tomato and toss gently to mix. Let vegetable mixture set aside but keep warm.

Melt butter over moderate heat in a sauté pan and cook lamb fillets (noisettes) until medium-rare. Transfer to heated platter and reserve. Add wine to the pan and cook until reduced by one-half. Whisk in heavy cream and mustard, and cook until reduced by one-fourth. Whisk in butter a bit at a time.

Lamb Flambé

Serves four

2 cups cooked lamb roast, cubed
2 tablespoons butter
½ cup sliced fresh mushrooms
½ cup black pitted olives, sliced
1 teaspoon Worchestershire sauce

1 tablespoon flour
½ cup beef stock
1½ tablespoons red currant jelly
½ ounce White Creme de Menthe liqueur
1 ounce Cognac
Salt and fresh ground pepper to taste

Melt butter over moderate heat and sauté mushrooms until tender. Add olives, Worchestershire, salt and pepper to taste. Add lamb roast and currant jelly. Pour Cognac and White Creme de Menthe towards the front of the pan and ignite. When flame has extinguished, add beef stock and flour. Cook, stirring constantly until sauce is thickened. Serve with rice pilaf.

Lamb Curry Flambé

Serves two

2 cups cooked lamb cubes
2 tablespoons butter
1 medium onion, chopped
1½ ounces Metaxa Brandy
¼ cup beef stock

2 cups plain yogurt
1 teaspoon curry powder
1 tablespoon lemon juice
Salt and fresh ground pepper to taste

Sauté onion in butter in a skillet over moderate heat until transparent. Add lamb cubes and salt and pepper to taste. Pour Metaxa towards front of pan and pull back to ignite. Reduce heat to low, add beef stock, yogurt, lemon juice and curry powder. Stir mixture until well blended. Serve with boiled rice.

Crown Rack of Lamb

Serves four

2–8 rib lamb roasts (about 6 pounds)	2 tablespoons butter
½ cup olive oil	1 large onion, minced
¼ cup white wine	1 ripe tomato, chopped
¼ teaspoon crushed mint	½ teaspoon oregano flakes
Juice of one lemon	1 cup tomato juice
6 garlic cloves, minced	8 medium tomatoes
1 teaspoon salt	3 cups cooked rice
2 tablespoons fresh ground pepper	

Combine olive oil, wine, mint, lemon juice, garlic salt and pepper in a small bowl. Rub mixture into lamb roast. Invert roast so ribs are up and sew pieces together to look like a crown. Place crown in an open roasting pan and bake at 400° F. for 30 minutes, then reduce heat to 300° F. and cook for 1 hour longer.

One half hour before lamb is ready to serve, melt butter in a skillet over moderate heat and sauté onion until lightly browned; add chopped tomato, parsley, oregano, tomato juice and salt and pepper to taste. Add cooked rice and mix well. Cut one inch off each tomato and scoop out core, making a cavity. Fill each tomato with the rice mixture. Place in a greased baking dish, cover with foil and bake in oven for 30 minutes. Remove lamb from oven and fill crown with stuffed tomatoes. Decorate ribs with paper frills and serve.

Lamb Papillots

Serves six

6 large loin lamb chops, 1½″ thick	¼ pound Feta cheese, cut in 6 slices
3 cloves garlic, pressed	Juice of one lemon
6 small carrots, peeled and sliced	¼ cup melted butter
6 small zucchini, sliced	6 large squares aluminum foil, 12″×12″
6 small onions, peeled and quartered	Salt, fresh ground pepper and oregano to taste

Season each lamb chop with salt, pepper and oregano and rub with garlic. Place each chop in a square of foil and arrange the carrot, zucchini and onion on top. Top with a slice of cheese and sprinkle lemon juice and butter over the vegetables. Season the vegetables with salt and pepper to taste. Fold the foil into an envelope, securing tightly so the juices will not escape. Place papillots on a greased cookie sheet and bake in a preheated 350° F. oven for 1 hour. Serve papillots on dinner plates and make a slit in the top to let the steam escape. Serve immediately.

Lamb L'Orange

Serves four

1 lamb shoulder, 1½ pounds	1½ ounces Brandy
Grated rind of one orange	1½ ounces Grand Marnier
1 cup orange juice	1 teaspoon cornstarch
1 tablespoon brown sugar	½ cup water
1 teaspoon dry mustard	Salt and fresh ground pepper to taste

Rub the lamb generously with salt and pepper and orange rind. Cook in a preheated oven at 350° F. for 45 minutes. Meanwhile mix the orange juice, brown sugar, mustard, Brandy and Grand Marnier together and pour over the lamb. Continue to bake the lamb until done medium-well, basting frequently. Transfer the cooked lamb to a heated platter and keep warm while making the sauce. Place the pan with the drippings on the stove over moderate heat and add the cornstarch dissolved in water to the drippings. Cook, stirring constantly until slightly thickened. At this time additional Grand Marnier may be added if desired. Slice lamb and serve with the sauce.

Lamb Kidney Flambé

Serves four

1½ pound lamb kidneys	Salt and fresh ground pepper to taste
2 tablespoons butter	
1 tablespoon oil	4 tablespoons chopped parsley
2 tblespoons flour	1½ ounce Cognac
1¼ cups half and half	
3 tablespoons Dijon-style mustard	

Cut kidneys into large pieces. In a large skillet melt butter with oil over moderate heat. Add kidneys and cook for 10 minutes turning occasionally. Pour Cognac towards the front of the pan and ignite. When flames have extinguished, transfer kidneys to a warmed platter.

Add flour to the remaining juices in pan and stir until a roux is formed. Stir in half and half and bring mixture to a boil. Simmer until thickened. Stir in mustard, salt and pepper to taste. Pour sauce over kidneys and sprinkle with parsley.

*Pastas, Rice &
Vegetables*

Stuffed Baked Potatoes

Serves four

5 baking potatoes	4 tablespoons bacon
½ cup butter	bits
½ cup sour cream	¼ cup Cheddar cheese
2 tablespoons chopped	bits
chives	Salt and pepper to taste

Allow one baked potato per person, plus one extra per four people. Scrub the potatoes, oil and bake them until done. Allow the potatoes to cool for 15 minutes. You will need a hot pad to hold the potatoes. With a sharp knife, slice ½″ across the top length-wise. With a small spoon scoop out the potato, being very careful not to break the skin. Place the potato meat in a bowl. Add butter and sour cream. Add salt and pepper to taste and chives. Whip the mixture with a rotary beater until light and fluffy. Refill the potatoes and sprinkle with bacon bits and cheddar cheese. When you have filled the potatoes, place the remainder of the potato mixture in a pastry tube and decorate the tops.

Reheat the potatoes in a 350°F. oven for 10 minutes before serving. The stuffed baked potatoes can be frozen and used when needed.

Stuffed Zucchini

Serves six

6 medium zucchini	1 teaspoon dried oregano
3 tablespoons olive oil	3 tomatoes, peeled,
2 cloves garlic, pressed	seeded and chopped
2 tablespoons minced	12 pitted black olives,
onion	chopped
½ pound ground beef	6 tablespoons bread-
2 tablespoons chopped	crumbs
chives	¼ cup white wine
1 tablespoon chopped	Salt and fresh ground
parsley	pepper to taste

Halve the zucchini lengthwise and scoop out some of the flesh. Heat 1 tablespoon olive oil in a medium fry pan over moderate heat and sauté onion and garlic until soft but not brown. Add ground beef and brown lightly. Drain off excess fat and add chives, parsley, oregano, tomatoes, and olives. Season with salt and pepper to taste. Fill the zucchini halves with this mixture and arrange in a baking dish. Sprinkle with breadcrumbs. Mix remaining olive oil and white wine together and pour over zucchini. Cover with foil and bake for 25 minutes in a preheated 350°F. oven. Serve hot.

Carrots Vichy

Serves four

1½ pounds carrots	1½ teaspoon sugar
trimmed, scraped and	¼ cup water
cut into very thin rounds	4 tablespoons butter
¼ teaspoon salt	1 tablespoon chopped
¼ teaspoon fresh ground	parsley
white pepper	

Place the carrots, salt, butter, pepper, sugar and water in a skillet. Cover the skillet with a round of buttered wax paper and cook the carrots over moderate to high heat. Shake the pan frequently to insure that the carrots do not burn. Cook until the carrots are tender and a light glaze is formed. Sprinkle with parsley before serving.

Zucchini Au Gratin

Serves four–six

2 large zucchini, sliced	2 eggs, beaten
6 tablespoons butter	Salt and fresh ground
½ cup heavy cream	pepper to taste
½ cup grated Parmesan	
cheese	

Boil zucchini in lightly salted water for 3 minutes. Drain in a colander. Heat butter in a large pan over moderate heat, and stir fry zucchini for 3 minutes. Add cream and eggs and stir until ingredients are well blended. Place zucchini in an oven proof casserole, sprinkle with Parmesan and brown lightly under the broiler. Season with salt and pepper.

Mushrooms with Grape Leaves

Serves four

16 large mushroom caps
16 grape or vine leaves
½ cup oil
3 cloves garlic, pressed
1 tablespoon oregano

Juice of ½ lemon
1½ ounce white wine
Salt and fresh ground
  pepper to taste

Brush grape leaves on both sides with oil and arrange them on an oven proof platter. Heat remaining oil in a saucepan over moderate heat; add garlic and oregano and saute' until garlic is golden brown. Stir in lemon juice and white wine. Brush mushrooms on both sides with oil mixture and arrange them—hollow side up on grape leaves. Season with salt and pepper to taste. Pour remaining oil mixture into hollows of mushrooms. Place platter in a preheated 350°F. oven for 15 minutes, or until mushrooms are tender. Turn mushrooms over before serving.

Green Beans Viniagrette

Serves four

4 cups chilled cooked
  fresh green beans
2 cups sliced celery
2 tablespoons minced
  onion
1 teaspoon salt
⅛ teaspoon fresh ground
  pepper
1½ tablespoons white
  tarragon vinegar

2 tablespoons white
  vinegar
2 tablespoons olive oil
2 tablespoons pickle
  relish
2 tablespoons minced
  parsley
1 tablespoon chopped
  chives
¼ teaspoon paprika

Combine green beans, celery and minced onion in an attractive glass bowl and set aside. Mix remaining ingredients and whisk until well blended. Pour over vegetables and toss to mix. Chill until ready to serve.

Green Beans with Sunflower Seeds

Serves four

1 pound fresh green beans
2 tablespoons butter
3 tablespoons minced
  onion
¼ cup sunflower seeds

2 tablespoons chopped
  parsley
½ teaspoon lemon juice
Salt and fresh ground
  pepper to taste

Cut ends off beans and cook in boiling salted water until tender. Drain and rinse under cold running water. Melt butter in a large skillet and saute' onion until tender. Add sunflower seeds and beans. Cook, stirring until beans are heated. Sprinkle with parsley, lemon juice, and salt and pepper to taste before serving.

Four Herb Green Beans

Serves four

1 pound fresh green
  beans, cooked and
  drained
3 tablespoons butter
½ teaspoon rosemary

¼ teaspoon basil
½ teaspoon curry powder
½ teaspoon oregano
Salt and fresh ground
  pepper to taste

Melt butter in a saute' pan, add seasonings and blend well. Add beans and toss until heated. Season with salt and pepper to taste.

Sweet and Sour Onions

Serves four

20 pearl or small white
 onions
3 slices bacon, chopped
1 clove garlic, pressed
2 tablespoons brown sugar

2 tablespoons chopped
 chives
½ cup white vinegar
1½ ounce dry white
 wine

Fry bacon over moderate heat until bacon is crisp; add garlic and cook until garlic is golden brown. Add onions and vinegar, cover pan and simmer onions for 20 minutes or until tender. Uncover and add remaining ingredients. Stir until sauce is slightly thickened and glazed.

Florida Beets

Serves four

¼ cup butter
2 tablespoons sugar
1 orange

1 16-ounce can sliced
 beets
Salt and pepper to taste

Melt butter in a heavy saucepan over moderate heat. Add sugar. Remove sections from orange and add to butter mixture. Add beets, salt and pepper to taste. Cook covered until ingredients are heated.

Broccoli William

2 pounds broccoli
½ cup olive oil
1 onion, minced
1 cup chopped pitted
 black olives
6 anchovies, chopped

1 cup grated Mozzarella
 cheese
2 cups red wine
1 cup croutons
Salt and fresh ground
 pepper to taste

Trim stalks of broccoli, and slice thick stalks in half lengthwise, making all stalks roughly the same size and thickness. Oil a large heavy pan and arrange 1/3 of onion, olives, anchovies, and cheese on top of broccoli. Continue to do this 2 more times. Season with salt and fresh ground pepper. Gently pour wine over entire mixture and bring mixture to a boil over moderate heat. Simmer for 25 minutes or until broccoli is tender. *Do not stir* mixture. Sprinkle with croutons before serving.

Snow Peas and Grapes

Serves four

½ cup orange juice
¼ cup honey
⅛ teaspoon grated ginger
⅓ cup olive oil
1 pound fresh or frozen
 snow peas

½ cup seedless green
 grapes
1 tablespoon chopped
 parsley
¼ teaspoon salt

In a medium sauce pan over moderate heat, combine orange juice, honey, ginger, olive oil and salt. Stir until mixture comes to a boil, cover and simmer for 15 minutes. Meanwhile steam snow peas until crisp. Add grapes to sauce and cook for 4 minutes. Drain snow peas and add to sauce. Sprinkle with parsley before serving.

Braised Snow Peas

Serves four

2 tablespoons butter
1 medium onion, minced
¼ cup minced lean ham
2 pounds fresh snow peas

4 tablespoons water
Salt and white pepper to
 taste

Melt butter in a large pan over moderate heat. Add onion and saute' until transparent. Add ham, peas, water and salt and pepper to taste. Cover tightly and cook over low heat for 15 minutes. Uncover and simmer for 15 minutes longer. Serve immediately.

Peas Francais

Serves four

10 ounce package frozen peas
1 tablespoon butter
3 tablespoons chopped onion
¼ cup sliced fresh mushrooms
⅛ teaspoon marjoram
¼ teaspoon salt
¼ teaspoon fresh ground pepper
½ cup whipping cream
1 ounce Madeira wine

Cook peas as directed on package. Melt butter in a medium saucepan over moderate heat. Add onion and mushrooms, cooking until onion is tender. Add marjoram, salt and pepper and whisk in whipping cream. When ingredients are well blended, add peas and wine. Stir well before serving.

Coconut Rice

Serves eight

3 cups raw rice
3 cups grated fresh coconut
2 cups milk
2 cups half and half
2 tablespoons sesame oil
3 scallions, minced
2½ teaspoon salt
1 cup water

Combine the coconut, milk and half and half in a saucepan. Scald the mixture and remove from heat. Allow coconut to soak for 30 minutes. Drain coconut, squeezing juice from pulp. Discard the coconut pulp.

Heat oil over moderate heat in a skillet. Add scallions and sauté until tender. Add rice, water, coconut milk and salt. Cover the skillet and cook over low heat until rice is light and fluffy.

Buttered Peas and Radishes

Serves four

1 package (10 ounce) frozen baby green peas
½ cup thinly sliced radishes
1 tablespoon butter
Salt and fresh ground pepper to taste

Cook peas as directed on package. Two minutes before the end of cooking time, add radishes; cook until radishes are thoroughly heated but still crisp. Drain and stir in butter. Season with salt and pepper to taste.

Deviled Brussels Sprouts

Serves six

½ cup butter
2 teaspoons mustard
1½ teaspoon Worchestershire sauce
¼ teaspoon salt
⅛ teaspoon cayenne pepper
2 packages (10 ounce) frozen or 1½ pounds fresh Brussels sprouts, cooked and drained

Melt butter, blend with mustard, Worchestershire sauce, salt and cayenne. Pour over hot Brussels sprouts.

Fettucini Carbanara

Serves four

¼ pound butter	1 tablespoon pimento strips
3 tablespoons chives, chopped	1 cup fresh sliced mushrooms
3 large garlic cloves, pressed	12 ounces spinach noodles, boiled and drained
½ pound thinly sliced ham, cut in julienne strips	½ cup Parmesan cheese
1 teaspoon Worchester-shire sauce	2 eggs
1 large green pepper, sliced in julienne strips	Salt and fresh ground pepper to taste
½ cup chopped onion	

Melt butter in a sauté pan along with chives, garlic and Worchestershire. Add ham, green pepper, mushrooms, onions and pimento, and sauté until onion and green pepper are soft. Add noodles and toss mixture well. Add Parmesan cheese, salt and pepper to taste and toss again. Break eggs into noodles and toss once more until eggs are blended into mixture. (Toss quickly so eggs do not set.) Serve as an entree or in place of a vegetable.

Rice L'Orange

Serves six

3 tablespoons butter	1 cup orange juice
½ cup chopped green onions	½ ounce Grand Marnier
1 cup chopped celery	1½ cup water
1 cup long grain rice	½ teaspoon salt
	⅛ teaspoon nutmeg

Melt butter over moderate heat in a medium sized sauté pan; add onions and celery. Sauté until tender and light brown. Combine celery-onion mixture with remaining ingredients and place in a baking dish, cover tightly. Bake at 350° F. for 35 minutes or until water is absorbed. Fluff rice with a fork before serving.

Fettucini with Proscuitto and Chicken

Serves four

6 tablespoons unsalted butter
½ cup whipping cream
2 ounces grated Parmesan cheese
1 tablespoon minced parsley
½ cup cooked chicken, cubed

12 ounces fettucini noodles, cooked and drained
⅛ pound proscuitto ham, thinly sliced and cut into thin strips
2 tablespoons pine nuts
Fresh ground black pepper to taste

Melt butter in a saute' pan over low heat. Add cheese, whipping cream, and blend well. Add parsley, chicken and noodles. Toss to heat all ingredients. Season with pepper to taste. Place noodle mixture on serving plates, and decoratively top with proscuitto ham. Sprinkle with pine nuts and serve.

Fettucini La Casa

Serves two as an Entree'
Serves four as a Side Dish

¼ cup butter
1½ tablespoon dried chives
3 cloves garlic, pressed
¼ cup green onion, chopped
¼ cup green pepper, cut in julienne strips

½ cup fresh sliced mushrooms
1 pound Fettucini noodles, cooked and drained
½ cup Feta cheese
¼ cup Parmesan cheese
2 eggs
Salt and pepper to taste

In a chafing dish or skillet, place butter, chives and garlic. Add onion and green pepper; saute' until tender. Add the mushrooms and noodles, and cook for two minutes stirring constantly. Add Feta and Parmesan cheese, salt, and pepper to taste and cook for another three minutes. Add the eggs and stir a few more times. Serve immediately.

Pasta Al Pesto

Serves four

2 cloves garlic, pressed
5 sprigs fresh basil
4 teaspoons salt
1½ tablespoons finely chopped pine nuts
5 tablespoons grated Romano cheese

⅛ teaspoon cayenne pepper
¼ cup olive oil
1 pound pasta (macaroni, pasta shells, spirals or fettucini)

Cook pasta in boiling salted water until al dente'. Meanwhile, place nuts, garlic, basil, cheese and cayenne pepper in a mortar and crush until a fine paste is formed. Gradually beat in 5 tablespoons olive oil to form a creamy sauce. Drain and toss pasta with remaining oil. Spoon pesto over pasta and serve.

Mixed Vegetables Flambé

Serves four

¼ cup butter
1 pound chopped carrots
½ pound cauliflower florets
½ pound small white onions

½ teaspoon fresh ground black pepper
2 tablespoons brown sugar
1½ ounces Brandy
½ teaspoon salt

Melt butter in a large frypan over moderate heat. Add carrots, cauliflower and onions and shake pan to coat them with butter. Add salt, pepper, brown sugar and stir. Reduce heat to low, cook for 25 minutes, covered, stirring occasionally. Place vegetables in a serving bowl. Heat Brandy in a small saucepan until hot. Remove pan from heat and ignite. Pour flaming Brandy over vegetables and serve.

Potatoes New Orleans

Serves four

4 large Idaho potatoes, peeled and diced
1 clove garlic, pressed
4 tablespoons butter
½ teaspoon chopped parsley
Salt and pepper to taste
Oil for frying

Heat oil over high heat in a deep fryer and fry potatoes until golden brown. Meanwhile melt butter over moderate heat in a skillet and sauté garlic until golden. Season with salt and pepper to taste. Add potatoes and parsley and mix well.

Artichokes with Mustard Sauce

Serves four

4 artichokes
½ cup mayonnaise
4 tablespoons Dijon style mustard
Salt and fresh ground pepper to taste

Steam artichokes in boiling water until tender. Cut in half lengthwise and clean. Fill cavity of artichokes with mustard mayonnaise mixture. Season with salt and pepper to taste and serve.

Mushroom Rice

Serves six

1 10-ounce can beef consommé
1¼ cup wild rice
¼ cup butter
¼ cup chopped green onion
1 tablespoon lemon juice
¼ cup chopped fresh parsley
1 cup fresh sliced mushrooms

Combine consommé with 2 cups water in a large saucepan and bring to a boil. Add rice and stir well. Reduce heat and cover; simmer for 20 minutes or until liquid is absorbed. Meanwhile melt butter in a small sauté pan. Add onions and sauté until tender. Toss mushrooms with lemon juice and sauté with onions until tender. Add mushroom-onion mixture and parsley to rice and toss before serving.

Potato Croquettes

Serves four

4 large potatoes
2 tablespoons butter
¼ cup grated Parmesan cheese
2 tablespoons chopped chives
2 egg whites
⅛ teaspoon nutmeg
2 egg yolks, lightly beaten
1 cup dry breadcrumbs
Oil for deep frying

Peel and wash potatoes cut in quarters and cook in boiling salted water until soft. Drain well and mash finely or rice. Add butter, chives, cheese, egg yolks, nutmeg and salt and pepper to taste. Shape mixture into croquettes or corkscrew shapes. Coat with egg whites and roll in breadcrumbs.

Heat oil until a bread cube dropped in it turns golden brown and floats to the top. Add croquettes and fry until golden brown. Remove from oil and drain on a paper towel. Serve immediately.

Potato Pyramids

Serves four

4 cups mashed potatoes
¼ cup butter
¼ teaspoon paprika
2 eggs
3 tablespoons milk
¼ cup melted butter
Salt and pepper to taste

Preheat oven to broil. Season potatoes with butter, paprika, salt and pepper. Beat in eggs. Add enough milk to make the mixture stiff enough to put in a pastry bag. Use a large rosette tip to form eight pyramids. Top with melted butter. Place under pre-heated broiler until golden brown.

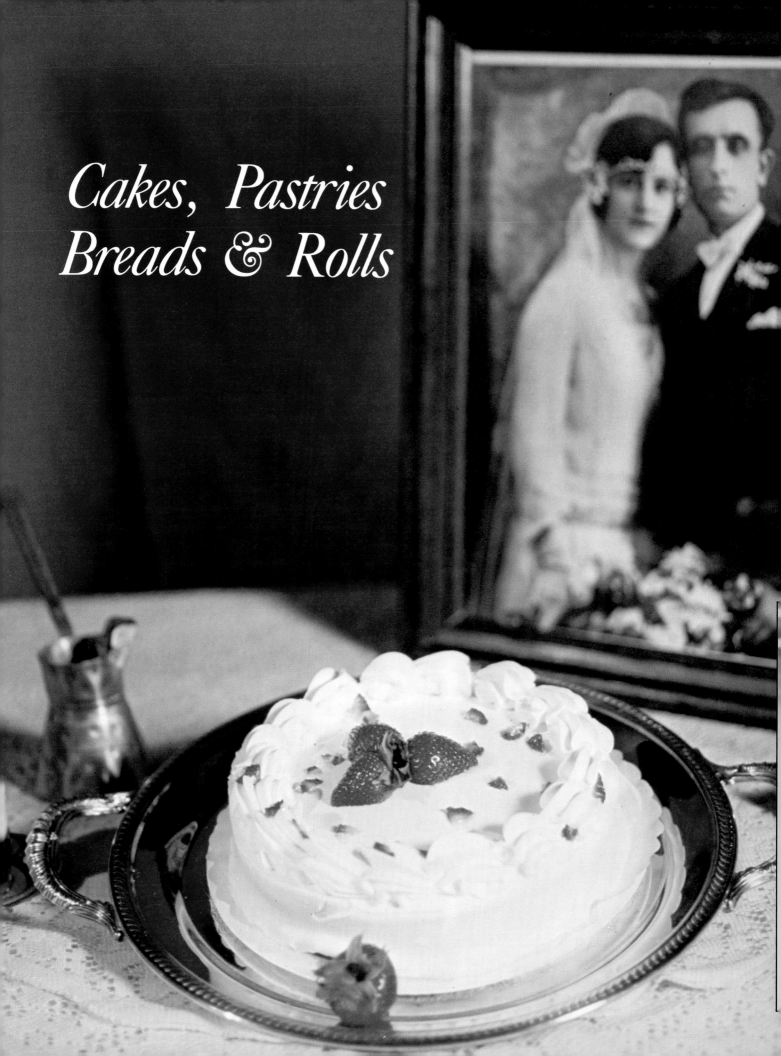

Cakes, Pastries
Breads & Rolls

Hard Rolls

Makes 18 rolls

4 cups all-purpose flour
2 packages active dry
  yeast
1 tablespoon sugar
1½ teaspoons salt

1 cup hot water (120°F.)
2 tablespoons vegetable
  oil
1 egg white
1 egg yolk

Combine one cup flour, yeast, sugar and salt in a large mixing bowl. Stir in water, oil and egg yolk. Beat mixture until smooth. Gradually stir in more flour to make a soft dough.

Turn dough onto a floured surface and knead until smooth and elastic. Cover dough with bowl and allow to rest 20 minutes.

Divide dough into 18 portions. Form each portion into a smooth oval and place on a greased baking sheet. Slash tops lengthwise ¼ inch deep. Cover and allow to rise until double in bulk. Meanwhile preheat oven to 400° F. Before baking, brush egg white on each roll. Bake in preheated oven for 20 minutes or until golden. If a crustier roll is desired place a shallow pan of boiling water on the lowest oven rack during baking.

Strawberry Walnut Cream Cake

4 eggs
½ cup sugar
1 tablespoon instant coffee
¾ cup sifted cake flour

½ cup finely chopped
  walnuts
1 pint strawberries, hulled
1 cup heavy cream

Grease an 8-inch springform pan and first sprinkle with sugar, then with flour. Preheat oven to 350° F. Beat eggs and sugar with instant coffee over a double boiler with a rotary beater, until mixture is thick and shiny. Remove from heat and whisk until cool. Sift flour and fold into egg mixture in 3 portions alternating with the walnuts. Pour into prepared pan and bake for 35 minutes or until cake springs back when lightly pressed with fingertip. Cool cake on a wire rack. Meanwhile, slice strawberries, reserving 8 for decorating. Whip cream until stiff. When cake has cooled, split in 3 layers. Fill layers with ⅔ of the cream, mixed with the sliced strawberries. Top cake with remaining cream and whole strawberries. Chill until ready to serve.

Bagels

Makes one dozen

4½ cups all-purpose flour
1 package active dry yeast
2 teaspoons salt

1½ cups hot water (120°F.)
2 tablespoons sugar
1 egg white

Combine 1 cup flour, yeast and salt in a mixing bowl. Stir in hot water and sugar; beat mixture until smooth. Stir in enough remaining flour to make a soft dough.

Turn dough out onto a floured surface and knead until dough is smooth and elastic. Cover with bowl and let rest 15 minutes.

Divide dough into 12 equal parts. Shape each into a flattened ball and then poke a hole into each center. Stretch and rotate until hole enlarges to 2 inches. Cover dough and allow to rise for 30 minutes.

Boil water in a large shallow pan about 2 inches deep. Add bagels and reduce heat. Simmer bagels for 7 minutes then remove from pan. Drain on a towel for 5 minutes. Place on a baking sheet, brush with egg white and bake in a preheated 375° F. oven for 30 minutes or until browned lightly on outside.

Croissants

Yield: 36

2 envelopes dry yeast
5 cups all-purpose flour
3 tablespoons sugar
¼ cup butter, room
temperature

2 cups milk
3 eggs, beaten
¾ pound butter, chilled
½ teaspoon salt

Egg wash: one egg yolk blended with 1 tablespoon
milk

Dissolve yeast in ½ cup warm water in a large
mixing bowl. Add one cup flour and stir to make a
smooth dough. Cover and let rise in a warm place until
doubled in size.

Combine remaining flour, sugar and salt in a large
mixing bowl. Add room temperature butter and milk,
stirring to make a smooth dough. Stir in egg and
combine with yeast dough. Cover and let rise in a
warm place for 20 minutes.

Cut cold butter into thin slivers. Roll out dough to
½-inch thick and place half of butter slivers over dough
surface. Fold ⅓ of dough over center and fold
remaining ⅓ over top to make 3 layers. Roll dough
again to ½-inch and repeat process. Fold dough and roll
out 3 more times. Roll dough into a ball and refrigerate
for one hour.

Roll chilled dough to ⅛-inch thick on a lightly floured
board. Cut dough in 5-inch squares. Cut squares diagonally
into 2 triangles each. Roll triangles from long side and
shape into crescents. Place on a lightly floured baking
sheet, cover and let rise in a warm place until double
in bulk. Brush surface with egg wash. Bake in a
preheated 375° F. oven for 20–25 minutes or until
golden brown.

Brioches

Yield: 24

1 package dry yeast
¼ cup warm water
5 cups all-purpose flour
½ cup butter, room
temperature

¼ cup sugar
½ teaspoon salt
6 eggs
2 cups scalded milk

Egg wash: one egg yolk blended with 1 tablespoon
milk

Dissolve yeast in warm water in a large mixing bowl.
Add 1 cup flour and mix to form a smooth dough.
Roll to form a smooth ball; place in a buttered bowl.
Cover and allow to double in bulk.

Combine remaining flour, butter, sugar and salt. Add
two eggs and half of milk, and mix to form a dough.
Knead dough until very smooth and elastic. Add
remaining milk and 2 eggs. Knead dough again until
very smooth and elastic. Add yeast dough and
remaining eggs and knead for 5 minutes. Place dough
in a buttered bowl; cover and let rise in a warm place
free of drafts until double in bulk.

Punch dough down and refrigerate 8 hours or
overnight.

Shape dough into balls large enough to fill small
brioche molds. Make a small incision in the top of
each and place smaller balls of dough over the
incisions, pressing firmly in place.

Cover molds and let rise in a warm place until
double in bulk. Brush surface of brioche with egg
wash. Place in preheated 375° F. oven and bake 20–25
minutes or until lightly browned.

Artichoke Pizza

Serves four

8 ounces puff pastry
dough
4 tomatoes, peeled,
seeded and cubed
16 canned, artichoke
hearts
16 pitted black olives

¼ cup grated Parmesan
cheese
1 garlic clove, pressed
1 tablespoon chopped
parsley
½ teaspoon dill weed
3 tablespoons olive oil

Roll puffed pastry out and use to line an 8-inch shallow
pan. Place tomatoes on puffed dough. Place artichoke
hearts and olives on tomatoes. Sprinkle with Parmesan
cheese. Blend olive oil with garlic, dill weed and
parsley. Brush oil mixture on ingredients. Bake in a
preheated 425°F. oven for 25 minutes.

Avocado Bread

Yield: one loaf

1 egg
½ cup mashed avocado
½ cup buttermilk
⅓ cup vegetable oil
2 cups all-purpose flour
¾ cup sugar

½ teaspoon baking soda
½ teaspoon baking
powder
¼ teaspoon salt
¾ cup chopped pecans
1 ounce Tequila

Preheat oven to 350° F. Grease and flour a 9″×5″
loaf pan. Mix avocado, egg, buttermilk and oil with a
hand mixer until well blended. Add flour, sugar,
baking soda, baking powder and salt. When mixture is
blended, add Tequila and pecans. Pour batter into
prepared pan and bake for 1 hour. Cool 10 minutes
on a wire rack before removing from pan. Serve warm.

Olive Nut French Bread

Two loaves

2 packages active dry
   yeast
1¼ cup warm water
   (105°–115°F)
3 tablespoons shortening
2 tablespoons sugar
1½ teaspoon salt

1 cup chopped pitted
   black olives
¾ cup chopped pecans
3½ cups all-purpose flour
1 egg white
2 tablespoons water

Dissolve yeast in warm water. Stir in shortening, sugar, salt, olives and pecans. Mix in enough flour to make dough soft and pliable. Turn onto a lightly floured board, knead until smooth. Place in a greased bowl, cover with a moistened cloth. Let rise in a warm place for two hours.

Punch dough down and let rise again, covered for 1 hour. Punch down once again and let rest, covered, for 15 minutes. Divide dough in half. Shape each half into a long loaf with tapered ends. Place on a lightly greased baking sheet. Make slashes 2 inches apart on tops of loaves. Let rise uncovered for 1 hour. Preheat oven to 375° F. Place a pan of hot water on top rack 30 minutes before baking bread. Leave pan in oven during baking. Brush bread with cold water. Bake for 20 minutes. Brush with egg white mixed with 2 tablespoons water. Return to oven and bake 25 minutes longer. Cool on a wire rack.

To quickly clean your pastry board: scrape off dough with a spatula, sprinkle board with salt and rub with a damp sponge or cloth.

Traditional Pizza

Serve four

1½ packages dry active
   yeast
2 cups all-purpose flour
½ teaspoon sugar
1¼ cups milk, warmed
6 tablespoons olive oil
5 tomatoes, peeled,
   seeded and diced
1 teaspoon fresh ground
   black pepper
2 teaspoons oregano
   flakes

4 ounces grated Parmesan
   cheese
6 anchovy fillets
5 capers chopped
1 onion peeled and sliced
   thin
1 green pepper seeded and
   cut julienne
¼ pound fresh
   mushrooms, sliced
½ teaspoon salt

Sift flour on a pastry board and make a well in the center. In a small mixing bowl blend 6 tablespoons milk (120°–130°F.), sugar and yeast with 1 tablespoon flour. Allow yeast mixture to become frothy. Pour frothy yeast mixture into flour well and allow to set for 30 minutes. Stir in remaining milk, 3 tablespoons oil and salt. Mix ingredients together and knead until a smooth elastic dough is formed. Roll dough out to form a 12-inch circle. Place on a greased baking sheet and turn edges up slightly. Mix tomatoes with pepper, oregano, anchovy and capers and place on dough. Scatter onions, pepper, mushrooms and cheese over tomatoes. Bake in a preheated 400° F. oven for 30 minutes.

Date Nut Bread

Two loaves

2 cups boiling water
3 tablespoons butter
3 eggs
2 cups sugar
5 cups sifted all-purpose
   flour

2 teaspoons baking soda
½ teaspoon salt
4 cups chopped, pitted
   dates
1 cup chopped walnuts
1 teaspoon vanilla extract

Preheat oven to 325° F. Grease 2 loaf pans 9"×5"×3". Pour boiling water over dates, add butter and stir until butter is melted. In a large mixing bowl beat eggs and sugar until light and fluffy. Sift flour with soda and salt and blend into egg-sugar mixture. Add dates, vanilla and nuts; stir until well blended. Pour into prepared pans and bake for 1 hour 15 minutes or until toothpick inserted in center comes out clean. Cool 10 minutes in pan, then place turned out breads on a rack to cool.

Beignets

Serves four

8 tablespoons butter
1 cup water
2 teaspoons sugar
1 cup all-purpose flour

2 eggs
1 egg yolk
Confectioner's sugar
Oil for frying

In a heavy saucepan bring butter, water and sugar to a boil. Add flour all at once and stir vigorously over heat until mixture leaves sides of pan. Place mixture in a mixing bowl and beat in eggs and egg yolks one at a time, beating vigorously after each addition. Spoon mixture into hot oil and fry until golden brown and puffy. Sprinkle with confectioner's sugar.

Tea Cakes

Makes 12 cakes

½ cup unsalted butter
½ cup granulated sugar
¼ teaspoon vanilla
½ teaspoon almond
  extract
1 tablespoon Jamaican
  Rum
Grated zest of 1 orange

¼ teaspoon salt
¾ cup all-purpose flour
1 cup finely ground
  unblached almonds
4 egg whites, stiffly
  beaten
3 tablespoons confectioner's
  sugar, sifted

Preheat oven to 375° F. Cream butter and sugar in a bowl. Add vanilla, almond extract, rum, orange zest, salt, flour and almonds. Mix well. Fold in ¼ of the egg whites and carefully fold in remaining egg whites. Pour into buttered 2-inch muffin tins and bake about 45 minutes, or until lightly browned. Remove from tins and cool on a rack. Sprinkle tops with confectioner's sugar.

Almond Fingers

Makes five dozen

1 package dry yeast
1 cup milk, warmed
4 cups all-purpose flour
½ cup butter
1 egg
¾ cup sugar
½ teaspoon grated orange
  rind

1 cup chopped almonds
½ cup unsalted butter
½ ounce Creme de
  Almond liqueur
1 cup confectioner's sugar
½ teaspoon almond
  extract

Mix yeast with three tablespoons warm milk, and allow to set for 10 minutes. Sift flour in mixing bowl and pour in yeast mixture. Melt ¼ cup butter in remaining warm milk and add to flour along with egg, ¼ cup sugar and orange rind. Form mixture into dough and knead for 5 minutes or until smooth and elastic. Spread dough on a greased baking sheet and allow to rise for 1½ hours in a warm place, free of drafts.

Melt remaining butter and stir in remaining sugar, Creme de Almond and almonds. Spread this mixture over dough and bake in a preheated 400° F. oven for 40 minutes. Cool and cut into 2″×4″ fingers. Split each finger in half and fill with filling made by creaming unsalted butter with confectioner's sugar and almond extract until light and fluffy.

Baklava Grand Marnier

Makes 36 pieces

2 pounds shelled walnuts chopped extra fine	1 teaspoon allspice
1 pound shelled walnuts, ground	⅔ cups sugar
2 teaspoons ground cinnamon	1 pound sweet butter, melted
	1 pound phyllo dough

Syrup:

2 cups honey	1 tablespoon grated orange peel
2 cups water	½ cup Grand Marnier
2 cinnamon sticks	

Combine all ingredients for the syrup in a saucepan, bring to a boil and simmer for 10 minutes, strain and cool. Combine the nuts with cinnamon, allspice and sugar. Brush a 9"×13"×2" pan with butter, lay a sheet of phyllo in the bottom, brush it with butter, cover with another sheet of phyllo, brush with butter and continue this process with 10 sheets. Spread a layer of nuts on the phyllo and continue with 10 more sheets of phyllo brushed with butter. Continue doing this until all nuts are used. Cover with remaining phyllo sheets, buttering each sheet. With a very sharp knife, cut the top sheets into diagonal triangles and bake at 350° F. for 1½ hours. When baklava is browned on the top, pour the cooled syrup over it and allow for cooling and penetration of the syrup of several hours before serving.

Raisin Casserole Bread

Makes two loaves

1 cup milk	2 packages active dry yeast
½ cup sugar	
¼ teaspoon cinnamon	2 eggs
1 teaspoon salt	4½ cups unsifted flour, or
½ cup butter	5 cups sifted flour
½ cup water (120°F.)	1 cup seedless raisins

Scald milk, stir in sugar, cinnamon, salt and butter; cool to lukewarm. Pour water into large bowl and sprinkle in yeast. Stir until dissolved. Stir in lukewarm milk mixture, egg and 3 cups flour. Beat until smooth. Stir in remaining flour to make a stiff batter. Cover and let rise in a warm place, free from draft until doubled (about 1 hour). After dough has doubled in bulk, stir batter down. Beat in raisins, and turn into a 1½ quart casserole, that has been greased. Bake immediately in a moderate oven at 350° for 40–45 minutes. Remove from casserole, cool on wire racks.

Tip: Coat raisins with flour before adding to dough, to make the stirring easier.

Hungarian Christmas Bread

Makes two poppy seed rolls

Dough:

2 packages active dry yeast	½ teaspoon salt
½ cup warm water (105°–115°F)	½ cup butter
	2 eggs
4½ cups all-purpose flour	2 egg yolks
¾ cup sugar	½ cup sour cream
	1 teaspoon vanilla extract

Filling:

2 tablespoons butter	2 egg whites
12 ounces poppy seeds, ground	½ cup sugar
	½ cup chopped citron
4 tablespoons honey	2 teaspoons grated lemon peels
2 teaspoons lemon juice	
½ cup white raisins	

Prepare dough by softening yeast in warm water in a small bowl. Mix flour with sugar and salt in a mixing bowl. Cut in butter with a pastry blender until mixture resembles fine crumbs. Beat eggs and egg yolks and mix with yeast mixture. Stir egg mixture into flour mixture. Add sour cream and vanilla extract and blend well.

Knead dough on a floured surface for 5 minutes or until smooth and elastic. Divide dough in half and roll each half into a 12-inch square. Cover dough and allow to rise.

To prepare filling melt butter in a large saucepan. Add poppy seeds and sauté for 3 minutes. Add honey, lemon juice and raisins to poppy seeds. Cover and set aside for 10 minutes. Beat egg whites until frothy and gradually add sugar continually beating until stiff. Fold in lemon peel and candied citron. Gently fold this into poppy seed mixture.

Spread half of filling over each dough roll. Roll up jelly roll style and seal edges well. Place on a greased baking sheet. Cover and let rise until double in bulk.

Bake at 350° F. for 45 minutes. Cool and if desired ice with a mixture of 1 cup confectioner's sugar and 2 tablespoons lemon juice.

Pecan Pie

1 9″ unbaked pie shell	1 teaspoon vanilla
3 eggs, beaten	1 ounce Praline liqueur
½ cup sugar	¼ cup unsalted butter, melted
1 cup dark corn syrup	
⅛ teaspoon salt	2 cups pecans

Blend eggs with sugar and corn syrup in a medium sized mixing bowl. Add salt, vanilla, and butter. Blend in Praline liqueur. Place pecans in the bottom of the pie shell. Gently pour filling over pecans. Bake in a preheated 350° F. oven for 60 minutes.

Creme Wafers à la Florence

Pastry:

1 cup lightly salted butter at room temperature	⅓ cup half and half
	2 cups all-purpose flour

Filling:

¼ cup butter at room temperature	1 tablespoon Kahlua
	Red food coloring
1 egg yolk	1¼ cup confectioner's sugar
¼ teaspoon peppermint extract	

In a medium sized mixing bowl, beat butter until creamy. Stir in cream and beat a few seconds longer. Mix in flour and blend thoroughly. Wrap the dough in wax paper and chill until firm (at least 2 hours). Heat oven to 350° F. Roll the pastry on a lightly floured board ¼ at a time to a ¼-inch thickness. Cut the pastry into 1½-inch rounds. Gather the trimmings together and chill before re-rolling. Place the cookies 1-inch apart on an ungreased baking sheet. Pierce 2 times and bake for 15 minutes. Cool on a wire rack.

For the filling, beat butter until creamy; add the egg yolks and beat until well blended. Add the sugar a little at a time, beating well after each addition. Mix the Kahlua and peppermint extract into the filling. Add 2–3 drops of red food coloring and beat the mixture until creamy. Spread filling between 2 wafers. Dust the finished wafers with confectioner's sugar if desired. Store in an air-tight container.

Strawberry Roulade

1 pint strawberries, hulled and quartered	½ cup all-purpose flour, sifted
⅓ cup sugar	6 tablespoons cornstarch, sifted
4 eggs, separated	
¾ cup confectioner's sugar	¾ cup whipping cream
	½ ounce Grand Marnier

Place strawberries in a bowl and sprinkle with Grand Marnier and 2 tablespoons sugar.

Beat egg yolks and remaining sugar until frothy. Beat egg whites in a separate bowl until frothy. Gradually add ½ cup confectioner's sugar to whites, beating until stiff. Fold egg whites into egg yolks with a whisk and quickly fold in cornstarch and flour. Spread mixture on a 9″×12″ jelly roll pan lined with baking paper. Bake in a preheated 400° F. oven for 12 minutes or until golden brown. Turn out carefully to a clean baker's paper and peel off first baker's paper. Roll with the clean paper inside and cool.

Meanwhile whip cream until thick and stiff, and fold in remaining confectioner's sugar. Unroll cake and place strawberries over cake. Spread whipped cream over strawberries and roll cake. Sprinkle with additional confectioner's sugar before serving.

Walnut Raisin Bread

Makes 2 loaves

1 package dry yeast
½ cup lukewarm water
  (105°–115°F.)
1 teaspoon sugar
1 cup milk
4 tablespoons unsalted
  butter
½ cup light brown sugar
2 cups whole wheat flour
4 cups all-purpose flour
2 teaspoons salt

3 teaspoons cinnamon
½ teaspoon nutmeg
2 eggs
2 cups white raisins
  plumped in ½ cup hot
  water for one hour
1 cup chopped walnuts
½ cup chopped citron peel
1 egg yolk stirred with
  2 tablespoons milk

Sprinkle yeast over water; add sugar and allow to become frothy.

Heat milk, butter and brown sugar over low heat until sugar dissolves. Sift together flours, salt, cinnamon and nutmeg. Beat yeast mixture and eggs together and add to flour mixture. Mix well, then knead dough on a floured board for 5 minutes. Place dough in an oiled bowl. Cover with a towel and allow to rise in a warm place free of drafts for 1½ hours.

Divide dough in halves and knead for a few minutes. Roll dough halves out to form long rectangles 10″×18″ each.

Drain raisins and toss in a bowl with nuts and citron. Press mixture into surface of dough, then roll up jelly roll fashion. Place in two, buttered, floured loaf pans. Allow to rise for 1 hour then bake at 375° for 50 minutes after brushing tops with egg yolk mixed with milk.

Irish Soda Bread

Makes 2 loaves

1 cup currants,
  plumped in
¼ cup hot water for
4½ cups all purpose flour
2 teaspoons salt

1½ teaspoons baking soda
1 teaspoon baking powder
2½ cups buttermilk
3 tablespoons cornmeal
2 teaspoons Kosher salt

Drain currants well. Sift 4 cups flour, salt, baking soda and baking powder together. Add 2 cups buttermilk and currants to flour and mix to form a soft dough. Knead on a floured dough board, adding more flour as necessary. Knead until smooth and elastic. Form into 2 loaves.

Spread cornmeal on baking sheet and place loaves on top of cornmeal. Brush with remaining buttermilk and sprinkle with salt. Cut a criss-cross cut in the top of each loaf and bake in a preheated 350°F. oven for 1 hour.

French Bread

Makes 3–4 loaves; depending upon desired size

2 cakes yeast, or 2
  envelopes active dry yeast
¼ cup warm water
½ cup milk
1 cup water

1 tablespoon sugar
1 tablespoon butter
2 teaspoons salt
5 cups unbleached,
  all-purpose flour

Dissolve yeast in ¼ cup warm water. Scald milk with 1 cup water and add sugar, butter and salt. Let mixture cool to warm and add the yeast and water. Gradually stir in flour and mix well. Toss the dough onto a floured board and knead it until it is smooth and springy and it does not stick to the board, adding more flour if needed. Place the dough in an oiled bowl, oil the top, cover the bowl and let the dough rise in a warm place until it doubles in size, about 1½ hours. Punch the dough down, pull the edges to the center making a firm ball, cover and let it rise again. When the dough has doubled again, about 30 minutes, toss onto the board again and divide into 3 or 4 parts. Shape each part into a long cylinder about 1¼ inches in diameter. Place the loaves onto a greased baking sheet, cover them with a towel, and let them rise in a warm place until double in size, about 30 minutes. Cut 6 or 7 diagonal slits, ¼-inch deep in size in top of each loaf when it is risen. Brush them with milk and bake in a hot oven (400° F.) until the crust is brown and the bread is done, about 20–25 minutes.

Chocolate Heart Cake

8 ounces bittersweet
  chocolate
8 ounces butter
  (at room temperature)
1 cup sugar

1 cup cake flour
6 eggs, separated
¼ cup chopped almonds
½ cup whipping cream

Melt chocolate in top of a double boiler simmering water. Allow to cool.

Beat egg whites until soft peaks form. In another bowl beat butter and egg yolks until thick and lemon colored. Add sugar gradually and beat until well blended. Add chocolate, almonds and flour gradually.

Fold chocolate mixture into egg whites with a whisk, using gentle strokes mixing just enough to blend.

Pour mixture into a buttered, floured, heart-shaped pan and bake in a preheated 400°F oven for 40–45 minutes or until cake just begins to pull away from sides of pan.

Whip whipping cream until stiff peaks form. Allow cake to cool and garnish with rosettes of whipped cream and chocolate curls if desired.

Petits Fours

4 ounces almond paste
1 cup sugar
8 eggs
1 cup butter
1 teaspoon vanilla

3 cups cake flour
3 teaspoons baking
  powder
Fondant Icing (recipe
  follows)

Garnish: Almond slivers, maraschino cherries, walnut halves and candied fruits

Combine almond paste with ½ cup sugar, add 1 egg and blend well. Cream butter with remaining sugar. Add remaining eggs, 1 at a time, beating well after each addition. Stir in vanilla and almond sugar mixture, beating until smooth. Sift flour with baking powder amd add ½ cup at a time blending after each addition. Spread batter evenly in a 10″×16″ sheet pan and bake at 350° F. until top is light brown and cake is firm. Cool cake in pan. Cut into small diamonds, squares or triangles. Ice with Fondant Icing.

Fondant Icing:

3 cups sugar
1½ cups water
Almond extract
Peppermint extract
Banana extract

Orange extract
⅛ teaspoon cream of tartar
Red, yellow and green
  food coloring

Combine sugar and water in a saucepan, place over medium heat and stir constantly until sugar has dissolved. Add cream of tartar and cook without stirring to soft ball stage (240°F.), wiping sugar crystals on side of pan with a pastry brush moistened with water. Remove from heat and place in four bowls. Place green food coloring and spearmint flavoring in one bowl, red food coloring and almond extract in another, red and yellow coloring to make orange with orange extract, and yellow food coloring with banana extract in the fourth bowl. Colors should be pastel.

Place bowls in a large pan of hot water. Spear the cut cake squares, triangles, or diamonds with a fork and dip one by one into fondant icing. Place on a cake rack to cool.

If fondant becomes too thick, add drops of boiling water and mix or replace water in pan holding bowls with fresh boiling water.

Garnish petits fours with walnut halves, candied fruits, almond slivers, maraschino cherries or any garnish you wish.

Cream Puff and Eclair Paste (Pate a' Chou)

In a saucepan, bring to boil 1 cup water, ½ cup butter, ½ teaspoon salt and 1 teaspoon sugar. Add all at once 1 cup flour and cook the paste over low heat, beating it briskly and constantly until the ingredients are combined throughly and the mixture rolls away from the sides of the pan. Remove the pan from the heat, cool 1-2 minutes, and beat in 4 eggs, 1 at a time. If the eggs are unusually small, add 1 extra egg.

Cream Puffs

To form cream puffs, drop the paste from the teaspoon or tablespoon, or force it through a pastry bag into balls on a greased baking sheet, allowing space for expansion between the shapes of the cream puffs. Fill with whipped cream, ice cream or custard.

Eclairs

To make eclairs, use a pastry bag with a plain round tube. Force the mixture through the bag to make strips 3½ to 4 inches long and 1 inch wide or 2 inches long and ½ inch wide, depending upon the size you desire. Fill with whipped cream, ice cream or custard.

Pear Coffee Cake

1 cup all-purpose flour	⅓ cup milk
½ teaspoon cornstarch	2 eggs
½ cup sugar	1½ teaspoons vanilla
1 teaspoon baking powder	½ cup sour cream
¾ teaspoon ground cinnamon	2 ripe pears
	Confectioner's sugar
2½ tablespoons butter, cut in bits	1 ounce Creme de Cassis

Preheat oven to 375°F. Butter a 9 inch pie plate. Sift flour, ¼ cup sugar, salt, baking powder and cinnamon. Work in butter with a pastry blender or a fork and knife until the mixture resembles corn meal.

In another bowl, blend milk, 1 egg and vanilla. Pour into flour-butter mixture and stir to blend. Spread mixture in the buttered pie plate.

In another bowl, whisk together sour cream, remaining sugar, cornstarch and egg. Pour over batter.

Core and peel pears. Cut into very thin slices and arrange, slightly overlapping, around edge of batter. Cover pie plate with foil and bake for 20 minutes. Remove foil and brush pears with Creme de Cassis and cook, uncovered, for 20 more minutes. Sprinkle with confectioner's sugar just before serving.

Apricot Galette

Yield: One Galette

Pastry:

2 tablespoons or 2 packages dry yeast	2 eggs
½ cup plus 2 teaspoons sugar	6 tablespoons unsalted butter, melted and 6 tablespoons softened butter
1 tablespoon grated lemon zest	4 cups all-purpose flour
	¼ cup Brandy

Filling and Glaze:

1½ pounds dried apricots	10 strawberries
½ cup sugar	½ cup apricot jam
	1 tablespoon Brandy

To prepare pastry, dissolve yeast in ½ cup warm water with 2 tablespoons of the sugar in a large mixing bowl. Allow to stand 10 minutes. Add lemon zest, eggs, 6 melted tablespoons butter, and Brandy to the yeast mixture. Stir until all ingredients are well blended. Stir in flour, adding only enough to make a soft but not sticky dough. Shape into a ball, and place in a buttered bowl. Allow to rise for 1 hour. Roll dough into a 16-inch circle and pinch up a decorative border. Place on a large pizza pan. Dot with remaining butter and sprinkle with remaining sugar. Bake in a preheated 475° F. oven for 12–15 minutes or until bottom is lightly browned. Remove pastry from oven and cool on a rack. Place on serving platter and set aside.

To prepare filling and glaze, place apricots in a saucepan and cover with water. Add sugar and simmer until apricots are soft. Drain apricots and arrange on pastry in overlapping fashion. Slice berries and arrange decoratively in the middle. Heat jam in a small saucepan. Add Brandy and stir. Strain and glaze the apricots with a pastry brush. Cut in wedges when ready to serve.

Madeleines

Makes 3 dozen

¼ pound unsalted butter, melted and cooled	⅔ cup superfine sugar
4 eggs	1 teaspoon almond extract
¼ teaspoon salt	1 cup sifted flour
	Confectioner's sugar

Preheat oven to 375° F. Grease and flour madeleine pans. Beat eggs, salt and sugar together until thick and lemon colored. Add almond extract. Fold in flour with a whisk. Mix in butter very gently. Spoon mixture into prepared madeleine pans and bake until golden, 10–12 minutes. Remove from pans and cool on wire racks. Sprinkle with confectioner's sugar.

Orange Savarin with Rum Syrup

Cake:

½ cup lukewarm milk	½ cup water
2 tablespoons sugar	¾ cup sugar
1 envelope dry yeast	¼ cup white corn syrup
2¼ cups all-purpose flour	¼ cup dark Jamaican Rum
4 eggs, beaten	1½ ounce Grand Marnier
Grated rind of 1 orange	
6 tablespoons unsalted butter, cut into ¼" pieces	

Syrup: (see above right column)

Filling:

1 cup whipping cream	Glaze:
3 tablespoons confectioner's sugar	½ cup marmalade, heated and strained
1 teaspoon vanilla extract	
Grated rind of 1 orange	

Heat milk until lukewarm, add sugar and stir until dissolved. Sprinkle yeast over surface and let stand 10 minutes.

Place flour into a large mixing bowl. Stir in milk-yeast mixture, eggs and orange rind. Mix with hands until dough is well blended and very soft and smooth. Cover dough with a damp towel and allow to rise for 1 hour. Beat in butter and transfer dough to a prepared 4-cup ring or savarin mold. Cover mold with damp towel and allow to rise for 1 hour. Bake in a preheated 350° oven for 45 minutes or until nicely browned.

Unmold cake and pierce it 20–25 times with a thin skewer. To prepare syrup place water, sugar and corn syrup in a small saucepan and cook, stirring constantly over low heat. When sugar has dissolved, cover saucepan and simmer for 5 minutes—do not allow syrup to boil. Uncover saucepan and simmer syrup for 4 minutes more. Add Rum and Grand Marnier and allow to cool to room temperature.

When syrup has cooled, pour it over pierced cake. Pour off excess syrup and repeat process until all sugar has been absorbed. Allow cake to rest at room temperature for 4 hours.

Beat cream until light and fluffy. Beat in powdered sugar 1 tablespoon at a time. Fold in vanilla and orange rind.

Cut cake in half lengthwise and fill with whipped cream mixture. Brush surface with warmed marmalade.

Flaming Baked Alaska

Serves eight

½ gallon ice cream (chocolate)	½ teaspoon cream of tartar
1 layer of a 9″ sponge cake	1½ cups sifted confectioner's sugar
8 egg whites (save 3 shell halves)	1 teaspoon vanilla extract
⅛ teaspoon salt	½ cup Kahlua
	½ cup 151 Proof Rum

Soften the ice cream, and then line a 2 quart mold with plastic wrap. Pack the ice cream in the mold and freeze until firm. Place the cake on a stainless steel platter, then trim the edge to ¾ inch large than the top of the ice cream mold. Pierce the cake with a fork and sprinkle with ⅛ cup Kahlua. Remove the ice cream from the mold and invert onto the cake. Remove the plastic wrap. Place the platter in the freezer until ice cream is very firm. Meanwhile combine egg whites and salt in a large mixing bowl. Beat with an electric mixer at high speed until foamy. Add cream of tartar and beat until soft peaks form. Add the sugar 1 tablespoon at a time, beating well after each addition. Beat in vanilla. Place ⅓ of meringue in a pastry bag with a large tube affixed and set aside. Remove platter from freezer and spread meringue very thickly over the entire surface, sealing well around the bottom edge of cake. Pipe swirls and rosettes over the Alaska with remaining meringue in the pastry bag. At this time place Alaska in freezer until serving time.

Just before serving, bake in a preheated oven at 450°F. for 2–3 minutes, or until meringue is lightly browned. Remove Baked Alaska from the oven and place egg shells on the top. Fill egg shells with 151 Rum and drizzle remaining Kahlua on the Alaska. Ignite the 151 Rum prior to presentation. Flaming mixture may be spooned over the meringue.

Strawberries in Puff Pastry

1 pound puff pastry dough	2 pints fresh strawberries, washed and hulled and halved lenthwise
½ cup red currant jelly	
1 tablespoon sugar	
½ ounce Grand Marnier	½ cup confectioner's sugar

Roll pastry ⅛ inch thick on a lightly floured table. Cut into 3-inch decorative shapes, such as "hearts" with cookie cutters. Mix jelly, sugar and Grand Marnier in the small saucepan and boil until a jelly glaze is formed. Place enough strawberries on each "heart" to fill and sprinkle lightly with confectioner's sugar. Place another pastry "heart" over these and crimp edges with a fork. Prick hearts 3 times each with a fork and place on an ungreased cookie sheet. Bake in a 425° F. oven for 12 minutes. Cool strawberry hearts and glaze with currant jelly mixture. Top with a small strawberry half.

Black Forrest Cake

4 ounces semisweet chocolate	2 cups whipping cream
½ cup butter	1½ pound can pitted bing cherries, drained
½ cup sugar	1½ ounces Cherry Herring liqueur
4 eggs	
¾ cup ground walnuts	12 maraschino cherries
½ cup all-purpose flour	Grated chocolate for garnish
½ cup cornstarch	
2 teaspoons baking powder	

Melt chocolate in top of a double boiler and cool. Meanwhile cream butter and sugar until light and fluffy. Beat in eggs 1 at a time, beating well after each addition, add walnuts and melted chocolate, sift in flour, cornstarch and baking powder with a folding motion, blending well. Pour batter into three greased and floured 7-inch layer cake pans. Bake in a preheated 350° F. oven for 25 minutes. Allow cakes to cool before removing from pan.

Whip cream until thick, and pat bing cherries dry with paper towels. Sprinkle cake layers with Cherry Herring. Sandwich cake layers together with cream and cherries. Spread remaining whipped cream on top and sides of cake and pipe a border around top of cake if desired. Decorate top of cake with cherries and chocolate shavings.

Raspberry Torte

6 egg whites	¼ cup all-purpose flour
¾ cup superfine sugar	1 cup whipping cream
½ cup almonds, chopped fine	2 tablespoons confectioner's sugar
2 tablespoons unsalted butter, melted	3 cups fresh raspberries
	2 tablespoons Triple Sec

Whip egg whites until stiff and gradually add sugar a tablespoon at a time, beating well after each addition. Fold in almonds, butter and flour. Grease three 10-inch layer cake pans and line bottom with baker's paper. Divide mixture evenly among cake pans and spread with a spatula. Bake in a preheated 350°F. oven for 15–20 minutes or until golden brown. Remove from oven and loosen at once with a knife. Peel off baker's paper gently and transfer to a wire cooling rack.

Meanwhile beat cream until slightly thickened and add confectioner's sugar and Triple Sec. Continue to beat until stiff peaks form; reserving 1 cup for top. Gently fold in ¾ of raspberries.

Sandwich the rounds with raspberry cream. Decorate with reserved whipped cream and place remaining raspberries around edge.

Dessert Cookies

Yield: six dozen

4 cups sifted pastry flour
2 cups unsalted butter,
  room temperature
2 egg yolks
2 cups ground toasted
  almonds

2 tablespoons Brandy
3 cups confectioner's
  sugar
1 teaspoon vanilla
1 teaspoon almond extract
¾ cup granulated sugar

Whip butter for 35 minutes with an electric beater until butter is white and fluffy. Add almonds, granulated sugar, egg yolks, vanilla, almond extract and Brandy; beat until well blended. Add sifted flour ½ cup at a time and beat until dough is easy to handle. Knead very lightly for a few minutes until dough forms a soft ball. Shape dough into walnut sized balls or crescents and place on an ungreased cookie sheet. Bake in a preheated 350° F. oven for 15 minutes or until lightly browned. Transfer cookies with a spatula and cover with powdered sugar. Place each cookie in a cupcake container and cover with more powered sugar.

Koulourakia

Yield: Approximately 72

3 sticks unsalted butter
2 tablespoons vegetable
  shortening
6 egg yolks
1 whole egg
4 teaspoons baking
  powder

Juice of one orange
Juice of one lemon
9 cups flour
1 ounce Brandy
2 egg yolks
½ cup sesame seeds

Cream butter and vegetable shortening until light and fluffy; about 20 minutes. Add sugar and egg yolks, mixing thoroughly. Sift in flour and mix well. Place baking powder in Brandy and juices and add quickly to mixture, blending well. Knead dough until smooth and firm. Roll the dough in the palms of your hands into cylinders ½-inch thick. Put ends together and twist twice. Place on a greased cookie sheet and brush with egg yolk. Sprinkle with sesame seeds and bake in a preheated 350° F. oven for 15 minutes or until lightly browned. Allow to cool slightly before removing from pan.

Cocktails
& Coffees

Cinnamon Iced Coffee

Serves four

3 heaping tablespoons
  decaffinated instant
  coffee
3 tablespoons sugar
1 cup boiling water

1 quart milk
¼ teaspoon ground
  cinnamon
4 iced glasses

Dissolve coffee and sugar in boiling water. Let mixture cool. Add milk and cinnamon. Serve over ice.

Café Athenia

Serves four

4 cups strong coffee
1 teaspoon sugar

2 ounces Metaxa Brandy
1 cup whipped cream

Pour coffee into a deep chafing dish or a regular coffee diablo pan. Add sugar, Metaxa brandy and ½ whipped cream. Bring to a boil. Pour coffee into water glasses that have been rimmed with sugar. Top with remaining whipped cream. Wrap a napkin around the glasses to prevent burning your hands, and to keep the Coffee Athenia warm.

Coffee Prunella

Serves two

¼ cup whipping cream
1½ tablespoons
  confectioner's sugar
1 cup strong coffee

2 cinnamon sticks
2 cooked prunes, pits
  removed
1½ ounces Cognac

Soak prunes with Cognac in a small bowl. Place cinnamon stick at the bottom of each cup. Heat coffee and pour over cinnamon stick.

Ignite prunes and spoon flaming prunes into coffee. Top with whipped cream sweetened with confectioner's sugar.

Coffee Chocolate

Serves four

2 ounces bittersweet
  chocolate
1 ounce Brandy

2 ounces Vodka
2 cups coffee
2 teaspoons sugar

Melt chocolate in a double boiler. Add Brandy, Vodka, coffee and sugar. Flame and serve in demitasse cups.

Café Brulot

Serves four

One continuous strip of
  lemon peel 10″ long
10 cloves
2 sticks cinnamon

8 sugar cubes
6 ounces French Cognac
4 cups strong black coffee

Stick the lemon peel with cloves and place the studded peel, cinnamon and sugar cubes in a fire-resistant bowl.

Heat the Cognac in a small pan and pour over the ingredients in the bowl. Grasp the end of the lemon peel between the tines of a fork and holding it 12″ from the bottom of the bowl, ignite the Cognac. Ladle the flaming Cognac over the lemon peel. When the flames are almost extinguished, pour the coffee into the bowl. Ladle into demitasse cups.

Daquiri

2 ounces Light Rum
½ ounce lime juice

½ teaspoon sugar
1 lime wedge

Place Rum, lime juice and sugar in a cocktail shaker with ice and shake well. Strain into a chilled glass and garnish with lime wedge.

Hot Buttered Rum

2 whole cloves
1″ stick of cinnamon
¾ teaspoon sugar
1½ ounce Light Rum,
  heated

½ ounce Dark Rum,
  heated
1 teaspoon butter
2 ounces boiling water

Place cloves, cinnamon stick and sugar in a heated mug with 1½ tablespoons boiling water. Allow to seep for 5 minutes. Add the hot rum and 2 ounces boiling water. Stir in butter until it is dissolved.

Gin Sour

1½ ounces Gin
½ ounce lemon juice
½ ounce orange juice

1 teaspoon sugar
½ slice orange
1 maraschino cherry

Place Gin, lemon juice, orange juice and sugar in a cocktail shaker with ice and shake well. Strain into a chilled glass and garnish with orange slice and maraschino cherry.

Rusty Nail

1 ounce Scotch
1 ounce Drambuie

Pour Scotch and Drambuie into a chilled glass over ice cubes. Stir well.

Whiskey Sour

2 ounces blended Whiskey   ½ slice orange
½ ounce lemon juice   1 maraschino cherry
1 teaspoon confectioner's
  sugar

Place Whiskey, lemon juice and sugar in a cocktail shaker with ice. Shake well then strain into a chilled glass. Garnish with orange slice and maraschino cherry.

Vodka Martini

2½ ounces Vodka
½ ounce Dry Vermouth
Green olive or lemon twist

Place Vodka and Dry Vermouth in a mixing glass with ice and stir. Strain into a chilled cocktail glass and garnish with olive or lemon twist.

Bull Shot

4 ounces chilled beef   1½ ounces Vodka
  consommé   1 slice lemon

Pour consommé and Vodka into a tall glass over ice cubes. Stir well and garnish with the lemon slice.

Old Fashioned

½ teaspoon sugar   2 ounces Whiskey
1 dash Angostura bitters   ½ orange slice
2 teaspoons water   Maraschino cherry

Mix together sugar, bitters and water in a chilled glass until the sugar is dissolved. Fill glass with ice and pour in Whiskey. Garnish with cherry and orange slice.

Rob Roy

2 ounces Scotch   1 dash Angostura bitters
½ ounce Sweet Vermouth   1 maraschino cherry

Stir the Scotch, Vermouth and bitters with ice in a mixing glass. Strain into a chilled glass. Garnish with maraschino cherry.

Orange Blossom

2 ounces Gin
1½ ounce orange juice
½ slice orange

Pour Gin and orange juice in a cocktail shaker with ice and shake well. Strain into a sugar-frosted glass and garnish with orange rind.

Pink Lady

1½ ounce Gin   1 teaspoon grenadine
1 teaspoon cream   ¼ egg white

Place above ingredients in a cocktail shaker with ice and shake well. Strain into a sugar-frosted glass.

Screwdriver

1½ ounces Vodka
2 ounces orange juice

Place Vodka and orange juice in a cocktail shaker with ice and shake well. Strain into chilled cocktail glass.

Cuba Libre

1½ ounces Golden Rum   Cola
½ ounce lime juice   Lime wedge

Fill tall glass half full of ice. Pour in Rum, lime juice and fill with cola. Mix gently and garnish with lime.

Spritzer

4 ounces Rhine, Moselle,
  Chablis or white wine
4 ounces soda water

Place 3 to 4 ice cubes in a tall glass and add wine and soda water.

Bacardi Cocktail

2 ounces Bacardi Light   3 dashes grenadine
  Rum   ½ ounce lime juice
½ teaspoon sugar

Place above ingredients into a cocktail shaker with ice and shake well. Strain into a chilled cocktail glass.

Between the Sheets

½ ounce White Rum   ½ ounce Cointreau
½ ounce Brandy   ½ ounce lemon juice

Pour above ingredients in a cocktail shaker with ice and shake well. Strain into a chilled cocktail glass.

Jack Rose

1½ ounces Apple brandy
3 dashes grenadine
½ ounce lime juice

Pour above ingredients into a cocktail shaker with ice and shake well. Strain into a chilled cocktail glass.

Manhattan

2½ ounces Whiskey
½ ounce Sweet Vermouth
1 maraschino cherry

Pour Whiskey and Vermouth in a mixing glass with ice and stir. Strain into a cocktail glass and garnish with cherry.

Dubonnet on the Rocks

Fill an old fashioned glass with ice. Fill glass with Dubonnet, add strip of peel.

Sloe Gin Fizz

1 ounce Sloe Gin   Soda water
1 ounce Gin   1 slice orange
½ ounce lemon juice

Pour Sloe Gin, Gin and lemon juice in a cocktail shaker with ice. Shake well and strain into a tall glass. Add ice to fill 3/4 full and soda water to fill. Garnish with orange slice.

Tom Collins

2½ ounces Gin   Soda water
1 teaspoon sugar   1 slice orange
1 ounce lemon juice   1 maraschino cherry

Pour Gin, sugar and lemon juice in a cocktail shaker with ice. Shake well and strain into a tall glass. Add ice to fill 7/8 full and soda water to fill and stir. Garnish with orange slice and cherry.

Grasshopper

1 ounce White Creme de
  Cacao
1 ounce Green Creme de
  Menthe
1 ounce cream

Pour the Creme De Cacao, Creme De Menthe and cream into a cocktail shake with ice. Shake well then strain in a chilled glass.

Gin Martini

2½ ounces Gin
¼ ounce Dry Vermouth

Place Gin and Vermouth in a mixing glass with ice. Stir gently and strain into a chilled cocktail glass. Garnish with a twist of lemon or an olive.

Gibson

2½ ounces Gin
¼ ounce Dry Vermouth
1 cocktail onion

Place Gin and Vermouth in a mixing glass with ice. Stir gently and strain into a chilled cocktail glass. Garnish with a cocktail onion.

Gimlet

2 ounces Gin
½ ounce Rose's lime juice

Place Gin and lime juice in a mixing glass with ice and stir. Strain in a chilled glass.

Gin Fizz

2 ounces Gin   Soda water
½ ounce lemon juice   1 slice lemon
1 teaspoon sugar

Place Gin, lemon juice and sugar in a cocktail shaker filled with ice. Shake very well then strain in a tall glass filled half way with ice. Add soda water and stir. Garnish with lemon slice.

Brandy Alexander

1 ounce Brandy   1 ounce cream
1 ounce Creme De Cacao Nutmeg

Pour Brandy, Creme De Cacao, and cream in a cocktail shaker with ice. Shake well then strain in a chilled glass. Sprinkle with nutmeg.

Mint Julep

| 16 fresh mint leaves | 3 teaspoons water |
| 1 teaspoon sugar | 2½ ounces Bourbon |

Crush 10 mint leaves and place in a tall glass with sugar and water. Stir to dissolve the sugar. Fill glass 3/4 full with crushed ice and add Bourbon. Stir well and garnish with remaining mint leaves.

Hot Eggnog

1 egg	6 ounces half and half
Pinch of salt	2 ounces Bourbon
1½ tablespoons sugar	Nutmeg

Beat egg well with salt and sugar. Slowly add hot half and half. Beat in Bourbon and pour in a heated mug. Sprinkle with nutmeg.

Apricot Brandy Sour

1½ ounce Brandy	½ ounce sugar syrup
½ ounce Apricot Brandy	1 orange slice
½ ounce lemon juice	1 maraschino cherry

Pour Brandy, Apricot Brandy, lemon juice and sugar syrup in a cocktail shaker with ice. Shake well then strain into a sugar frosted glass. Garnish with cherry and orange slice.

Brandy Manhattan

| 2 ounces Brandy | 1 dash bitters |
| ¼ ounce Sweet Vermouth | 1 maraschino cherry |

Stir Brandy, Vermouth and bitters with ice in a mixing glass. Strain into a chilled glass. Garnish with maraschino cherry.

Sidecar

1 ounce Brandy
1 ounce Cointreau
1 ounce lemon juice

Pour Brandy, Cointreau and lemon juice in a cocktail shaker with ice. Shake well then strain into a chilled glass.

Stinger

1½ ounce Brandy
1½ ounce White Creme
   de Menthe

Pour Brandy and Creme De Menthe into a mixing glass with ice. Stir and strain into a chilled glass.

Bloody Mary

1½ ounces Vodka	Dash hot red pepper sauce
Dash Worchestershire sauce	3 ounces tomato juice
Dash each of salt and pepper	1 lime wedge

Fill a highball glass half way with ice cubes and add above ingredients except lime. Stir well and garnish with lime.

Marguerita

1½ ounce Tequila	Salt
½ ounce Triple Sec	Lime wedge
½ ounce lime juice	

Rub rim of cocktail glass with lime peel. Dip rim in salt and set aside. Pour Tequila, Triple Sec and lime juice into cocktail shaker with ice and shake well. Strain into salted glass.

Champagne Cocktail

| 1 lump sugar | ½ split Champagne |
| 3 drops Angostura bitters | One lemon twist |

In a chilled Champagne glass, saturate sugar lump with bitters. Add an ice cube and fill glass with Champagne. Add lemon twist.

Hot Toddy

1 teaspoon sugar	2 ounces boiling water
3 whole cloves	2 ounces Bourbon, heated
1 inch cinnamon stick	Nutmeg
1 slice lemon	

Place sugar, cloves, cinnamon stick and lemon slice in a warmed mug. Pour in boiling water and allow to steep for 5 minutes. Add hot Bourbon and stir. Sprinkle with nutmeg and serve.

Glogg (Holiday Punch)

Serves 12

1 quart Port	½ cup currants
2 cups Brandy	1 cup sugar
2 cups Rum	3 sticks cinnamon
10 whole cloves	Grated rind of one orange
1 cup blanched almonds	10 cardamom seeds
1 cup raisins	

Place above ingredients in a large saucepan and bring to a boil. Remove from heat and cool slightly before serving. Ladle into glass cups making sure to include a few raisins, almonds and currants.

Desserts

Easy Caramel Flan

4 eggs, well beaten
½ cup caramel sundae
  topping
½ teaspoon salt
½ ounce Jamaican Rum
2½ cups milk, scalded
8 tablespoons caramel
  sundae topping

Preheat oven to 350°F. Blend eggs, ½ cup caramel topping, salt, milk and Rum. Place 1 tablespoon caramel topping in each of 8 custard cups. Pour custard over topping. Place custard cups in a baking pan and fill pan with very hot water to within ½ inch of cup tops. Bake for 45 minutes, remove from pan and chill. Unmold onto dessert dishes, champagne or sherbet glasses.

Chocolate Mousse

Serves four

½ pound semisweet
  chocolate
½ ounce unsweetened
  chocolate
4 tablespoons hot water
2 tablespoons Jamaican
  Rum
1 teaspoon vanilla extract
5 egg yolks, beaten
5 egg whites

In the top of a double boiler over hot water melt semisweet and unsweetened chocolate. Add hot water and Jamaican Rum and stir until mixture is velvety. Add egg yolks and vanilla extract and blend well. Beat egg whites until they are stiff and gently fold into chocolate mixture with a whisk. Pour mousse into 4 individual coupes or dessert glasses and chill for 6 hours before serving.

Pears Hélène

Serves four

4 pears, stems on
Juice of 1 lemon
2 cups sugar
3 cups water
¼ teaspoon cinnamon
2 teaspoons vanilla
8 scoops vanilla ice
   cream, frozen until
   ready to use

4 ounces bittersweet
   chocolate
2 tablespoons Creme de
   Cassis
4 mint leaves

Peel pears leaving stem on. Place sugar, lemon juice, water, cinnamon and vanilla in a saucepan and mix until blended. Add pears to pan and poach pears, covered, over moderate heat until tender. Remove pears with a slotted spoon and allow to drain.

Meanwhile, prepare chocolate sauce by melting chocolate over hot water in the top of a double-boiler and whisking in Creme de Cassis.

Place 2 scoops of ice cream in the bottom of individual compotes or serving coupes, center pear in middle with stem up and drizzle with chocolate sauce. Garnish with mint leaf and serve immediately.

Strawberries Romanoff

Serves six

2 quarts fresh, hulled
   strawberries
1 pint vanilla ice cream

1 cup whipped cream
1 cup sugar
½ cup Grand Marnier

In a chilled large mixing bowl, toss strawberries with sugar and set aside. In another large chilled mixing bowl, whip ice cream with a hand mixer or mash with 2 forks until smooth. Fold whipped cream into ice cream and add Grand Marnier. Blend in strawberries mashing a few with a fork to add extra flavor and color. Spoon into dessert dishes and serve immediately.

When buying strawberries, examine container on all sides for over-ripeness. Green and white tips indicate under-ripeness and lack of the tart, sweet flavor. Store strawberries unwashed in the refrigerator. Do not soak in water before hulling because this dilutes the flavor. Dip berries in a bowl of water and drain immediately in a colander to clean.

Bing Cherry Fritters

Serves six

2 eggs
½ cup flour
2 tablespoons
   confectioner's sugar
⅛ teaspoon salt
1½ tablespoons Cherry
   Herring liqueur

1½ cups vegetable oil
1 pound firm Bing
   cherries with stems on
Additional confectioner's
   sugar

Mix eggs, salt, flour, 2 tablespoons confectioner's sugar and Cherry Herring in a mixing bowl until smooth. Heat oil in a frying pan over high heat. Dip cherries into the batter and stand them up in the oil; frying until golden brown on all sides. Transfer to a plate lined with paper towels. Sprinkle with confectioner's sugar and serve.

Blueberry Flambé

Serves four

1 quart blueberries
1 tablespoon butter
½ cup brown sugar
Juice of 1 lemon

1½ ounce Blackberry-
   flavored Brandy
¾ cup sour cream

In a saute' pan over moderate heat, melt butter. Add brown sugar and stir until sugar begins to carmelize. Squeeze juice of 1 lemon into pan and stir until well blended. Add blueberries and heat thoroughly. Pour Brandy towards the front of the pan and ignite. When flames have extinguished, spoon blueberries into serving dishes. Top with a dollop of sour cream and serve.

Hungarian Rhapsody Flambé

Serves four

1 tablespoon butter
¼ teaspoon cinnamon
4 tablespoons light brown sugar
Juice of ½ orange
2 bananas, quartered lengthwise
8 canned or fresh apricot halves
½ cup bing cherries, drained

½ cup pineapple pieces, drained
¼ cup pineapple juice
1 ounce 151 Proof Rum
2 ounces Anisette liqueur
1 ounce Grand Marnier or Triple Sec
4 scoops vanilla ice cream
2 tablespoons slivered almonds, toasted

Melt butter in a pan. Add cinnamon and brown sugar, stirring constantly until the mixture begins to carmelize. Squeeze orange juice into the mixture and stir well. Add bananas, apricots, cherries, pineapple and pineapple juice, stirring until fruits are heated thoroughly. Push mixture to the side of the pan, pour liqueurs on the empty side of the pan and ignite. When the flame is extinguished, place equal amounts of fruits and juice on the ice cream scoops. Top with almonds.

Pêche Melba

Serves four

4 slices pound cake
4 scoops vanilla ice cream
4 peach halves

1 cup grenadine syrup
⅔ cup chopped roasted almonds

Place a slice of pound cake at the bottom of each of 4 dessert coupes or bowls. Top each with a scoop of ice cream, then a peach half, cut side down. Pour grenadine syrup over the peaches and sprinkle with almonds.

Glaceéd Strawberries

2½ cups sugar
¾ cup water
1 pint strawberries

Place sugar and water in a heavy saucepan and swirl until dissolved. (Do not stir). Place pan over moderate heat and continue to swirl mixture until clear. Raise heat to high, cover pan and boil for 3 minutes. Insert candy thermometer and continue to boil until hard ball stage is reached (265° F).

Dip strawberries into sugar glaze and place on a baking sheet greased with vegetable oil. Store in a cool dry place until ready to serve.

Cherries Jubilee

Serves two

12 pitted black cherries—reserve ¼ cup cherry juice
2 tablespoons sugar
Juice of ½ orange

⅛ teaspoon ground cinnamon
1½ ounce Cognac
1 ounce Cherry Brandy
2 scoops vanilla ice cream

Place cherry juice and sugar in a flat skillet or chafing dish over a moderate flame. Stir constantly until mixture begins to carmelize. Add the cherries and squeeze the juice of one-half orange onto the cherries. Add the cinnamon and stir well. Pour the Cognac towards the front of the pan and ignite. Add the Cherry Brandy. Place the cherries and sauce in equal amounts of the ice cream. Serve immediately.

Bread Pudding with Figs

Serves six

½ pound dried figs
4 ounces pitted prunes
1 cup sweet red wine
3 slices white bread, crusts removed, broken into small pieces
1 teaspoon cinnamon

⅔ cup light cream
1 cup sugar
4 tablespoons unsalted butter
Grated zest of 1 lemon
2 ounces Grand Marnier
⅓ cup chopped walnuts

Preheat oven to 375°F. Butter a 1½ quart casserole. Place figs, prunes and wine in a medium-size saucepan and simmer for 15 minutes over low heat, or until tender. Soak bread briefly in cream and add to the saucepan, along with the rest of the ingredients, except the walnuts. Stir until blended and pour mixture into prepared casserole; bake for 15 minutes. Sprinkle with chopped walnuts and bake for 15 minutes longer. Cool before serving.

Crepes Suzette

Serves four

½ cup butter	½ ounce 151 Proof Rum
4 tablespoons superfine sugar	½ ounce Grand Marnier
1 orange	1 ounce Curacao
	12 dessert crepes

Grate the zest of the orange and set aside. Place the butter and sugar in a flat skillet or a chafing dish and stir as it melts. While the butter is melting, add orange zest to the mixture. When the mixture begins to carmelize, squeeze the juice of the orange into the pan. Add the crepes one at a time and, using a fork and large spoon, turn each crepe over in the sauce, then fold into quarters. When the crepes are coated with sauce and folded into quarters, push them gently to the side of the pan, add the 151 Rum and ignite. Add the Grand Marnier and Curacao before the flame has extinguished. Serve hot.

Bananas au Rhum Flambé

Serves four

8 bananas, peeled	1 tablespoon butter, melted
1 cup Light Rum	12 macaroons, crushed
2 tablespoons sugar	½ cup slivered almonds
½ cup whipping cream	

Place bananas, Rum and sugar in a sauté pan over moderate heat and cook until bananas are thoroughly heated. Ignite Rum; when flames have extinguished, place bananas in a baking casserole. Top with cream, melted butter, macaroons and almonds. Bake in a preheated 500° F. oven for 5 minutes. Serve immediately.

Pears Cherise Flambé

Serves four

2 cinnamon sticks	12 maraschino cherries
½ cup slivered almonds	½ ounce 151 Proof Rum
½ cup brown sugar	2 ounces Cherry Flavored
½ cup water	Brandy
⅛ teaspoon ground	1 ounce Anisette liqueur
cinnamon	4 scoops vanilla ice cream
4 pears, peeled, cored and	1 cup whipped cream
quartered lengthwise	

Place cinnamon sticks and almonds in a hot pan, over moderate heat. Stir until cinnamon aroma is released and almonds are lightly browned. Reserve half of almonds for garnish. Add brown sugar, water, cinnamon and stir until slightly carmelized. Add pears and cherries and simmer until pears are tender. Remove cinnamon sticks. Pour the 151 Rum towards the front of the pan and ignite. Add Cherry Brandy and Anisette. When flames are extinguished, place pears and sauce in equal amounts on ice cream. Top with whipped cream, cherries and remaining almonds.

Crepes Kahlua Flambé

Serves four

½ cup butter	1½ ounce Kahlua
½ cup sugar	½ ounce Brandy
½ cup macaroon crumbs	8 crepes

Melt butter over moderate heat, add sugar and stir until dissolved. Add macaroon crumbs and place 3 tablespoons of mixture in each crepe and roll. Add Brandy and Kahlua. Ignite and spoon flaming mixture over crepes. Serve immediately.

Mincemeat Flambé

Serves two

½ cup ready-to-use	1½ ounce Jamaican Rum
mincemeat	4 scoops vanilla ice cream
½ cup chopped pecans	

Heat mincement with pecans in a chafing dish. Add Rum and ignite. When flames have extinguished, pour mixture over ice cream. Serve immediately.

Champagne Mousse

Serves four

2 tablespoons unflavored	1 cup sugar
gelatin	2 cups Champagne
¼ cup hot water	1 cup whipping cream
7 eggs	

Dilute gelatin in water. Separate 4 eggs and beat yolks until smooth. Place remaining yolks in a double boiler and beat in sugar and Champagne with a whisk until thick and frothy. Add gelatin and let mixture cool. Beat egg whites until stiff. In a separate bowl, whip whipping cream until stiff. Gently fold egg whites and whipping cream into Champagne mixture. Place mousse in Champagne glasses and chill.

Chocolate Amaretto Fondue

Serves Four

6 ounces bittersweet	½ pint fresh strawberries
chocolate	washed and hulled
⅓ cup whipping cream	2 bananas, peeled and
2 tablespoons Amaretto	sliced into 1-inch rounds

Melt chocolate in the top of a double-boiler over simmering water. Whisk in cream and Amaretto.

Pour chocolate fondue into fondue pot or chafing dish. Dip strawberries and bananas into chocolate with wooden skewers.

Oranges Romanoff Flambé

Serves eight

8 large thick skinned	½ cup sugar
oranges	1 pint vanilla ice cream
1 pint strawberries, hulled	1½ cups whipped cream
(reserve 8 whole	8 sugar cubes
strawberries)	½ ounce 151 Proof Rum
2 ounces Grand Marnier	

Cut off ⅓ of each orange top and remove all the fruit pulp and juice. (This can be used in a fruit salad.) Place the strawberries, Grand Marnier, sugar and ice cream in a blender and frappe for 1 minute. Scoop the mixture into the oranges, and top with whipped cream and a whole strawberry. Serve immediately, topped with a sugar cube that has been soaked in 151 Rum and ignited.

Homemade Yogurt

½ quart milk
½ quart half and half
2 tablespoons yogurt with
  active cultures

Bring the milk and half and half to a boil slowly over a low fire, stirring constantly to prevent sticking. Simmer for 10 minutes, remove from the fire and cool. Dilute the yogurt in a little of the milk and then blend it well with the rest of the milk. Pour into small jars or one bowl, cover and leave in a warm place overnight. When yogurt is set, store in refrigerator. Serve plain, with your favorite fresh fruit or with honey sauce as follows.

Spicy Honey Sauce

1 cup honey
½ cup water
2 ounces Triple Sec
1 cinnamon stick
2 teaspoons grated orange
  peel
1 teaspoon vanilla extract

Bring all ingredients except vanilla to a boil. Simmer for 8 minutes over low heat. Add vanilla. Remove from fire and cool. Serve over yogurt.

Trifle Romano

Serves eight

12 macaroons
2 ounces Galliano
1 teaspoon grated orange
  zest
2 cups milk
½ teaspoon vanilla extract
4 eggs beaten
3 tablespoons sugar
2 cups whipping cream
2 tablespoons chopped
  pistachio nuts

Break macaroons into small pieces and place in a decorative serving bowl (preferrably glass or crystal). Moisten with Galliano and sprinkle with orange zest.

Heat milk over low heat until bubbles begin to form around edges; then transfer to a double boiler of simmering water. Add eggs, sugar and vanilla and cook , stirring constantly until mixture thickens and coats the back of a wooden spoon. Do not allow mixture to boil or it will curdle. Pour into a clean bowl and allow custard to cool. Meanwhile whip whipping cream until stiff. Pour cooled custard over macaroons, then pile whipped cream over custard. Sprinkle the pistachios on top and chill until ready to serve.

Mandarin Caramel Trifle

Serves four

2 poundcakes, cut in
  slices ½" thick
2 tablespoons Grand
  Marnier
2 tablespoons orange juice
1¼ cups sugar
1¼ cups vanilla pudding
⅔ cup whipped cream
2 cups mandarin orange
  sections

Sprinkle cake slices with Grand Marnier and orange juice. Melt sugar in a heavy pan over low heat until it turns golden brown. Remove from heat and place over a pan of hot water.

Arrange ⅓ soaked cake slices in a glass serving bowl. Spoon over ⅓ pudding. Layer ⅓ mandarin sections and drizzle ⅓ caramel in a thin stream. Repeat this 2 more times. Decorate top of trifle with whipped cream rosettes before serving.

Dried Fruit Compote

Serves six

4 cups mixed dried fruits
1 cup sugar
2 cups Champagne
½ teaspoon cinnamon
1 can (16 ounce) cherry
  pie filling

Place fruit in a deep baking casserole. Mix sugar, champagne and cinnamon together and pour over fruit. Cover with canned cherries and bake in a preheated 350° F. oven for 3 minutes.

Baked Pears Cassis

Serves four

4 ripe Anjou pears
4 tablespoons sugar
6 tablespoons
  half and half
2 tablespoons Creme de
  Cassis
1 tablespoon butter

Preheat oven to 375° F. Peel each pear, cut in half and remove seeds. Generously butter a baking dish and sprinkle with 2 tablespoons of sugar. Place pears core side down in dish. Sprinkle with remaining sugar and Creme de Cassis. Bake for 15 minutes. Remove from oven and pour half and half over pears.

Bake for 15 minutes longer and serve with cream spooned over pears.

Instant Orange Mousse

⅔ cup hot water
2 envelopes unflavored
  gelatin
½ cup sugar

6 ounce can frozen orange
  juice concentrate
2 cups crushed ice

Place hot water and gelatin in a blender and blend on high speed for 30 seconds. Add sugar and blend for 5 seconds at high speed. Add orange concentrate and crushed ice and blend at high speed until all ingredients are thoroughly blended. Spoon into serving dishes and serve immediately.

Grape and Yogurt Crepes

Serves four

8 dessert crepes
2 cups plain yogurt
2 cups green seedless
  grape halves

¼ teaspooon ground
  cinnamon
½ teaspoon ground
  cardamom seed

Combine 1½ cups yogurt with grapes, cinnamon and cardamom. Fill each crepe with mixture and fold over. Dot with remaining yogurt and serve.

Spirited Pineapple

2 fresh ripe pineapples
1 cup dark Rum
¼ cup brown sugar

1 pint strawberries,
  washed and hulled
3 dashes bitters

Slice the tops off the pineapples and reserve for later use. Cut the pineapples in half lengthwise and scoop out the fruit with a small melon baller. Soak the pineapple balls in Rum and brown sugar. Wash the pineapple tops and place on a bed of ice and then attach the pineapple balls and strawberries which have been speared with a toothpick. Strain the juice left over from the pineapple. Add the bitters to this and pour over the spears.

Sugar Glazed Grapes

1 cup light corn syrup
½ cup sugar
1 teaspoon cinnamon

½ teaspoon ground
  cardamom seed
1 pound seedless grapes

In small saucepan heat corn syrup to hard ball stage. In a small bowl mix sugar, cinnamon and cardamom. Cut grapes into small clusters. Dip grapes, holding by tongs into corn syrup, then roll in sugar mixture until well coated. Refrigerate on waxed paper until ready to serve.

Peaches Flambé

Serves four

2 tablespoons butter
3 tablespoons sugar
¼ cup orange juice
Juice of ½ lemon
1 ounce Curacao or Triple
  Sec

8 canned peach halves
1 ounce Cognac
4 scoops vanilla ice
  cream

Melt butter over moderate heat and add sugar. Stir constantly until sugar begins to carmelize. Blend in orange and lemon juice and let simmer until sauce thickens. Add Curacao. Place peaches in the pan and let cook a few minutes. Flame with Cognac. When flames have extinguished, spoon over ice cream scoops. Serve immediately.

Note: Puncture peaches with a fork. This allows the sauce to penetrate.

Sherry Trifle

Serves four

8 slices poundcake
  (½″ thick)
3 tablespoons cream Sherry
1 package vanilla pudding

1 can (13 ounce) crushed
  pineapple, well drained
1 cup whipped cream
¼ cup almond slivers

Place 2 slices poundcake on each dessert dish. Sprinkle with Sherry. Prepare pudding as directed on the package. Layer pineapple and pudding on poundcake slices. Refrigerate until chilled and top with whipped cream and almonds.

Alaskan Pineapples Flambé

Serves four

1½ ounce butter	½ ounce 151 Proof Rum
2 ounces granulated sugar	4 maraschino cherries
Juice of 1 orange	1 banana sliced in ½-inch
Juice of ½ lemon	pieces
8 pineapple slices	4 scoops vanilla ice cream
1½ ounces Brandy	2 teaspoons shredded
	coconut, toasted

Place butter and sugar in a skillet or chafing dish over high heat. Allow it to carmelize. Add the fruit juices and simmer until creamy and slightly thickened. Spread the pineapple slices in the pan and heat them on both sides. Pour the Brandy and Rum over the fruit and ignite. When the flames have extinguished, add the cherries and banana pieces. Cook for 2 minutes.

To serve, place a pineapple slice on a dessert plate or bowl, place a scoop of ice cream in the middle and another pineapple slice on top. Garnish with cherries and banana slices. Pour the remaining sauce over the Alaskan pineapples. Sprinkle with coconut. Serve immediately.

Cheese Chocolate Cherries

Makes two dozen

2 cups powdered sugar	1 10-ounce jar maraschino
½ cup cream cheese	cherries with stems on
2 tablespoons cocoa	(drained)
1½ teaspoon vanilla	½ cup finely crushed
1½ cups flaked coconut	chocolate wafers
2 teaspoons Amaretto	Dash salt

Mix sugar, cream cheese, Amaretto, vanilla and salt together. Stir in coconut and cocoa. Wrap about 2 teaspoons mixture around each cherry. Roll in chocolate wafer crumbs. Refrigerate.

Tia Maria Meringues Flambé

Serves six

6 large egg whites	1½ teaspoons cocoa
1 cup superfine sugar	4 scoops chocolate
	ice cream

Beat the egg whites in a large mixing bowl with an electric mixer at the highest speed until stiff but not dry. Sprinkle ⅛ cup sugar over the egg whites and beat for 3 minutes longer at high speed. Sprinkle remaining sugar one tablespoon at a time until all has been added. Add the cocoa. Drop the meringue by heaping tablespoons on oiled brown paper placed on a baking sheet 2-inches apart. Bake immediately in a 250°F. oven for 55 minutes. Immediately remove from the paper to cooling racks. Arrange the cooled meringues in a compote pyramid in which the base has been filled with the ice cream. Top with Tia Maria sauce that follows.

Tia Maria Sauce

¼ cup brown sugar	2 ounces Tia Maria
1 teaspoon instant coffee	1 ounce light Creme de
½ cup water	Menthe liqueur
½ cup butter	1 ounce 151 Proof Rum
1 teaspoon cornstarch	

Dissolve sugar and instant coffee in water over low heat. Add butter and stir until well blended. Mix the cornstarch in 1 tablespoon water and add slowly to the mixture, stirring constantly until slightly thickened. Pour over the meringue pyramid and sprinkle with 151 Rum and ignite. When the flames have extinguished, sprinkle with Tia Maria and Creme de Menthe.

The meringue part of this recipe can be prepared ahead of time and frozen until ready to use.

Crepes Crèole Flambé

Serves two

1 banana, sliced	1 ounce Creme de Banana
1 tablespoon lemon juice	Liqueur
1½ tablespoon butter	4 dessert crepes
½ cup brown sugar	4 small scoops chocolate
¼ cup slivered almonds	ice cream
2 ounces Jamaican Rum	Cinnamon

Toss the banana with lemon juice. Combine the butter and brown sugar together in a sauté pan over moderate heat. Add the almonds as the mixture begins to carmelize. Add the Rum and ignite. When the flame has extinguished, add the Creme de Banana. Swirl crepes in mixture and place ¼ of the banana mixture inside each crepe. Place a scoop of ice cream in the middle and quickly fold crepe in thirds. Transfer to serving dishes and sprinkle very lightly with cinnamon. Pour remaining juices over crepes and serve immediately.

Dessert Crepes

Yield: 24 Crepes

3 cups sifted flour	2 tablespoons sugar
4 eggs	1 teaspoon salt
4 egg yolks	¼ cup clarified butter
1 quart milk	

Mix the flour, eggs and egg yolks together with a whisk. Add the milk, sugar and salt and beat until all the ingredients are well blended. Heat a crepe pan and brush it with the clarified butter. Spoon in 1 tablespoon of the batter and tilt the pan immdiately so that the batter coats the entire pan and cook until the crepe starts to turn golden brown on the bottom. Using a spatula, turn the crepe over to "set" the other side. (Do not allow it to brown.) Place the finished crepes between sheets of waxed paper.

Russian Apple Cream Dessert

Serves eight

2½ pounds cooking apples	1 teaspoon vanilla extract
½ cup water	1 tablespoon Jamaican
½ cup sugar	Dark Rum
2 envelopes unflavored	1 tablespoon Applejack
gelatin	liqueur
1 cup cold water	2 egg whites, beaten stiff
1 teaspoon grated lemon	1 cup whipping cream,
peel	whipped stiff
2 tablespoons lemon juice	1 recipe Rum Custard Sauce

Peel, core, and quarter apples. Place in a large saucepan with ½ cup water. Cover and simmer until apples are tender, adding more water if necessary. When apples are tender, place in blender and pureé. Measure 3 cups apple pureé and add sugar. Soften gelatin in 1 cup cold water. Dissolve over boiling water. Add to apple pureé mixture. Cool. Stir in lemon peel and juice, vanilla, Rum and Applejack. Fold gently into egg whites. Chill until mixture begins to set. Fold in whipped cream. Place in a lightly greased 2 quart mold. Chill until firm. Serve with Rum Custard Sauce (Recipe follows).

Rum Custard Sauce

2 egg yolks	1 cup milk
3 tablespoons sugar	1 tablespoon Jamaican Rum
Dash of salt	

Mix egg yolks, sugar and salt together. Scald milk. Gradually stir into egg mixture. Cook over a double boiler until mixture thickens, beating constantly with a whisk. When mixture coats a wooden spoon, it is thickened. Remove from heat and stir in Rum. Serve spooned over Russian Apple Cream. (May be chilled before serving.)

The best cooking apples are colorful juicy Greenings, Northern Spy, Pippin or Golden Delicious apples.

Banana Fritters Flambé

Serves four

¾ cup flour	1 egg white
3 tablespoons sugar	4 ripe bananas, peeled
1 tablespoon melted butter	1 tablespoon Light Rum
¼ cup warm water	2 tablespoons lemon juice
½ cup Cognac	1½ ounce 151 Proof Rum
⅛ teaspoon salt	Oil for deep frying
1 egg yolk, beaten	Confectioner's sugar
1 tablespoon Light Rum	

Sift flour and 1 tablespoon sugar into a bowl and stir in melted butter. Add water and Cognac to flour, stirring to make a batter. Add egg yolk and salt and blend well. Beat egg white until stiff and fold into batter.

Cut bananas into lengthwise halves and cut crosswise at 2-inch intervals. Mix banana pieces with lemon juice, Light Rum and remaining sugar.

Heat oil over high heat. To make fritters: dip banana pieces into batter and drop into hot oil. Fry until golden brown and puffed. Drain fritters on paper towels. Before serving, place fritters on a serving platter and dust with confectioner's sugar. Sprinkle with 151 Rum and ignite. Serve flaming.

Oven Apple Pancake Flambé

Serves four

6 eggs	¼ teaspoon cinnamon
1 cup flour	¼ cup butter
1½ cup milk	2 apples, peeled, cored
1 teaspoon vanilla extract	and sliced ¼ " thin
½ ounce Applejack	3 tablespoons brown sugar
½ teaspoon salt	

In a large mixing bowl blend eggs, flour, milk, sugar, vanilla, salt and cinnamon until blended but small lumps remain. Melt butter in a 12-inch quiche dish. Place apple slices in bottom. Pour batter over apples. Sprinkle with brown sugar. Bake in middle rack of a preheated 425° F. oven for 20 minutes or until puffed and golden brown. Heat Applejack in a small pot and ignite. Pour flaming Applejack over apple pancake and serve flaming.

Bananas Foster Flambé

Serves four

1 tablespoon butter	1 ounce 151 Proof Rum
½ cup brown sugar	2 ounces Banana Liqueur
3 bananas, peeled and	4 scoops vanilla ice cream
quartered	

Melt butter in a chafing dish or flat skillet. Add brown sugar and stir until sugar begins to carmelize. Add bananas and pierce with a fork. Cook for 3 minutes. Pour 151 Rum towards the front of the pan and ignite. Add the banana liqueur before the flame is extinguished. Serve over ice cream.

Chocolate Paté

Serves six

3 ounces semi-sweet chocolate	2½ tablespoons unsalted butter
3 ounces bittersweet chocolate	2 teaspoons Brandy
¾ cup whipping cream	¾ cup chopped pistachios

Melt the chocolates in the top of a double-boiler over simmering water. Place cream in a saucepan and heat until scalded. Whisk melted chocolate and butter into cream until well blended and slightly thickened. Stir in Brandy and pistachios. Spoon chocolate mixture into a cheese crock or attractive serving dish and place a piece of waxed paper over surface to prevent a "skin" from forming. When cooled to room temperature, serve with shortbread cookies, sweet biscuits and wafers, spreading mixture with a small knife.

Ice Cream Balls with Chocolate Sauce & Chocolate Raspberry Sauce

Serves four

1 pint vanilla ice cream
1 egg white, lightly beaten until frothy
6 ounces semi-sweet chocolate
1 cup chopped toasted almonds
Vegetable oil for deep frying
½ ounce Raspberry Brandy

Using an ice cream scoop, shape ice cream into balls. Roll balls in egg white then in almonds. Place ice cream balls in freezer until ready to use.

Melt chocolate in a double boiler over hot water. Stir in Raspberry Brandy.

In a deep fryer, heat 4 inches of oil. Using a slotted spoon, lower ice cream balls in oil and fry for 25 seconds. Remove from fryer and drain on a paper towel.

Place ice cream balls in individual serving dishes and top with chocolate raspberry sauce.

Chocolate Orange Ice Cream

Yield: One Quart

6 egg yolks
1 cup half and half
½ cup sugar
¼ teaspoon salt
4 tablespoons unsalted butter
1½ cups whipping cream
2 tablespoons light Creme de Cacao
2½ tablespoons Grand Marnier Liqueur
3 ounces bittersweet chocolate, coarsely grated
Grated zest of 1 orange

Place egg yolks, sugar, half and half and salt in a saucepan over low heat and cook, stirring constantly until mixture thickens and coats the back of a wooden spoon. Remove pan from heat and stir in butter until thoroughly blended. Place a piece of paper over the "custard" surface and cool in refrigerator.

Place cooled mixture in an ice cream maker along with whipping cream, Creme de Cacao, Grand Marnier, orange zest and chocolate and churn according to the manufacturer's instructions. Pack in container and freeze until ready to serve.

Coconut Bananas

Serves four

4 ripe bananas, peeled
4 tablespoons lemon juice
6 ounces semi-sweet chocolate
½ ounce Jamaican Rum
1½ cup shredded coconut

Cut bananas in half. Place lemon juice and coconut in separate bowls. Melt chocolate with Rum in a double boiler over hot water. Dip bananas in lemon juice, then in chocolate, then roll in coconut. Place on a baking sheet lined with waxed paper. Cover and refrigerate until ready to serve.

Baked Apples Flambé

4 large baking apples, peeled and cored
1 cup mince meat
½ cup brown sugar
¾ cup Sauterne wine
½ cup half and half
2 tablespoons sugar
1½ ounces 151 Proof Rum

Place apples in a greased baking dish. Fill centers with mince meat and sprinkle with brown sugar. Pour Sauterne into dish and bake in a preheated 350° F. oven for 40 minutes or until tender. Transfer apples to a heated serving platter. Add remaining mince meat and half and half to baking dish. Cook sauce until blended and slightly thickened and pour around apples. Sprinkle apples with sugar and 151 Rum. Ignite and serve flaming.

Napkin Folding

Blossom Napkin Fold

1. Open napkin.
2. Pick up napkin in exact center with thumb and index finger. Shake napkin a few times.
3. Pull napkin through cupped hand and twist the bottom four inches tightly.
4. Place blossom in a large wine glass or water goblet.

1

2

3

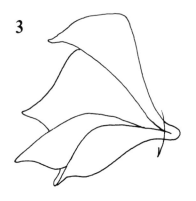

4

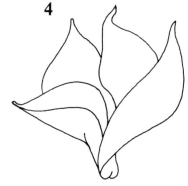

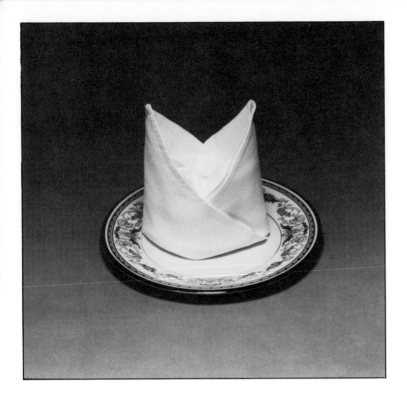

Bishop's Mitre

1. Fold napkin from top to bottom.
2. Fold left top corner down to the middle and lower right corner up to the middle.
3. Fold in half along line A.
4. Secure the two top points so they are not tucked in the fold.
5. Bend one side and tuck into the other side.
6. Bend the remaining side and tuck into the folded side.
7. Fluff out and place on table or base plate.

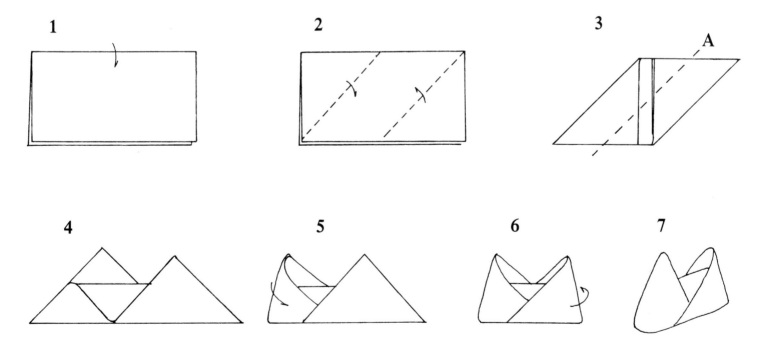

1   2   3

4   5   6   7

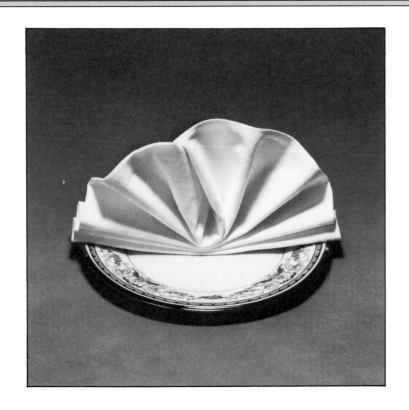

Japanese Fan Fold

1. Fold napkin in half lengthwise and crease with your hands.
2. Repeat above process again.
3. Fold into accordion pleats.
4. Press pleats together firmly.
5. Place on base plate and fan out holding bottom tightly.

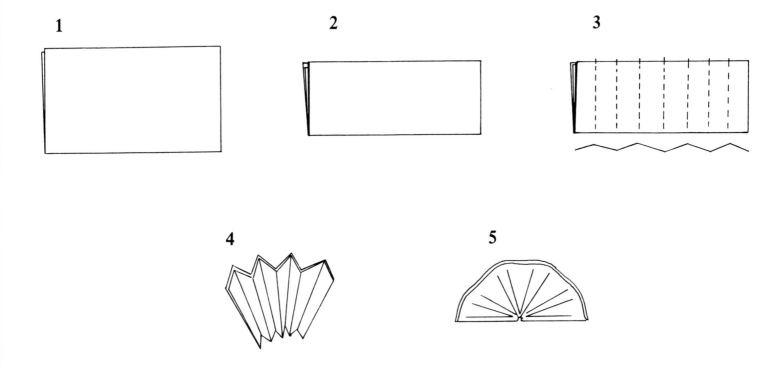

1

2

3

4

5

Tiara Fold

1. Make two accordion pleats, one from the top to the middle, and one from the bottom to the middle.
2. Fold back each pleat along the exact middle, so three open edges are on the top side.
3. & 4.
   Accordion pleat once from both sides to meet the middle. Hold corners of pleat with thumb and forefinger at Point A. Fold up to Point B reversing the crease of the flap forming a triangle as in 4.
5. Make triangles with each flap by reversing the crease in the middle of each pleat. Press each pleat with your fingers.
6. Place on a base plate or table.

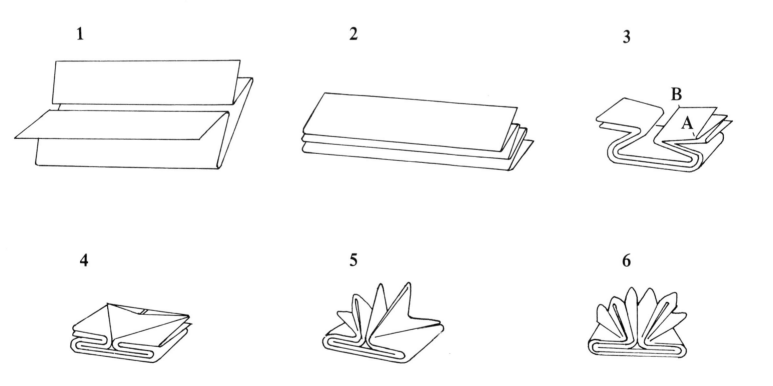

1

2

3

B
A

4

5

6

Sailboat Napkin Fold

1. Fold napkin into quarters. Fold quartered napkin into a triangle.
2. Fold left and right sides in to meet the middle.
3. Fold bottom corners up towards the back.
4. Fold in half and hold together with one hand so points pop upwards as in 5.
5. With other hand pull loose points up individually.
6. Place on table or base plate.

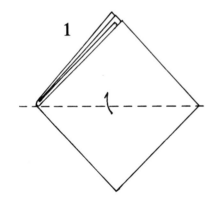

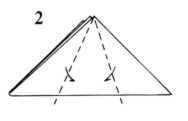

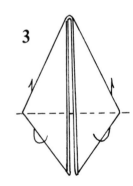

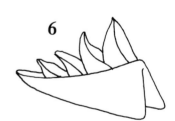

Silverware Pocket Fold

1. Fold napkin into quarters by folding the bottom to the top and the left to the right with open edges at the upper right corner.
2. Fold the upper right corner down so that the point meets with the exact center of the square.
3. Roll line A so that the fold is even with the diagonal of the napkin.
4. Fold the next corner back and fold the edge into the pocket of the first corner.
5. Fold the left and right thirds of the napkin to the back so that they meet evenly.
6. Place silverware inside the napkin.

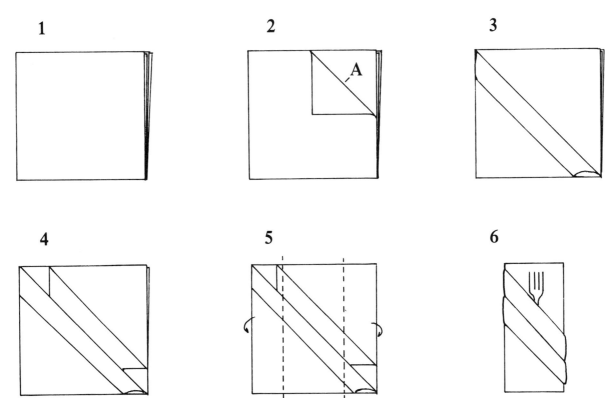

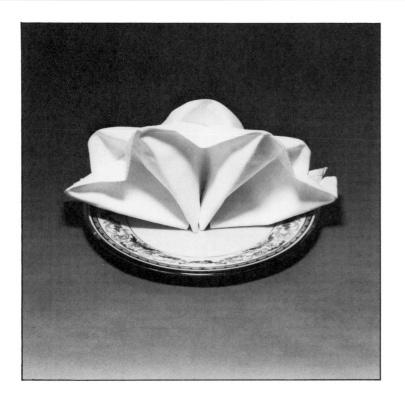

Double Japanese Fan Fold

1. Fold napkin from bottom to top.
2. Fold again from bottom to top.
3. Make accordion pleats from the left to the right, pressing together to crease with your hands.
4. Fold top indentations of pleats down on both sides as per diagram.
5. Fold base and fan out top part of the fan.
6. Place on base plate or table, allowing sides to touch base.

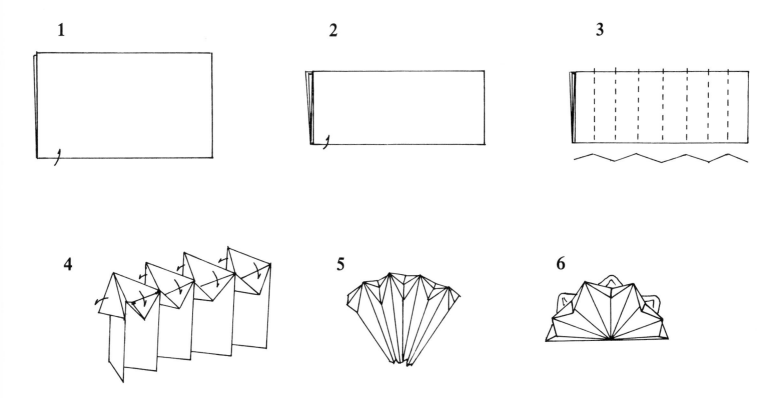

Water Lily Fold

1. Place napkin on a flat working surface and fold in all corners to meet in the middle.

2. Fold all corners in again to meet in the middle.

3. Repeat process one more time. Turn napkin over.

4. Fold corners up to meet the middle and firmly hold them in the middle with one hand.

5. With the other hand, one by one, pull corner flaps on the bottomside up to form petals.

6. Continue this process until all eight flaps or "petals" are pulled up.

7. Pull single "leaf" flaps from underneath and fluff out.

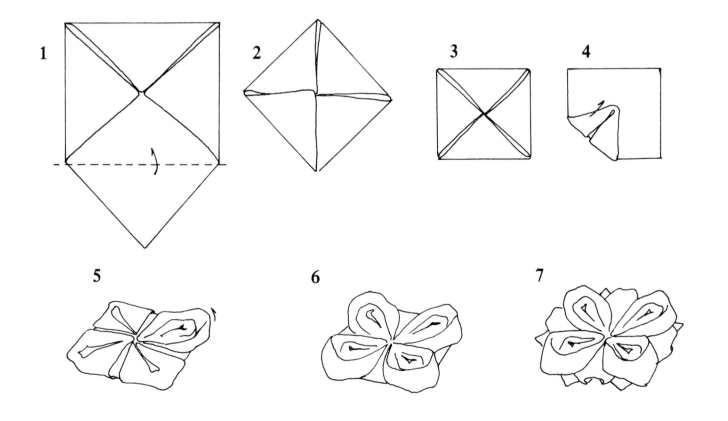

1 2 3 4

5 6 7

Swan

1. Open napkin flat on working surface.
2. Bring left and right corners in to form a long triangle.
3. Roll right corner inwards to meet the middle.
4. Roll left corner inwards to meet the middle.
5. Fold in half lengthwise and insert fold in water goblet or wine glass.
6. Form beak and tail as shown in Diagram 6.

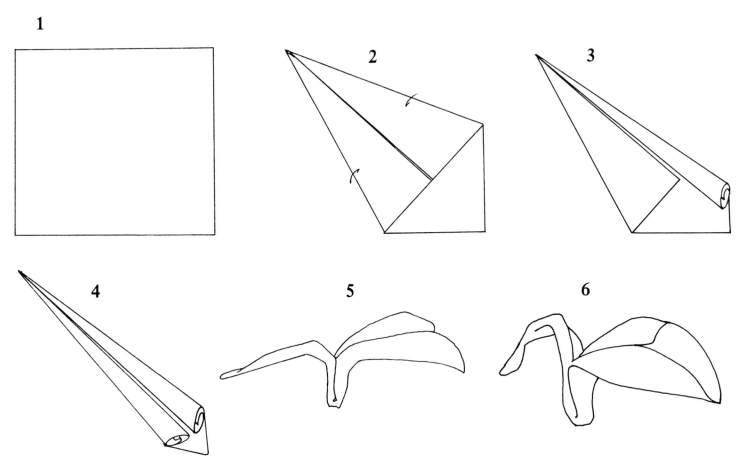

1

2

3

4

5

6

Fleur-de-Lis

1. Fold the upper corner of the napkin to the opposite bottom corner.

2. Fold the two upper left and right corners down to meet the middle, forming a square.

3. Fold the two bottom points up to meet the top.

4. Fold the bottom corner up so it meets the diagonal center of the square.

5. & 6.
   Roll bottom edge up so it overlaps the lengthwise diagonal by one inch forming a collar, as in Diagram 6.

7. & 8.
   Bend the napkin from front to back and insert one point of the collar into the other to secure them together.

9. Turn down the two loose points and tuck them into the collar.

10. Arrange on a base plate or table.

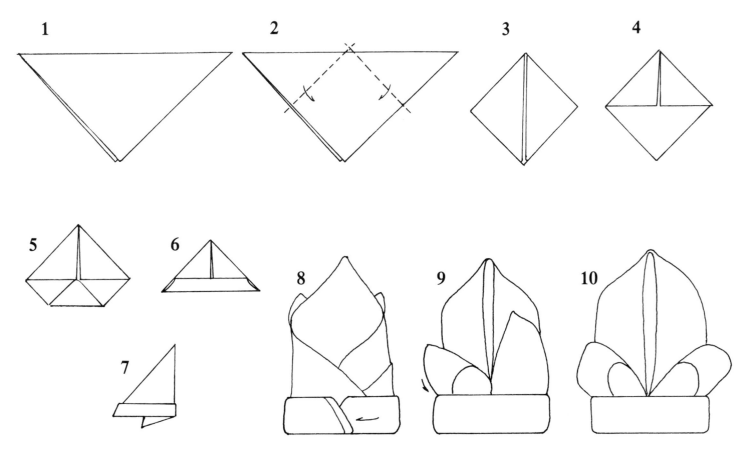

1   2   3   4

5   6   8   9   10

7

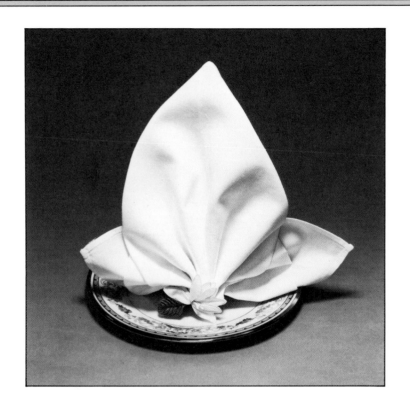

Peacock Fold

1. Fold napkin in half lengthwise from bottom to top.
2. Fold single upper corners in to meet the middle.
3. Turn the napkin over and fold the entire top edge flush with the bottom.
4. Fold the bottom right hand corner of the napkin up and do the same with the bottom left hand corner. Turn the napkin over once again. Press creases firmly with your hands.
5. Accordion pleat from the left to the right and place the bottom edges in a flat bottomed napkin ring.
6. Fan out top edges and place on table or base plate.

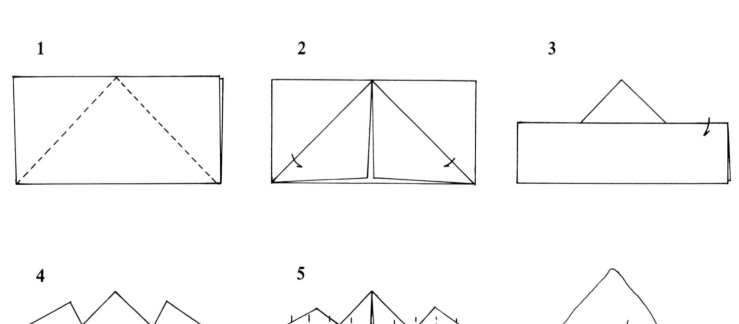

Triangle Fold

1. Fold napkin from bottom to top and left to right so that it is in quarters with open edges at the top right side.
2. Fold down the top right corner to the bottom left corner.
3. Fold same corner back to meet the very middle.
4. Fold next top right corner to meet very middle.
5. Fold top left and bottom right corners under to meet the middle back.
6. Place on base plate or table.

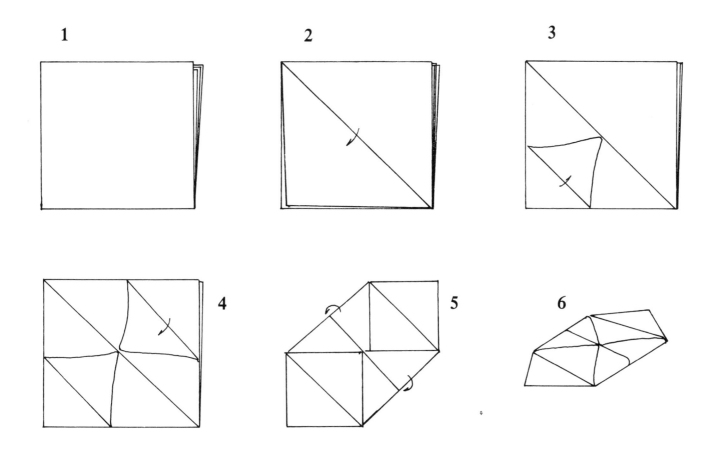

1 2 3

4 5 6

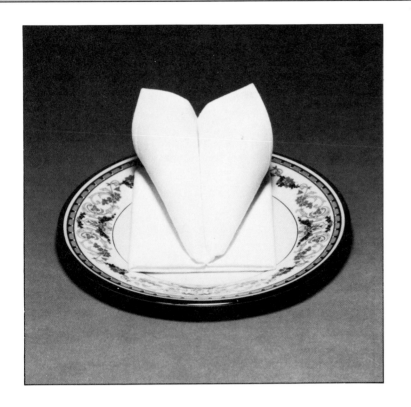

Butterfly Fold

1. Fold napkin in half lengthwise with fold at bottom.
2. Fold again from bottom to top. Mark middle of napkin.
3. Make one pleat to center of napkin on the left and repeat process on the right.
4. Roll top points under to form a raised triangle and fluff up to form wings.
5. Place on base plate.

1

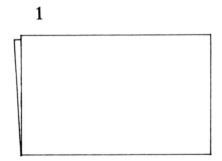

2

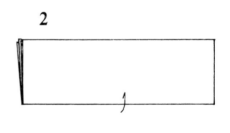

3

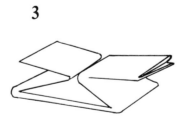

4

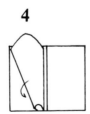

5

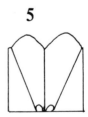

Helpful Hints

How to Flambé

FLAMBÉ!!! The thought of it is mouth-watering . . . tender filet or crisp chicken with a touch of brandy or delicious desserts and sauce flavored with liqueurs. It is our belief that if the evening is planned as a dinner party that the main event of the evening should be the dinner itself. Food should be the setting and ideally should include the preparation as well as the consumption. Flambéing is not only pleasing to the palate, but also a welcome sight to your guests and simple to do. Before you begin flambéing, please read the following hints and tips.

You will need a sauté pan or crepe pan and a source of heat. First move the pan over the heat or fire allowing the base of the pan to become evenly heated. Make sure you have enough heat prior to flaming. The more sauce there is in the pan, the longer it takes the alcohol to burn. If possible, tilt the sauce away from the front of the pan before flambéing.

If you are using an electric range, place your liquor towards the front of the pan and quickly ignite with a match.

If you are using a gas range, a brazier or rechaud, pour the liquor towards the front of the pan, and then withdraw your pan from the heat source until the flame leaps over the rim of the pan, igniting the evaporating alcohol.

Always remember to keep your body slightly back from the pan and heat soure when flambéing. When using 151 Proof Rum or any liquor, you must be very careful not to pour while a flame is present.

If there is a lot of liquid in the pan, tilt it slightly and pour where there is no liquid. After the spirits have ignited place the pan back in the burner in its horizontal position. Shake the pan slightly to allow the flames to spread.

Have fun with your flambé cookery.

Liqueurs Used in Flambé

Anisette - Anise seed flavored liquer.

Applejack - American term to describe apple brandy.

Aquavit - a potato based liqueur from Scandinavia, flavored with caraway.

Benedictine - brandy based liqueur.

Calvados - apple brandy from Normandy, France.

Cherry Herring - cherry flavored liqueur.

Cointreau - brand name for orange flavored liqueur.

Creme de Cacao - chocolate flavored liqueur.

Creme de Cassis - black currant liqueur.

Creme de Menthe - peppermint flavored liqueur; white or green colored.

Creme de Noyauxe - brandy based liqueur flavored with apricot and peach kernels.

Curacao - rum based liqueur flavored with orange peel.

Drambouie - brand name of whiskey based liqueur from Scotland.

Dubonnet - a sweet french apertif, either blonde or red in color.

Grand Marnier - a brand name of an orange flavored liqueur.

Grenadine - pomegranate flavored syrup.

Kirsch - colorless cherry brandy.

Kummel - German liqueur flavored with anise seed and cumin.

Lillet - a French apertif.

Madeira - a fortified wine from the island of Madeira.

Marsala - A sweet Italian dessert wine.

Ouzo - an anise seed flavored Greek liqueur.

Pernod - a French anise seed flavored aperitif.

Sake - Japanese rice wine.

Strega - an Italian liqueur.

Triple Sec - Orange flavored liqueur.

Basic Bar Stock

1 fifth Bourbon	2 quarts club soda
1 fifth Gin	2 quarts mineral water
1 fifth Vodka	2 quarts ginger ale
1 fifth Scotch	2 quarts tonic water
1 fifth Rum	2 quarts cola
1 fifth Blended Whiskey	2 quarts diet soda
1 10th Dry Vermouth	1 quart each tomato juice
1 10th Grenadine	and orange juice
1 10th Sweet Vermouth	attractive ice bucket &
1 fifth Tequila	tongs
1 fifth Cointreau	oranges, lemons, limes
1 fifth Cognac	green olives, anchovy olives
1 fifth Grand Marnier	cocktail onions
1 fifth Kahlua	maraschino cherries
1 fifth White or Dark	lemon zester
Creme de Menthe	sharp knife
1 fifth Amaretto	corkscrew
1 fifth Dubonnet or Lillet	blender
2 bottles each Red and	pitcher
White Wine,	jigger
Champagne	salt
1 case Beer - an	Worchestershire sauce
assortment of light,	Tabasco sauce
dark and imported	

Food and Wine Pairings

Hors d'Oeuvres and Canapes
Dry white wine such as Rhine, Chablis, Chenin Blanc or Pinot Chardonnay.
Rosé such as Rosé d'Anjou or Necta Rosé.
Light red such as Beaujoulais or Zinfandel.

Salads
Dry white wine such as Pouilly Fuisse, Soave or Corvo.

Soups
Wine is not normally served with soup. However, a dry Sherry or Madeira may be served with consommés.

Light Meats
Pork
Medium sweet white such as Graves, Vouvray, or White Anjou.
Rosé such as Mateus or Rosé d'Anjou.

Veal
Dry white such as Montrachet, Pinot Chardonnay or Chenin Blanc.
Light red such as Zinfandel, Valpollicella or Gamay Beaujoulais.

Ham
Rosé such as Rosé d'Anjou, Lancers or Necta Rosé.
Light red such as Macon or Mouton Cadet Red.

Dark Meats
Beef, roasted or broiled
Bordeaux such as St. Julien, Chateau Lafite Rothschild, Chateau La Tour, St. Emilion or Cabernet Sauvignon.

Beef casseroles and stews
Red Burgundy such as Chateauneuf du Pape or Pommard.
Heavy reds such as Hungarian Egri Bakiver or Pinot Noir.

Lamb
Bordeaux such as Margaux, a light Italian wine such as Bordolina or Chianti

Game
Bordeaux such as St. Emilion, Chateau Haut Brion or Medoc

Venison
Strong reds such as Chateauneuf du Pape, Cotes du Rhone or Chateau Haut Brion

Fish
Broiled or Lightly Poached
Light dry wine such as Chablis Pouilly Fumé or Green Hungarian
Fish in rich cream sauces
Meursault, Montrachet, Chateau Y'quem
Dry Rhine Wine or Niersteiner

Shellfish
Light white wines such as Muscadet, Soave, Vouvray Pinot Chardonnay or Corvo

Poultry
Chicken
White such as Hungarian Reisling, Dry Semillion, Pinot Blanc or White Burgundy
Light red such as Beaujoulais or Zinfandel.

Duck
Heavy white Burgundy such as Meursalt, or Rosé such as Zinfandel Rosé

Turkey
White wine such as Montrachet, Rhine or Pouilly Fuisse

Dessert
Sauterne, German Auslese or Spatlese, Hungarian Tokay, or White Anjou

After-Dinner
Port, Madeira, Hungarian Tokay, Cream Sherry or Muscatel

Equivalents

Liquid Measures
1 cup = ½ pint = 8 fluid ounces = 16 tablespoons
1 tablespoon = ½ fluid ounce
1 teaspoon = ⅙ fluid ounce
1 pint = 16 fluid ounces
1 quart = 2 pints = 32 fluid ounces
1 gallon = 4 quarts

Solid Measures
1 pound = 16 ounces
1 ounce = 28 grams
1 tablespoon = 3 teaspoons
1 bushel = 4 pecks

Bread
2 slices = 1 cup breadcrumbs
1 pound loaf = 10 cups cubed

Butter or Margarine
1 ounce = 2 tablespoons
1 stick = ½ cup = ¼ pound

Cheese
¼ pound = 1 cup shredded

Cream (heavy or whipping)
1 cup = 2 cups whipped cream

Chocolate
1 ounce = 1 square

Eggs
4–6 whole = 1 cup
8–10 whites = 1 cup
12–14 yolks = 1 cup

Flour, all purpose
1 pound = 3½ cups

Flour, cake
1 pound = 4 cups

Lemon
1 lemon = 3 tablespoons juice
1 lemon = 1 tablespoon grated rind

Onion
1 medium = ¾ cup chopped

Orange
1 medium = ½ cup orange juice
1 medium = 2 tablespoons grated rind

Potatoes
1 pound = 3 medium

Raisins
1 pound = 3 cups

Sugar
Granulated, 2¼ cups = 1 pound
Super fine, 2½ cups = 1 pound
Brown, 2¼ cups packed = 1 pound
Confectioners', 4 cups = 1 pound

Tomatoes
1 pound = 3 medium

Walnuts, shelled
4 cups = 1 pound

Fish Tips

- Fish are very perishable, so they must be refrigerated at all times.
- Frozen fish must be kept frozen and never refrozen.
- Fresh fish should be kept below 40°F. The best way to accomplish this is to keep the fish on crushed ice. This keeps the surface of the fish moist. Normal refrigeration causes the surface of the fish to dry and possible dehydration which will lead to spoilage.

It is important to recognize the following characteristics when purchasing fresh fish at the market.

- The fish should smell fresh, not excessively fishy, and have no strange odors.
- The eyes should be clear and bulging.
- The scales should be bright and not falling off.
- When pressed with the finger-tips, the fish should spring back into shape.
- The gills should be surrounded by a reddish-pink color.

Cutting Terminology

Chop
Cut food into smaller pieces, use a knife and cutting board. Hold the knife tip on the board with one hand and move the blade up and down with the other hand, cutting through the food. Pieces should be about the size of peas.

Mince
Cutting food in pieces smaller than chopped in the same manner as chopping. Mincing can also be done with scissors. Minced means very finely chopped.

Cube
Cut food into solid cubes from ½" to 1" thick.

Dice
Cutting food into cubes smaller than ½ " using a sharp knife or dicing gadget.

Julienne
Cutting food into match-like pieces

Shred
Cut or tear into small long narrow pieces.

Grate
Tearing off coarse to very fine particles of food with a hand grater.

Herbs and Spices

Capers
Taken from a shrub, as unopened flower buds, used to flavor salads, fish and sauces.

Caraway
Seeds of small white and yellow flowers, used in breads and cheeses for their pungent flavor.

Cardamom
Used in desserts, curry and in sauces.

Chervil
Used for fines herbes and in soups, salads and sauces.

Cinnamon
In stock and ground form. Used for spicy flavor in fruit dishes, beverages and baked goods.

Chives
Can be grown very easily indoors. Used in soups and egg cookery.

Cloves
An onion stuck with a clove is used to season soups and stews. Also used in sweet dishes and beverages.

Curry Powder
Curry is not obtained from a single plant, but is a blend of several spices such as: cardomom, cayenne, cloves, coriander, cumin, ginger, mace, pepper and tumeric.

Dill
Leaves used in flavoring fish, vegetables, sauces, soups, salads and tomato cookery.

Garlic
Bulb composed of multiple cloves. Used to flavor meats, salad dressings, tomato cookery and stews.

Ginger
Used in desserts and some meat dishes, especially Eastern cuisine. Comes in root, powdered and crystallized form.

Marjoram
Used in vegetables, chicken cookery, fish, soups, eggs and tossed salads. Enhances poultry dressings also.

Mustard
Seed or ground form, for hot sauces or salad dressings.

Mace
Mace is the outer covering of nutmeg. Used primarily in baking.

Nutmeg
The seed of mace, used primarily in sauces, fruits and vegetable cookery.

Parsley
French, Curly and Italian (flat) varieties. Used as an ingredient of fine herbs, sauces, soups and as a garnish.

Paprika
Powder made from dried sweet red peppers. Used in Hungarian and fish cookery.

Pepper
Dried berries of the tropical pepper vine. Whole black peppercorns are the whole under-ripe berries that have been dried and cured. They are used for sauces, salad and dark meat cookery.

Whole white peppercorns are the dried ripe berries in which the dark outer shell has been removed. White pepper is not as pungent as black pepper and has a finer, more aromatic flavor. White peppercorns are used in cooking white fish, cream sauces, eggs, cream soups, veal and poultry.

Cayenne
Cayenne is very strong red pepper which is used sparingly in cooking. Cayenne gives zest to sauces, especially Hollandaise and Veloute.

Basil
Leaves of basil are used in tomato sauces, soups and salads.

Bay Leaf
Used in soups, fish, vegetables, stews and is an ingredient in bouquet garni.

Oregano (wild marjoram)
Flakes used in tomato sauces, lamb, salads and beef soups.

Sage
Used in poultry stuffings, dressings and paté.

Thyme
Used in bouquet garni, stews, fish and egg cookery.

Tarragon
Dark green leaves used in salad dressings, sauces and chicken and fish cookery.

Saffron
Bright spicy powder from crocus. Used in Mediterranean and fish cookery.

Vanilla
Bean and extract form. The bean comes from the long pod of a tropical vine and extract is formed by mashing pods with alcohol. Vanilla will impact a rich flavor to creams and desserts.

Equipment For The Complete Kitchen

Apple Corer:
Wooden handle with stainless steel corer attached.

Blender or Food Processor:
Not essential, but will save you much time in the kitchen.

Cutting Board:
For chopping, a large wooden one is best. Make sure the wood is smooth so dirt will not catch and form bacteria. Lucite is very easy to clean.

Bowl:
A large earthenware bowl for breads and pastas.
A large metal or copper tin lined bowl for whipping cream and egg whites.
A wooden salad bowl, large enough for tossing salads.
Nested mixing bowls made of stainless steel or pyrex.

Cake Rack:
Two small or one large for cooling cookies, pastries and cakes.

Cake Plate:
Round china, glass or silver with or without a stand.

Cake Pans:
Made of ovenproof glass or metal: Three 9″ layer cake pans, one springform pan and two loaf pans.

Fork:
Three-prong used only when carving meat, as food should never be pierced while cooking.

Funnel:
For pouring liquid into narrow openings.

Garlic Press:
Two piece metal, squeeze action. For keeping pulp out of recipe, and extracting juice of garlic.

Grater:
A sturdy stainless steel grater that has fine to coarse surfaces.

Ice Pick:
For breaking ice, hard chocolate and testing vegetables for doneness.

Tea Kettle:
A sturdy easy to handle kettle that is either whistling or brewing always on the back burner!

Well and Tree Carving Board:
A large wooden oval with grooves to catch the meat juices. Used for fowl and meat.

Casseroles:
One large and small with tight fitting lids, made of suitable material for stove top and oven cookery.

Colander:
A large colander for draining liquid from food.

Corkscrew:
Preferable combination knife-corkscrew and bottle opener.

Cookie sheets:
Three good heavy cookie sheets, can also be used for roulades, and bread baking.

Custard cups or ramekins:
For oven cooking and can also store small amounts of leftovers or ingredients used in a recipe.

Dish cloths and towels:
Look for thick, plain cloths; 6 of each cloth and towel is great.

Double Boiler:
Copper bottom and glass top so you can see the water boiling in the bottom.

Perforated Spoon:
For lifting meat from juices or food from deep fryer.

Knives:
Knives made of carbon steel are better than stainless steel when it comes to sharpening. Keep your knives sharp. Never let them sit in water; but rather wipe with a damp cloth after use and dry immediately. Sharpen professionally when dull and use a carborundum for touch-ups.

Cake knive:
For cutting cake and pie

Chef's knife:
8″ blade for chopping, cutting, slicing and mincing.

Paring knife:
For cutting and trimming vegetables.

Narrow blade slicing knife:
For thin slices of ham, roast beef and turkey.

Stainless steel serrated knife:
For cutting fruit, vegetables, bread and angel food cake.

Boning knife:
For poultry, fish and meat.

Flat cleaver:
For heavy chopping, slicing and pounding veal and chicken slices very thin. Also used to gather ingredients.

Carving knife:
A 10-14″ blade used for carving roasts.

Sauce Boat:
China or silver for serving gravies and sauces.

Timer:
If your stove does not have a timer, purchase a one-hour timer with a bell.

Tin-lined Copper Saucepan:
2 quart size used exclusively for saucemaking because it provides even heat and will not scorch.

Tureen and Ladle:
To bring soup piping hot to the table.

Pot Holders:
Thick asbestos backed.

Potato or Vegetable Peeler:
For potatoes and carrots. Will also peel thin skinned fruits. One with a floating blade will do the best job.

Refrigerator and Storage Jars:
Square plastic that can be stacked works the best and can also be used in the freezer.

Rechaud or Chafing Dish:
Used for tableside cookery—the type of fuel used is strictly a matter of preference. Available in stainless steel, silver-plate and copper. Some rechauds have a cannister for butane fuel, others have a holder for sterno and liquid fuel.

Rolling Pin:
A long thin rolling pin is best because it enables you to work with a large delicate piece of pastry at one time.

Roasting Rack:
For holding meat up from its juices.

Salad Spinner or Basket:
A small cage which you can shake dry or spin your freshly washed greens. Remember water will spoil any dressing.

Scissors:
For cutting string, twine, paper and cheesecloth.

Rubber Scrapers:
For food that is not cooking, getting in corners or almost-empty jars, and for scraping bowls.

Skewers:
Wooden or metal for brochettes.

Pots and Pans:
Choose pans with flat, tight-fitting lids

Aluminum saucepans:
Choose a 1 quart, 2 quart and 5 quart pan

Miniature copper pot:
For melting butter or heating Brandy and Liqueurs for flaming.

Roasting pans:
Uncovered shallow, rectangular pans in stainless steel or aluminum.

Frying pans:
Heavy cast aluminum or iron in several sizes. One with a basket for deep frying.

Omelette pan:
Heavy cast iron or aluminum with a rounded base. Wipe out with a clean dry cloth after each use—do not immerse in water.

Ladle:
Select one each for soups and sauces.

Lemon or Orange Juicer:
For fresh squeezed orange juice in the morning and when your recipe calls for orange or lemon juice.

Measuring Cups:
A glass one quart graduated liquid measuring cup and one set of aluminum ¼, ⅓, ½ and 1 cup sizes.

Measuring Spoons:
1 teaspoon and 1 tablespoon are the most important sizes.

Melon Baller:
For scooping melons or potatoes.

Mixer:
A hand mixer and an electric mixer for heavy work if possible with a deep bowl.

Molds:
Brioche tins, savarin mold, madeleine molds.

Mortar and Pestule:
Essential for pesto and for grinding quantities too small for the blender or food processor.

Needle and Thread:
A large needle and coarse cotton thread for kitchen use only. For poultry, meat and fish.

Pastry Bag and Tips:
Buy a canvas bag with plastic lining with a round, star and rose tip. Clean bag in hot soapy water and rinse and dry after each use.

Pastry Board:
A large thin pastry board to fit on your counter.

Pastry Brushes:
A couple good brushes made of nylon and/or goosedown. Wash in warm soapy water and air dry after each use.

Pepper Mills:
One for black, white & green peppercorns.

Platters:
Glass or silver, oval and round in various sizes.

Souffle Dish:
1 quart and 2 quart porcelain with fluted sides and a ridge at the top.

Metal Spatulas:
One large and one small for turning and lifting food.

Wooden Spoons:
For tossing salads, or stirring sauces over heat.

Metal Spoons:
Large spoon for coating with sauce, slotted spoon for draining.

Strainers:
One very small and one large stainless steel. One cone shaped strainer for fine sauces and fats. Large strainer can double as a colander or steamer basket.

String:
One ball of string for trussing fowl and tying meat.

Terrine:
For pates—one quart rectangular earthenware size is best.

Thermometers:
Oven thermometer and one for meat and one for candy are essential.

Tongs:
To be used in turning meats and vegetables so they are not pierced.

Wire Whisks:
For beating, folding and whipping. One large, medium and small wire whisk will work much better than any mixer.

Cheese Guide

Brie	semisoft, mild
Bleu	semisoft, sharp
Camembert	soft, pungent
Caraway	hard, spicy
Cheddar	semihard, may be mild or sharp
Cream	soft, mild
Edam	semisoft, mild
Gouda	semihard, mild
Greyere	semihard, mild
Meunster	soft, mild
Monterey Jack	hard, sharp
Neufchatel	soft, mild
Port Du Salut	semihard, sharp
Provolone	hard, sharp
Roquefort	semisoft, sharp
Swiss	hard, sweet

Egg Whites

- Egg whites whip to a greater volume at room temperature.
- Eggs separate easier when they are chilled.
- When separating eggs, remove every trace of egg yolk from the whites. If there is even one spec of egg yolk remaining, the fatty substance will prevent the whites from whipping past the frothy stage.
- If there is any grease on the beaters or any water in the mixing bowl, the whites will not whip stiffly.
- A mixing bowl of stainless steel, glass or glazed pottery is good for whipping egg whites.
- Aluminum tends to discolor egg whites—plastic retains a greasy film.
- Don't lose your patience when beating egg whites! They take a long time to reach the stiff stage. A pinch of salt may speed the whipping.
- Use the egg whites immediately after whipping or they will lose their volume. Fold them very gently into another mixture with a spatula or whisk.

For Emergencies Only!!!

(If you are out of an ingredient!)

1 cup cake flour =
    1 cup minus 2 tablespoons all-purpose flour

1 tablespoon cornstarch =
    2 tablespoons flour or 4 tablespoons quick cooking tapioca

1 whole egg =
    2 egg yolks

½ cup butter or margarine =
    ½ cup shortening and ¼ teaspoon salt

1 cup whole milk =
    ½ cup evaporated milk and ½ cup water
                OR
    1 cup reconstituted nonfat dry milk plus 2 teaspoons butter

1 cup sour milk or buttermilk =
    1 tablespoon lemon juice plus sweet milk to make one cup—let stand 5 minutes

1 small fresh onion =
    1 tablespoon instant minced onion rehydrated

Kitchen Hints

- To prevent fruits from browning and discoloring, brush them with lemon juice.
- To cut fresh baked bread easily, use a hot knife.
- Run cold water while peeling onions to keep your eyes from watering.
- To keep parsley, mint and watercress from wilting, wash thoroughly, shake off excess water and place in a covered glass jar in refrigerator.
- Add one tablespoon vegetable oil to boiling water when cooking noodles or spaghetti to keep them from sticking together and prevent water from boiling over.
- To keep cheese from molding, wrap in a vinegar dampened cheesecloth and store in a cool place or refrigerator.
- Rinse saucepan with hot water before using to keep scalding milk from scorching.
- Rub your hands with a slice of lemon to remove fish odors or vegetable stains.
- To skin a tomato easily, place a fork through the stem end and plunge into boiling water for 3 seconds and immediately into cold water.
- Drain deep fried foods and bacon on absorbent paper towels before serving.
- To hold egg white and yolks together while poaching add a few drops of lemon juice to the water.
- To ripen avocados, place in a brown paper bag in a warm place for 1–2 days.
- Salt added to pork before cooking will toughen it.
- When cream will not whip add the white of an egg to cream and chill for ½ hour, then rewhip.
- To prevent a dark ring from forming on the bottom of your double-boiler, add ½ teaspoon vinegar to the water.
- To keep the cut edges of a frosted cake or torte from drying out, cover them with a piece of bread fastened with tooth-picks.
- To cut dried fruits, dip scissors or blade of knife in confectioner's sugar before cutting.
- To keep steel wool pads from rusting, store them in a small clay saucer or pot.

Menus For Special Occasions

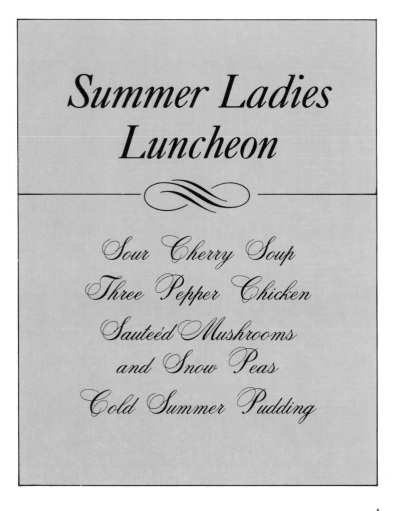

Summer Ladies Luncheon

Sour Cherry Soup
Three Pepper Chicken
*Sautéed Mushrooms
and Snow Peas*
Cold Summer Pudding

Sour Cherry Soup

Serves four

1 pound pitted sour
cherries
7½ cups water
½ teaspoon ground
cinnamon

1¼ cups sugar
4 cloves
1 egg, beaten
Juice of ½ lemon
⅔ cup sour cream

Combine cherries, water, sugar, cinnamon, and cloves in a large saucepan. Bring to a boil and simmer for 30 minutes or until cherries are tender. Set aside.

Combine egg and sour cream in a large bowl, blending well. Slowly ladle in the cherry mixture, blending well. Squeeze in lemon juice and blend. Chill before serving.

Three Pepper Chicken

Serves four

4 boneless breast of
chicken
2 tablespoons butter
¼ teaspoon paprika
¼ teaspoon fresh ground
black pepper

¼ teaspoon fresh ground
green pepper
½ teaspoon salt
½ cup chicken stock
2 onions, peeled and
sliced

Blend butter with paprika, black and green pepper and salt. Rub generously on chicken breasts. Place chicken in a baking casserole along with chicken stock and onions. Preheat oven to 450°F and bake for 20–25 minutes, or until chicken is tender inside and crisp outside, basting occasionally.

Sautéed Mushrooms and Snow Peas

Serves four

½ pound fresh snow peas
½ pound fresh sliced
mushrooms
3 tablespoons oil

1 teaspoon soy sauce
1 teaspoon sesame seeds
Juice of ½ lemon

Heat oil with soy sauce in a skillet over moderate heat and cook sesame seeds until golden. Add mushrooms and snow peas and cook until mushrooms are tender. Squeeze lemon juice over all and serve.

Cold Summer Pudding

10 slices day-old bread
1 pound raspberries
1½ cups sugar
1 cup water

1½ cups sliced, peeled
and cored, apples
2 cups light cream

Trim crusts from the bread and slice into 3-inch fingers. Line a bowl with 2 layers of the bread fingers. Simmer the berries and apples in a saucepan with sugar and water for 10 minutes. Spoon the fruit into the bread lined bowl. Place a plate on the top of bowl rim and weight it down. Place in refrigerator at least 4 hours before serving. To serve, invert onto a platter and serve with cream.

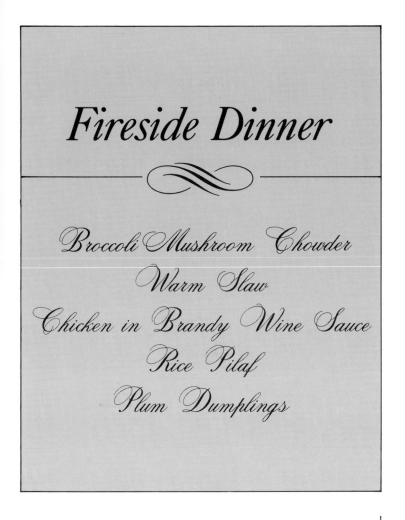

Fireside Dinner

Broccoli Mushroom Chowder

Warm Slaw

Chicken in Brandy Wine Sauce

Rice Pilaf

Plum Dumplings

Warm Slaw

Serves six

½ pound bacon
1 tablespoon poppy seeds
½ cup vegetable oil
1 pound green cabbage
  finely shredded
1 pound red cabbage
  finely shredded

1 teaspoon salt
½ teaspoon fresh ground
  green pepper
1½ cup sour cream
Juice of ½ lemon

Sauté bacon over high heat until crisp. Remove bacon and place on paper towels to drain. Crumble bacon when cooled.

Heat vegetable oil over moderate heat and cook cabbage until tender, stirring constantly. Stir in poppy seeds, sour cream, salt, pepper and bacon. Squeeze lemon juice over all and blend well. Serve warm.

Broccoli Mushroom Chowder

Serves six

1 pound fresh broccoli,
  cut in ½" pieces
½ pound fresh sliced
  mushrooms
½ cup butter
½ cup flour

6 cups chicken stock
6 cups half and half
½ teaspoon salt
½ teaspoon fresh ground
  white pepper
⅛ teaspoon nutmeg

Steam broccoli in ½ cup water until tender and set aside. Melt butter over moderate heat. Sprinkle flour over butter and cook stirring constantly until mixture is golden. Whisk in chicken stock 1 cup at a time and bring mixture to a boil. Reduce to a simmer and add broccoli, mushrooms, half and half, salt, pepper and nutmeg. Stir well until all ingredients are blended thoroughly and mushrooms are tender. Serve in heated soup crocks or bowls.

Chicken in Brandy Wine Sauce

Serves four

2 pounds chicken,
  disjointed
4 cloves garlic, pressed
2 ounces Brandy
1½ cups dry white wine
2 green peppers, seeded
  and cut in julienne strips
⅔ cup chopped onion
½ teaspoon oregano
½ cup olive oil

8 medium tomatoes,
  peeled, seeded and
  chopped
1 teaspoon basil
1 tablespoon chopped
  parsley
1 bay leaf
Salt and fresh ground
  pepper to taste

Season chicken with salt and fresh ground pepper to taste. Heat ⅓ cup olive oil over moderate heat and sauté green pepper until tender. Remove green pepper and reserve. Add remaining oil to pan. Add chicken and cook until browned on all sides and opaque. Transfer chicken to a serving platter. Sauté onion in remaining oil until tender and transparent. Add oregano, parsley, basil, bay leaf, garlic, wine and Brandy and cook until mixture is reduced by one-half. Add tomatoes, and simmer uncovered for 20 minutes. Remove bay leaf and return chicken and green pepper to pan and simmer for 10 minutes before serving.

Rice Pilaf

Serves four

½ cup long grain rice
1 cup chicken stock
½ teaspoon salt
3 green onions, chopped

¼ cup butter
Fresh ground pepper to
  taste

Melt butter over moderate heat in a heavy saucepan and sauté onion until tender. Add rice, chicken stock, salt and pepper and increase heat to high to bring mixture to a boil. Cover with a tight fitting lid and lower heat to simmer. Cook for 15–20 minutes. Fluff with a fork before serving.

Plum Dumplings

Serves four

2 cups mashed potatoes
1 egg
½ teaspoon salt
5 tablespoons unsalted
  butter
½ cups brown sugar

20 Italian plums, pitted
  and quartered
Grated zest and juice of
  1½ lemons
½ teaspoon cinnamon
½ cup Madeira wine

Place brown sugar, plums, lemon juice and zest, cinnamon and Madeira wine in a non-aluminum saucepan and simmer until plums are tender. Drain plums and set aside, reserving juice.

Mix potatoes with the egg, salt and 1 tablespoon butter. Add the flour and knead the dough well on a floured surface. Stretch dough to ½-inch thickness square. Cut dough into 16 squares.

Place a tablespoon of the plum mixture in the center of each square of dough. Pull the corners together to make a dumpling out of each square, making sure filling is completely enclosed in dough.

Fill a large saucepan with water and bring to a boil. Gently drop dumplings into boiling water. When dumplings rise to the surface, remove with a slotted spoon. Melt remaining butter and pour over dumplings. Transfer dumplings to individual serving dishes and top with remaining plum sauce.

Special Celebration Dinner

Oriental Romaine Salad
Filet Cordon Bleu
Carrots Vichy
Chestnut Snow Peak
Dessert Dusan

Cafe Alexandria

Oriental Romaine Salad

Serves four

1 head Romaine lettuce
1 tablespoon sugar
½ teaspoon
  Worchestershire sauce
½ teaspoon Dijon-style
  mustard
1 tomato, peeled and
  chopped

Juice of ½ lemon
¼ cup olive oil
½ teaspoon basil
6 scallions, chopped
4 tablespoons chopped
  pimentos
1 cup croutons
¼ pound alfalfa sprouts

Wash Romaine and tear into bite sized pieces. Mix lemon juice, sugar, Worchestershire sauce, mustard and basil together and set aside.

Heat oil in wok or skillet over high heat and sauté scallions until tender. Add tomato, pimento and lemon juice mixture and heat to boiling. Add Romaine and toss lightly until Romaine is slightly wilted and coated with dressing.

Transfer Romaine to salad plates and top with croutons and alfalfa sprouts before serving.

Filet Cordon Bleu

Serves four

4-6 ounce filets, 1″ thick
6 tablespoons butter
1 cup fresh sliced
  mushrooms
¾ cup Bearnaise sauce
2 ounces Brandy

4 thin slices cooked ham,
  4″×4″
4 thin slices Swiss cheese,
  4″×4″
Salt and fresh ground
  pepper to taste

Season filets with salt and fresh ground pepper to taste. Melt butter in a skillet over moderate heat and sauté mushrooms until tender, and set aside. Sauté filets in remaining butter until medium-rare. Top each filet with equal portion of mushrooms, a slice of ham and a slice of cheese. Pour Brandy around the perimeter of the skillet and ignite. Spoon juices over cheese until it has melted. Lace with Bearnaise sauce.

Carrots Vichy

Serves six

1½ pounds carrots
  trimmed, scraped and
  cut into very thin rounds
¼ teaspoon salt
¼ teaspoon fresh ground
  white pepper

1½ teaspoon sugar
¼ cup water
4 tablespoons butter
1 tablespoon chopped
  parsley

Place the carrots, salt, butter, pepper, sugar and water in a skillet. Cover the skillet with a round of buttered wax paper and cook the carrots over moderate to high heat. Shake the pan frequently to insure that the carrots do not burn. Cook until the carrots are tender and a light glaze is formed. Sprinkle with parsley before serving.

Chestnut Snow Peak Dessert Dusan

Serves six

1½ pounds fresh chestnuts
4 cups milk
1¼ cups sugar

1 cup heavy whipping cream
3 tablespoons dark rum

Cut a criss-cross on the pointed end of each chestnut, then boil in water for 15 minutes. Drain and peel. Combine chestnuts with milk in a saucepan and cook over low heat for 30 minutes. Drain and mash until a smooth paste is formed. Beat in sugar. Place mixture in a potato ricer and force mixture on 4 dessert dishes in a mound. Chill until ready to serve.
Meanwhile, whip cream until stiff peaks form and blend in rum and place on chestnut mounds.

Cafe Alexandria

Serves two

2 ounces chocolate syrup
1½ cups strong coffee
½ ounce 151 Proof Rum
2 ounces Vodka
½ cup whipped cream

⅛ teaspoon powdered
  cinnamon
Chocolate shavings
1 Orange wedge
Sugar to rim glass

Two tempered glass water goblets.
*Note: It is imperative to use tempered glass, otherwise glass could crack or explode.

Place a diagonal slice in orange and fit on rim of glass. Rub around perimeter. Place sugar in a dish and dip glass in sugar to "frost" edge. Drizzle 151 Rum in each glass and ignite. Turn glasses so flame carmelizes sugar on rim. Pour in Vodka when flame has extinguished. Pour in chocolate syrup and coffee. Top with dollops of whipped cream, a sprinkling of cinnamon and chocolate shavings. For a special touch, wrap goblets in a cloth napkin by folding a napkin in lengthwise quarters and tying around roundest part of goblet. (This prevents burned fingers.)

Autumn Dinner

Snow Peas with Herbed Cheese

Hot Bacon and Endive Salad

Roast Duckling with Cabbage

Baked Apples in Red Wine

Amaretto Cheesecake

Snow Peas with Herbed Cheese

Makes 24

24 tender young snow peas
4 ounces whipped cream
  cheese
Pinch cayenne pepper
1 teaspoon chopped dill
1 teaspoon minced fresh
  mint

Remove the stem end from each snow pea, and blanch in boiling water for 30 seconds. Rinse immediately with ice cold water. With a small sharp knife, slit open the straight seam of each snow pea. Mix cream cheese, with mint, cayenne and dill and place in a pastry bag. Affix a small round tip to the bag and pipe the herbed cheese into the pea slits. Garnish each tip with a small sprig of fresh dill if desired.

Hot Bacon and Endive Salad

Serves four

2 heads Belgium endive,
  cleaned
6 slices bacon
1 tablespoon oil
1 tablespoon vinegar
Fresh ground black pepper

Cut bacon into small pieces. Heat oil in a fry pan over moderate heat and add bacon. Cook until bacon is crisp. Place endive leaves in a warmed salad bowl and add bacon. In skillet in which bacon fat remains add oil, vinegar and pepper to taste. Mix well and pour over endive. Toss gently and serve.

Roast Duck with Cabbage

Serves four

2 ducklings, 3 pounds each
1 tablespoon cumin
1 head white cabbage,
  shredded
4 chopped onions
¼ cup vinegar
Salt and pepper to taste
Sugar to taste

Season ducklings with salt and pepper to taste inside and out. Place in a roaster with ¼ cup water and roast at 375°F until golden brown. Transfer to a heated platter and keep warm.

Sauté onion in 3 tablespoons of duck drippings and vinegar. Season to taste with cumin, sugar, salt and pepper and serve with duck.

Baked Apples in Red Wine

Serves four

4 apples, cored
½ cup brown sugar
½ cup cherry preserves
½ teaspoon mace
1 cup red wine
½ teaspoon vanilla

Butter a baking casserole and place apples in casserole. Fill each core with cherry preserves. Mix brown sugar with mace, wine and vanilla. Pour wine mixture over apples and cover casserole. Bake in a preheated 350°F. oven for 45 minutes.

Amaretto Cheesecake

2 cups crushed macaroons
⅓ cup melted butter
3 8-ounce packages cream
  cheese at room
  temperature
1½ cups granulated sugar
4 eggs
2 ounces Amaretto liqueur
1½ cups sour cream
½ teaspoon almond
  extract
½ cup toasted sliced
  almonds

Blend macaroon crumbs and butter together. Press crumb mixture on side and bottom of a greased springform pan.

Beat cream cheese and sugar until light and fluffy. Add eggs one at a time. Blend in Amaretto and whip mixture for 15 minutes.

Pour mixture into crumb crust and bake in a preheated 325° F. oven for 50 minutes. Remove from oven and cool for ½ hour.

Meanwhile blend sour cream and almond extract together and pour over cooled cheesecake. Top with almonds and bake 10 minutes longer.

Mexican Fiesta

Avocado Soup with Nachos
Sherried Fruit
Beef Acapulco
Curried Tomatoes
Chocolate Flan
Coffee with Kahlua

Avocado Soup

Serves four

4 avocados, peeled and mashed
4 cups chicken stock
1 tablespoon butter
1 small onion, minced
½ bunch watercress, chopped

1½ cups peeled, seeded and chopped tomato
½ teaspoon red hot pepper sauce
½ teaspoon salt

In a heavy saucepan melt butter over moderate heat and sauté onion until tender and golden brown. Add watercress and cook until wilted. Pour in chicken stock. Bring to a boil and remove from heat. Add mashed avocado, tomato, salt and red hot pepper sauce. Pureé one cup at a time in a food processor or blender. Chill before serving if desired or serve hot.

Sherried Fruit

Serves four

2 papayas
4 seedless oranges
½ cup sugar

¼ cup Sherry
Mint leaves

Cut papayas in half lengthwise. Remove and discard seeds. Cut each papaya half into ¼-inch wedges. Peel oranges, removing white membrane. Slice into ½-inch rounds. Arrange papaya and orange slices on a decorative platter. Sprinkle with sugar and Sherry and chill. Garnish with mint leaves before serving.

Beef Acapulco

Serves four

1 pound tenderloin tips
1 fresh hot chili, seeded and minced
3 green onions, minced
3 teaspoons greated fresh ginger

Juice of ½ lemon
½ teaspoon salt
1 tablespoon cornstarch
2½ tablespoon soy sauce
3 tablespoons vegetable oil

Combine all above ingredients and marinate for at least 4 hours, preferably overnight. Heat wok or large skillet over high heat and sauté beef until done medium to medium-rare, tossing constantly.

Curried Tomatoes

Serves four

4 tomatoes, peeled and diced
1 tablespoon olive oil
1 teaspoon curry powder
1 onion peeled and sliced

⅛ teaspoon Worchestershire sauce
¼ teaspoon fresh ground pepper
¼ teaspoon basil

Heat oil over moderate heat in a skillet and sauté onions with curry powder until tender. Add tomatoes, Worchestershire and pepper. Cook, stirring constantly, until tomatoes are heated. Sprinkle with basil and serve.

Chocolate Flan

Serves four to six

1 quart chocolate milk
6 egg yolks
1 whole egg

2 cups sugar
1 tablespoon vanilla

Preheat oven to 350°F. Fill a large pan with 1½-inches of hot water and place in oven. Place 1½ cups of sugar in a heavy pan over high heat until sugar dissolves. As sugar turns light brown, remove from heat and place in a 1½-quart souffle dish, rotating to spread caramel over bottom and sides. Set aside.
To make custard, whisk egg and egg yolks in a large bowl until blended. Whisk in remaining sugar, vanilla and milk. Pour this mixture into the caramel coated souffle dish and then set it in the baking pan filled with water. Bake 45 minutes. Remove from oven, take out of water and allow to cool to room temperature, then place in refrigerator to chill. Unmold onto a rimmed serving dish at serving time.

Summer Dinner

Cheese Puffs

Salad Melba

Salmon in Dijon Mustard Sauce

Champagne Sorbet

Cheese Puffs

Serves four

1½ cups milk
4 tablespoons butter
1 teaspoon salt
½ teaspoon fresh ground white pepper
¼ teaspoon nutmeg

⅛ teaspoon cayenne pepper
1 cup flour
4 eggs
1 cup Cheddar cheese, grated

Reserve 2 tablespoons of milk. Heat milk in a saucepan until scalded, stir in butter and seasonings and continue to stir until milk and butter have blended together.

Reduce heat to low and add flour. Vigorously stir until mixture pulls away from the sides of the pan. Remove pan from heat and beat in eggs one at a time, blending thoroughly after each addition. Add grated cheese and mix well.

Butter a cookie sheet and drop batter by tablespoons onto baking sheet, spacing evenly. Brush each mound with reserved milk. Bake in a preheated 375°F oven for 40 minutes or until puffed and golden brown. Do not open oven door during baking or your puffs will deflate!! Serve hot or at room temperature.

Salad Melba

Serves four

8 leaves Belgium endive
12 leaves Romaine lettuce
¼ cup alfalfa sprouts
½ cup fresh sliced mushrooms

4 cooked artichoke hearts, cut in half
½ cup fresh raspberries
½ cup Viniagrette dressing (see page 52)

Mix raspberries with viniagrette dressing and set aside. Arrange Romaine lettuce and Belgium endive on chilled salad plates. Decoratively arrange sliced mushrooms and artichoke hearts on lettuce. Top with alfalfa sprouts and spoon raspberry viniagrette over all.

Salmon in Dijon Mustard Sauce

Serves four

2 tablespoons oil
2 tablespoons butter
4 scallions finely chopped
4 salmon filets, cleaned and washed
¾ cup dry white wine
5 tablespoons whipping cream

2 tablespoons Dijon-style mustard
4 tablespoons fresh chopped dill
Salt and fresh ground green pepper to taste

Season salmon with salt and fresh ground pepper to taste. Heat butter and oil over moderate heat in a large fry pan. Add scallions and sauté until tender. Add sauté salmon and white wine. Slowly bring to a boil, then simmer for 20 minutes, turning salmon once. Transfer to a heated serving platter and keep warm.

Stir juices in pan over high heat until reduced by one-fourth. Add mustard and whisk in cream. Reduce heat and stir until well blended. Pour over salmon and sprinkle with dill.

Champagne Sorbet

Serves six

1 bottle Brut Champagne
2½ cups corn syrup
Juice of 1½ lemons

Combine all ingredients and place in freezer trays. Freeze for 45 minutes, remove and beat well. Return to freezer for at least 4 hours. Serve in champagne flutes.

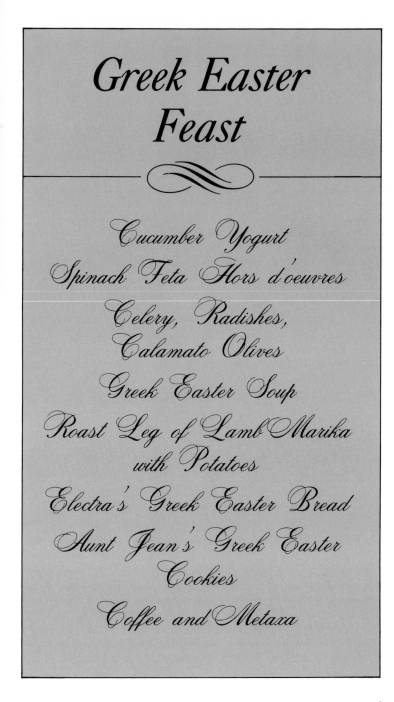

Greek Easter Feast

Cucumber Yogurt

Spinach Feta Hors d'oeuvres

Celery, Radishes, Calamato Olives

Greek Easter Soup

Roast Leg of Lamb Marika with Potatoes

Electra's Greek Easter Bread

Aunt Jean's Greek Easter Cookies

Coffee and Metaxa

Cucumber Yogurt

1 quart yogurt
1 cucumber, peeled
½ teaspoon salt
2 cloves garlic pressed

Grate cucumber, salt it and let it stand in a sieve for ½ hour to drain. Squeeze out excess moisture by pressing with your hands. Add drained cucumber to yogurt and garlic, blend well and place in an attractive serving dish. Refrigerate until ready to serve. Serve with pita breads or toasted French bread.

Spinach-Feta Hors d'oeuvres

Makes 20

1 pound chopped fresh spinach
2 onions, minced
2 cups bread cubes, moistened with ½ cup half and half
4 ounces Feta cheese, crumbled
¼ cup butter
½ teaspoon salt
1 teaspoon garlic powder
½ tablespoon thyme
½ teaspoon fresh ground pepper
6 eggs, well beaten

Melt butter over moderate heat and saute onion with thyme, garlic powder and pepper until tender and transparent. Add spinach and cook until spinach is tender and slightly wilted, tossing lightly. Place onion-spinach mixture in a large mixing bowl and add remaining ingredients. Blend well and shape mixture into walnut sized balls. Bake on a greased cookie sheet in a preheated 375° F. oven for 20 minutes. Serve hot.

Greek Easter Soup

Serves four to six

1 lamb lung
1 lamb heart
1 lamb liver
1 cup chopped green onions
4 teaspoons olive oil
½ cup chopped celery
½ cup raw rice
4 eggs
Juice of 2 lemons
Salt and fresh ground pepper to taste

Wash lung, heart and liver and place in a pot with 10 cups of water. Bring to a boil and simmer for 45 minutes. Strain broth, reserving meat. Remove cartilage and meat and then chop into small pieces. Return broth to pot.

Heat olive oil over moderate heat in a saute pan and saute green onions and celery until transparent. Add meat and brown lightly. Season with salt and pepper to taste. Add this mixture to broth. Add rice and bring to a boil. Simmer until rice is tender.

Beat eggs well and gradually beat in lemon juice. Add one cup hot broth slowly to egg-lemon mixture, beating constantly. Stir egg-lemon mixture into soup, blending well. Do not allow soup to boil or egg will separate.

Roast Leg of Lamb Marika

Serves four to six

5-6 pound leg of lamb	1 teaspoon oregano
4 cloves garlic, chopped	Salt and fresh ground
One lemon	pepper to taste
¼ cup butter	

Preheat oven to 350° F. Wash leg of lamb in cold water and pat dry with paper towels. Make several incisions 1-1½ inches deep and insert chopped garlic in incisions. Squeeze lemon juice over lamb. Rub lamb with butter. Season lamb with salt and pepper to taste and sprinkle with oregano. Rub seasonings into the lamb with your hands. Place lamb in a roasting pan along with 1 cup water and cover tightly. Bake for 2 hours or until lamb is cooked to desired doneness, basting occasionally.

Electra's Greek Easter Bread

Yield: Three Loaves

5 pounds flour	3 teaspoon powdered
1 tablespoon salt	mastica (spice from
4 packages dry yeast	Syria, purchased in
4 cups lukewarm milk	specialty stores)
10 eggs, beaten well	3 egg yolks, beaten
4 cups sugar	⅓ cup sesame seeds
1 pound unsalted butter,	5 hard-boiled eggs, dyed
melted	red

Dissolve yeast with 1 cup milk. Sift flour with mastica, salt and place 4 pounds only in a large bowl, making a well in the center. Add yeast, eggs and sugar and mix well. Add butter and remaining milk, mixing thoroughly; adding more flour if necessary to make a firm mixture.

Place dough on a floured board and knead until smooth and elastic. Place dough in a buttered bowl, turn over to coat top of dough and cover with towels. Set in a warm place, free of drafts and allow to rise until double in size. Knead again and allow to rise until double in dize. Repeat this process once again.

Divide dough into 9 sections, and roll each section into a rope. Braid 3 ropes pressing ends together forming separate loaves. Form each braid into a wreath pressing ends together. Brush wreaths with egg yolks and sprinkle with sesame seeds and press 3 eggs into each braid. Bake on a greased baking pan at 350° F. for 1 hour or until golden brown.

Aunt Jean's Greek Easter Cookies

Yield: Approximately 72

3 sticks unsalted butter	Juice of one orange
2 tablespoons vegetable	Juice of one lemon
shortening	9 cups flour
6 egg yolks	1 ounce Brandy
1 whole egg	2 egg yolks
4 teaspoons baking	½ cup sesame seeds
powder	

Cream butter and vegetable shortening until light and fluffy; about 20 minutes. Add sugar and egg yolks, mixing thoroughly. Sift in flour and mix well. Place baking powder in Brandy and juices and add quickly to mixture, blending well. Knead dough until smooth and firm. Roll the dough in the palms of your hands into cylinders ½-inch thick. Put ends together and twist twice. Place on a greased cookie sheet and brush with egg yolk. Sprinkle with sesame seeds and bake in a preheated 350° F. oven for 15 minutes or until lightly browned. Allow to cool slightly before removing from pan.

Marinated Mushrooms

Serves four to six

1½ pounds large white	2 tablespoons minced
mushrooms	pimento
1¼ cups wine vinegar	2 garlic cloves, pressed
¾ cup olive oil	1 teaspoon salt
½ teaspoon fresh ground	1 tablespoon minced
pepper	parsley

Remove stems from mushrooms and discard. Wipe mushrooms gently and place in a mixing bowl. In a separate bowl blend remaining ingredients. Add to mushrooms and mix gently. Chill until ready to serve.

A Night In Old Italy

Bagna Cauda with Raw Vegetables

Salad Italiano

Cioppino

Macaroon Peaches Flambé

Fresh Fruit and Cheeses

Expresso

Bagna Cauda with Raw Vegetables

Serves four

4 ounces unsalted butter
4 tablespoons olive oil
2 ounce can anchovies in
   oil, drained and chopped
5 garlic cloves, pressed
1 cup whipping cream

Broccoli florets,
   cauliflower florets,
   celery strips,
   green pepper strips,
   fresh mushrooms, and
   carrot sticks

Place butter, olive oil, anchovies and garlic in a saucepan and cook gently for 15 minutes. Whisk in whipping cream and transfer to a fondue pot. Dip raw vegetables into hot sauce.

Salad Italiano

Serves four

1 green pepper, seeded
   and cut in julienne slices
1 red pepper, seeded and cut
   in julienne slices
2 tablespoons chopped flat
   parsley
2 tomatoes, chopped
1 stalk celery, chopped
   fine
3 green onions, sliced

6 radishes, sliced thin
4 anchovies
2 tablespoons capers
2 cloves garlic, pressed
½ teaspoon salt
½ teaspoon fresh ground
   pepper
½ cup tarragon vinegar
½ cup olive oil
Juice of ½ lemon

Mash anchovy and garlic in a wooden salad bowl. Add salt, pepper, vinegar and lemon juice: Whisk in olive oil slowly. Add remaining ingredients and toss lightly before serving.

Cioppino

Serves four

1 cup chopped, fresh
   mushrooms
½ cup olive oil
2 onions, chopped
2 cloves garlic, pressed
1 green pepper, seeded
   and chopped
1½ cups canned tomatoes
1½ cups dry red wine

½ teaspoon saffron
1 bay leaf
2 teaspoons salt
⅛ teaspoon fresh ground
   black pepper
1 two-pound sea bass
1 pound shrimp
1 quart clams
1 pound lobster

Cut sea bass in serving size slices. Shell the shrimp and shuck the clams. Cut the lobster in chunks.

Heat olive oil over moderate heat in a deep, heavy saucepan. Add onion, garlic, mushrooms and green pepper and sauté until tender. Add tomatoes, red wine, bay leaf and saffron. Cover and simmer for 1½ hours. Add salt, pepper, sea bass, lobster and shrimp and simmer 20 minutes. Add clams and simmer five minutes longer. Serve in a shallow soup bowl.

Macaroon Peaches Flambé

Serves four

4 large fresh peaches
¾ cup crushed macaroon
   crumbs
½ cup ground almonds
Grated zest of one lemon

½ cup apricot preserves
2 tablespoons butter
4 ounces Amaretto
1 ounce Brandy

Peel peaches and cut in half, removing pits. Place in a lightly buttered baking dish. In a small mixing bowl, combine: macaroon crumbs, almonds, grated lemon zest and bind with apricot preserves. Spoon mixture into the peach cavities and dot with butter. Pour Amaretto into dish; cover and bake in a 350°F oven for 30 minutes. Before serving drizzle Brandy over peaches, ignite, and serve immediately.

Breakfast In Bed For One Or Two

Mimosas

Chocolate Omelette

Toast or Croissants with Jellies, Preserves and Unsalted Butter

Sour Cream Coffee Cake

Viennese Coffee

Mimosa

Serves two

1 cup fresh-squeezed
  orange juice
1 cup Champagne
2 strawberries with stems on

Pour orange juice and Champagne simultaneously in saucer-type or fluted champagne glasses. Make a small incision midway, in each strawberry and insert on rim of glass.

Viennese Coffee

Serves two

2 cups strong hot coffee
½ cup whipping cream
1 teaspoon confectioner's
  sugar

Whip cream until peaks begin to form. Add confectioner's sugar and continue to whip until stiff. Pour coffee in cups and top with a dollop of sweetened cream.

Chocolate Omelette

Serves one

2 tablespoons butter
⅓ cup whipped cream
3 large eggs
4 tablespoons granulated
  sugar
10 bing cherries, drained
8 strawberries, hulled and
  sliced
½ cup crushed pineapple,
  drained
1 tablespoon cocoa mix
⅛ teaspoon ground
  cinnamon
Confectioner's sugar
Chocolate shavings
1½ ounce Grand Marnier

Mix fruits with Grand Marnier and set aside.

Beat eggs with cinnamon, sugar and cocoa mix until light and fluffy. Melt butter in an omelette pan over moderate heat. Pour eggs in pan and cook, lifting edges to allow unset eggs to run to the bottom. Flip omelette and then place fruit mixture in center. Fold in half and slide omelette onto a heated platter.

Top with a sprinkling of confectioner's sugar, dollops of whipped cream and chocolate shavings.

Sour Cream Coffee Cake

Serves six

8 tablespoons butter
2 eggs beaten
2 cups flour
1 teaspoon baking soda
1 teaspoon baking powder
¼ teaspoon salt
1 cup sour cream
½ teaspoon almond extract
½ cup sugar
½ cup chopped almonds
1 teaspoon cinnamon

Cream butter in a mixing bowl and then add 2 eggs, mixing until well blended and light and fluffy. Sift flour, baking powder, soda and salt together, and add to creamed mixture alternately with sour cream and almond extract, beating well after each addition. In a separate bowl mix sugar, cinnamon and nuts. Pour half of batter in a greased 9-inch tube pan. Sprinkle with half of sugar and nut mixture and add remaining batter. Top with remaining sugar and nut mixture. Bake in a preheated 350°F oven for 35–40 minutes or until toothpick inserted in coffeecake comes out clean. Serve warm.

Afternoon Soiré

30-40 guests

Stir Fried Pork

Beef Calcutta

Fried Won Ton

Shrimp Hawaiian

Crabmeat Hors d'oeuvres

Oriental Wing Dings

Escargots in Puffed Pastry

Shrimp Rolls

*Oysters Fromage on a
Half Shell*

Pineapple Scallops

Sables

Apricot Pastries

Rum Currant Cookies

Apple Cake

Lime Champagne Punch

Stir Fried Pork

1 pound pork loin cut in 1½″ strips	1½ tablespoons cornstarch
2 cloves garlic, pressed	1 teaspoon lemon juice
6 tablespoons vegetable oil	2 tablespoons soy sauce
4 scallions, chopped	½ cup beef stock
½ pound fresh sliced mushrooms	2 ounces cooking Sherry
½ pound miniature baby whole corn, drained	Fresh ground pepper to taste

Mix cornstarch, lemon juice, soy sauce, beef stock, and Sherry and set aside. Season pork with fresh ground pepper to taste.

Heat oil over high heat in a large skillet and stir fry pork until lightly browned. Add mushrooms, onion, and sauté until onion is tender. Add corn and sauce mixture and cook, stirring constantly until corn is thoroughly heated and sauce is slightly thickened.

Beef Calcutta

1½ pounds tenderloin tips	½ teaspoon tumeric
½ cup butter	½ teaspoon paprika
2 onions, minced	½ teaspoon ground pepper
2 cloves garlic, pressed	¼ teaspoon ground ginger
1 tablespoon ground coriander	½ teaspoon chili powder
½ teaspoon ground cumin	1½ cups sour cream
	Juice of one lemon

Blend coriander, cumin, tumeric, pepper, paprika, ginger and chili powder with 2 tablespoons of sour cream.

Melt butter over moderate heat in a large skillet and sauté onion and garlic until tender and transparent. Add tenderloin tips and sauté until cooked medium-rare. Stir in spice paste and blend well. Add remainder of sour cream and squeeze in juice of lemon. Blend, stirring constantly until all ingredients are thoroughly heated.

Fried Won Ton

Makes 40

1 pound lean ground pork	3 green onions, sliced thin
½ cup drained water chestnuts, thinly sliced	1 tablespoon soy sauce
2 cloves garlic, pressed	1 teaspoon cornstarch
2 canned green chilies, minced	1 egg, beaten
½ teaspoon grated ginger root	40 egg rolls skins
	Oil for frying
	Hot mustard

Brown pork and garlic, stirring constantly in a skillet over high heat. Remove pan and discard excess fat. Stir in chestnuts, green chilies, ginger root and onion. Return pan to moderate heat and cook until onion is tender. Mix cornstarch with soy sauce and stir into pork mixture. Cook stirring constantly until thickened. Cool slightly. Place egg roll skin with one point towards you. Spoon one generous tablespoon of mixture across the center. Fold bottom point of skin over filling tucking point over filling. Fold side corners to center overlapping slightly. Roll up towards remaining point; moisten point with beaten egg and press firmly to seal. Repeat with remaining egg roll skins. Heat oil over high heat and fry egg rolls 6 at a time until golden. Serve with hot mustard.

Shrimp Hawaiian

Makes 40

2½ pounds medium-sized shrimp, peeled and deveined	½ teaspoon ground ginger
1 cup whipping cream	1 tablespoon cornstarch
1 cup milk	3 pineapples, sliced in 1″ rounds
3 cups fresh shredded coconut	4 coconut halves, halved
½ shredded sweet coconut, toasted	Salt and fresh ground pepper to taste
	4″ wooden skewers

Place milk and cream in a saucepan and scald. Add the fresh coconut and simmer for 10 minutes. Remove from heat and set aside for 1 hour. Drain liquid from coconut and discard the coconut. Add ginger, cornstarch, salt and pepper and shrimp to coconut milk. Cook over moderate heat stirring constantly until sauce thickens slightly. Place shrimp mixture in coconut shells. Slice each pineapple round into quarters. Skewer one piece of pineapple on each skewer and lay around coconut shells. Sprinkle toasted coconut over all.

Crabmeat Hors d'oeuvres

Makes 40

1½ pounds Snow crabmeat	2 tablespoons ground walnuts
8 bananas, peeled and sliced in ½″ rounds	¼ teaspoon nutmeg
1 green pepper, chopped fine	½ teaspoon fresh ground white pepper
1 medium onion, minced	¼ teaspoon cayenne pepper
10 slices day-old bread, crusts removed	⅔ teaspoon salt
2 tablespoons butter	3 eggs
2 tablespoons pimento, minced	½ cup milk
	Oil for frying (peanut oil preferably)

Melt butter over moderate heat and sauté onion and green pepper until tender. In a mixing bowl blend: crabmeat, pimento, ground walnuts, nutmeg, white pepper, cayenne pepper, salt, eggs and onion-green pepper mixture.

Moisten bread in milk and then squeeze out excess. Add to ingredients in mixing bowl and blend well.

Roll 1 tablespoon of mixture at a time into round balls. Dust with flour. Heat oil over high heat and deep fry crab balls until golden.

Cover a platter with palm or pineapple leaves. With frill toothpicks, skewer a crab ball with a banana slice on bottom and place on platter.

Oriental Wing-Dings

2 pounds chicken wings, tips discarded	Grated zest of one orange
¾ cup Sake	½ cup cornstarch
¼ cup hoisin sauce	Oil for frying
1 tablespoon grated ginger root	

In a large mixing bowl combine Sake, hoisin sauce, ginger root and orange zest. Marinate chicken wings in mixture for 20 minutes. Drain chicken, pat dry with paper towels and then dust with cornstarch. Heat oil over high heat and fry chicken wings until golden. Drain cooked wings on paper towels. Serve with additional hoisin sauce if desired.

Escargots in Puffed Pastry

Makes 40

40 pieces of 2"×2"
  puffed pastry
80 escargots
½ pound butter, melted
1 pound butter, room
  temperature
12 cloves garlic, pressed
2 teaspoons Worchester-
  shire sauce

1½ tablespoons minced
  parsley
1 tablespoon chopped
  chives
⅓ cup dry white wine
Juice of 1½ lemons
Salt and fresh ground
  pepper to taste

Whip butter in a mixing bowl. Add all remaining ingredients except escargots, melted butter and puffed pastry. Blend well and place in refrigerator until well chilled.

Lightly dust a pastry board with flour and place on piece of puffed pastry dough on the board. Top with 2 escargots and ½ teaspoon of the butter mixture. Top with another piece of puffed pastry. Using a fork, crimp edges to seal. Do this with the remainder of the ingredients. Place on a greased sheet pan and brush with melted butter. Bake in a preheated 375°F. oven for 10 minutes or until golden brown.

Shrimp Rolls

Makes 40

40 medium-size shrimp,
  boiled, peeled and
  deveined
20 slices bacon
8 ounce package cream
  cheese, room temperature
2 tablespoons dill weed

Juice of one lemon
½ teaspoon Worchestershire
  sauce
¼ teaspoon red hot
  pepper sauce
Salt and fresh ground
  white pepper to taste

Cut bacon in half crosswise and cook until lightly browned, but still limp. Whip cream cheese with lemon juice, red hot pepper sauce, Worchestershire sauce, and salt and fresh ground pepper to taste. Split shrimp in half lengthwise, and fill with cream cheese mixture, using a pastry bag with a plain tube affixed.

Wrap each shrimp with partially cooked bacon. Secure with a tooth pick. Broil for 3 minutes on each side, or until bacon is crisp. Sprinkle with dill before serving.

Oysters Fromage on a Half Shell

Makes 30

30 fresh oysters on ½
  shell
1 pound fresh spinach,
  steamed and drained
1 onion, minced
2 tablespoons horseradish
  sauce

8 ounces Greyeure
  cheese, grated
1 tablespoon butter
Salt and fresh ground
  pepper to taste
1 head red cabbage,
  shredded

Melt butter in a sauté pan over moderate heat and cook onion until tender and transparent. Remove pan from heat. Add spinach, horseradish sauce, cheese and salt and pepper. Blend well and place a teaspoon of mixture on each oyster. Line a large platter with shredded red cabbage and arrange oysters on platter. Serve chilled.

Pineapple Scallops

Makes 40

1 pound medium-size sea
  scallops
½ cup butter
Flour for dredging
2 cups fresh pineapple
  chunks

Juice of 1 lemon
Salt and fresh ground
  pepper to taste
4" skewers

Cut off pineapple top with leaves intact and place pineapple top with leaves on a platter.

Season scallops with salt and pepper to taste and dust with flour. Melt butter in a sauté pan over moderate heat and sauté scallops until lightly browned on all sides. Squeeze lemon juice over scallops. Skewer scallops and pineapple alternately and stick skewers in pineapple top.

Sables

Makes 5 dozen

1½ sticks (12 tablespoons) unsalted butter at room temperature	2 cups flour
⅔ cup sugar	¼ cup colored crystal sugar
2 egg yolks	1 egg yolk beaten with 1 teaspoon water

Beat butter and sugar until creamy and lemon colored. Add egg yolks one at a time, beating well after each addition. Add flour one cup at a time, blending well after each addition. Divide dough into thirds and wrap each third in plastic wrap and refrigerate until chilled.

Preheat oven to 350° F. Remove dough from refrigerator one third at a time and roll to ⅛-inch thick. Cut into 2-inch rounds and place on a buttered baking sheet. Chill until rest of dough has been rolled out and cut out.

Brush tops of each cookie with egg yolk mixture and sprinkle lightly with crystal sugar. Bake until golden and transfer to a wire rack to cool.

Apricot Pastries

Makes 72

1 pound dried apricots	4 egg yolks, well beaten
1 cup water	1 teaspoon almond extract
¾ cup sugar	8 to 10 tablespoons ice water
2 tablespoons lemon juice	3 slightly beaten egg whites
Grated zest of one lemon	
1 pound unsalted butter	Confectioner's sugar
4 cups all-purpose flour	

In a saucepan combine apricots, water, sugar, lemon juice and lemon zest. Bring mixture to a boil and simmer until apricots have absorbed water and are tender. Pureé mixture in a food processor or blender.

Meanwhile in a mixing bowl, cut butter into flour until mixture resembles crumbs. Add egg yolks and almond extract, stirring until mixture is well blended. Sprinkle ice water 1 tablespoon at a time over flour mixture and toss with a fork. Add enough ice water to moisten mixture to form a ball. Form dough into a ball, wrap in waxed paper and chill for 1 hour. Divide dough into quarters and roll on a lightly floured surface until ¼-inch thick. Cut into 3-inch squares, and place one teaspoon of apricot pureé in the center of each square. Bring up the two opposite corners to overlap slightly. Place on an ungreased baking sheet. Brush lightly with egg white and bake in a preheated 400°F. oven for 12 minutes or until pastry is golden brown. Cool on a wire rack. Sprinkle with confectioner's sugar before serving.

Rum Currant Cookies

Makes four dozen

1½ ounces Jamaican Rum	1 cup currants
1 cup flour	1 cup granulated sugar
4 eggs	¼ cup ground almonds
⅓ pound unsalted butter	

Whip butter until light and fluffy and add sugar. Add eggs, one at a time, blending well after each addition. Add ground almonds and mix well. Mix currants with flour and place in a food processor or blender container. Process until a pureé is formed. Add Rum and blend well. Fold currant pureé into almond-egg mixture. Place in a pastry bag with a star tip affixed. Make star rosettes on a greased baking sheet and bake in a preheated 325°F. oven until golden; about 12–15 minutes.

Apple Cake

Makes one

3 eggs	¼ teaspoon salt
1¾ cups granulated sugar	1 cup walnuts, chopped
1 cup vegetable oil	6 McIntosh apples, peeled, cored and sliced thin
2 cups all-purpose flour	
1 teaspoon baking soda	
1 teaspoon cinnamon	

Sift flour, salt, cinnamon and baking soda. Beat sugar, oil and eggs until light. Add flour mixture, 1 cup at a time, blending well. Add apples and walnuts and pour mixture into a 9″×9″ greased pan and bake in a preheated 350°F. oven. Allow to cool and cut into 1½-inch diamonds. Place in foil cupcake holders before serving.

Lime Champagne Punch

Serves 40

4 bottles semi-sec Champagne	2 limes
1 quart lime sherbet	1 lemon

Place sherbet in a punch bowl and pour Champagne over sherbet. Stir to blend. Slice limes and lemons paper thin and float on top of punch.

Acknowledgements

We would like to thank all of our family, business associates and colleagues for their support and enthusiasm in publishing *Carrots to Caviar*.

A special thank you to our dear friends Donna and Pierre for all the wonderful times we have spent together.

To Chris and Dr. Paul for all their support and encouragement and friendship which we value very much. "Confusion to our enemies!"

To Paul Russell for all his hard work, patience and dedication in publishing *Carrots to Caviar*.

To our friends Bill Baltas, Chef extraordinare, and his lovely wife Filio. Hope to relocate to your warm climate someday!

To my sister and very best friend, Juli. What a beautiful woman you have grown up to be!

To my little sister, Treena...it was so much fun watching you grow up to become the prettiest girl in Hubbard! You add a little sunshine to everyone's day.

To my father, Joseph Szanyi...nobody ever had a father as wonderful as mine. Thank you for all your gentle ways, patience, guidance and great childhood stories. I love you very much and think of you always.

To Phil Hartten and Ian. We always enjoy staying at Sawmill Creek. It seems like old times.

To Richard Fischer. It has been a long time since the Mayflower Donut Shop and Florida fishing. We wish you much success in your Food and Beverage position in Honolulu.

To our dear friend and Master Chef, Emmanuel Ortiz. You still have not given us your secret recipes.

To Tammy Fling and Barbara Anderson, my secretaries. Thank you for all your endless hours of typing, proofreading and retyping. If it was not for you this book would still be in my out-tray!

To Maria Callas. Thank you for all those lovely songs.

To Alan Stegman. Thank you for introducing us to the Hilton and Columbus.

To Kris and Arthena Tulupan and their two beautiful daughters. Thank you for all your help with our restaurant and the great meals we shared.

To Frank Sinatra. It has always been a pleasure working with you.

To my lovely daughters: Kristina, Peggy, Stephanie and Katrina. I wish we were living closer and could see each other more often. I love you very much.

To Mr. Billy Weinberger. Thank you for the invitation to your wonderful Park Place Hotel in Atlantic City. We thoroughly enjoyed your hospitality.

To Dale Cochran and the Hilton Staff. It has been a pleasure working for you at the Hilton Inn North. Thank you for making our employment fun. Wishing you great success.

To Debbie Boone and Jose Ferrar Jr. It was nice of you to have us cater your dinner at the Sheraton. We enjoyed doing it.

To Margaret Whiting, Rosemary Clooney, Rose Marie and Helen O'Connell. It was great cooking for you backstage.

To Mr. Harry Monfrans. Best wishes on your superlative new restaurant, The Galeon. We're sure you will soon have Chicago's finest.

The authors would like to express their gratitude to the following companies for the loan of accessories for photography. Overby's Emporium, The Continent, Columbus, Ohio, and The Glassery, Morse Road, Columbus, Ohio.

Index

183